The Doctrine of the Holy Spirit in the Major Reformed Confessions and Catechisms of the Sixteenth and Seventeenth Centuries

Yuzo Adhinarta

© 2012 by Yuzo Adhinarta

Published 2012 by Langham Monographs
an imprint of Langham Creative Projects

Calvin Theological Seminary, Dissertation 2010

Langham Partnership
PO Box 296, Carlisle, Cumbria, CA3 9WZ
www.langham.org

ISBNs:
978-1-907713-28-6   print
978-1-907713-29-3   Mobi
978-1-907713-30-9   ePub

Yuzo Adhinarta has asserted his right under the Copyright, Designs and Patents Act, 1988, to be identified as Author of this work.

All rights reserved. No part of this publication may be reproduced, stored in a retrieval system, or transmitted, in any form or by any means, electronic, mechanical, photocopying, recording or otherwise, without the prior permission of the Publisher or the Copyright Licensing Agency.

Unless otherwise stated, Scripture quotations are taken from the Holy Bible, New International Version. Copyright © 1973, 1978, 1984 by International Bible Society. Used by permission of Hodder & Stoughton, a division of Hodder Headline Ltd. All rights reserved. 'NIV' is a trademark of International Bible Society. UK trademark number 1448790.

British Library Cataloguing in Publication Data
Adhinarta, Yuzo.
  The doctrine of the Holy Spirit in the major Reformed
  confessions and catechisms of the sixteenth and seventeenth
  centuries.
  1. Holy Spirit--History of doctrines--16th century.
  2. Holy Spirit--History of doctrines--17th century.
  3. Reformed Church--Catechisms. 4. Reformed Church--
  Creeds.
  I. Title
  238.4'2'09031-dc23

ISBN-13: 9781907713286

Cover & Book Design: projectluz.com

Langham Partnership actively supports theological dialogue and a scholars right to publish but does not necessarily endorse the views and opinions set forth, and works referenced within this publication or guarantee its technical and grammatical correctness. Langham Partnership does not accept any responsibility or liability to persons or property as a consequence of the reading, use or interpretation of its published content.

Contents

Foreword	xi
Abbreviations	xiii
Abstract	xv

CHAPTER 1 1
Introduction
    Thesis Statement 2
    Present Status of the Problem 3
    The Studies of the Confessional Documents in
        Reformed Orthodoxy 10
    The Importance of Confessional Documents 16
    The Major Reformed Confessions of the
        Sixteenth and Seventeenth Centuries 18
    Proposed Method with Outline 21

PART ONE

CHAPTER 2 27
Doctrinal Themes Commonly Associated with the Holy Spirit in the Reformed Confessions and Catechisms – Part A
    The Holy Spirit and the Doctrine of Scripture 30
    The Holy Spirit and the Doctrine of the Trinity 44
    The Holy Spirit and the Doctrine of Christ 56

CHAPTER 3 67
Doctrinal Themes Commonly Associated with the Holy Spirit in the Reformed Confessions and Catechisms – Part B
    The Holy Spirit and the Doctrine of Salvation 68
    The Holy Spirit and the Doctrine of the Church 80
    The Holy Spirit and the Doctrine of Sacraments 85

PART TWO

CHAPTER 4   105
The Holy Spirit and the Doctrine of Creation And Providence
- The Holy Spirit and the Doctrine of Creation   107
  - Creation as the Work of the Whole Trinity   107
  - The Holy Spirit's Creational Activities   113
- The Holy Spirit and the Doctrine of Providence   117
  - Providence as the Work of the Whole Trinity   118
  - The Unique Role of the Holy Spirit in Providence   121
  - The Holy Spirit in the Special Providence over the Church   124
  - Human Ministers and Ministries as Outward Means   130

PART THREE

CHAPTER 5   137
The Holy Spirit and the Doctrine of the Church: The Church's Unity and the Diversity of Spiritual Gifts
- The Holy Spirit and the Church's Unity   137
  - Unity in Communion   139
  - Unity in Worship and Service   146
  - Unity under God's Rule and Government   148
  - Sacraments as Outward Means for Preserving Unity   151
- The Holy Spirit and the Diversity of Spiritual Gifts   158

CHAPTER 6   163
The Holy Spirit and the Doctrine of the Church: The Church's Evangelistic Mission
- The Church's Mission as the *Missio Dei*   167
- The Propagation of the Gospel by Human Ministries   175
  - The Preaching of the Gospel by the Ministers of the Word   176
  - The Living Testimony of the Gospel by All Believers   178

PART FOUR

CHAPTER 7   187
The Holy Spirit and the Doctrine of Good Works: Social Responsibility
    The Holy Spirit as the Cause of Good Works   188
    Acts of Good Works as the Manifestation of Social Concerns   198
        Keeping the Sabbath and Marriage Holy   198
        Care for the Common Good, the Poor, and the Afflicted   202

CHAPTER 8   211
Conclusion
    The Doctrine in Review   211
    Final Reflections on the Treatment of the
        Doctrine in the Reformed Confessions   216

Bibliography   223
    Sixteenth- and Seventeenth-Century Reformed
        Confessions and Catechisms   223
    Books, Articles, and Essays   225

To my beloved wife Yuliwaty
and our children, Jason and Janice

"We also believe that God has created all things by His eternal Word, that is, by His only-begotten Son, and preserves and strengthens all things by His Spirit, that is, by His power; and therefore, God sustains and governs all things as He created them."

The First Confession of Basel I

"ALL Saints, that are united to Jesus Christ their head, by his Spirit, and by Faith, have fellowship with him in his graces, sufferings, death, resurrection, and glory: And, being united to one another in love, they have communion in each others gifts and graces, and are obliged to the performance of such duties publick and private, as do conduce to their mutual good, both in the inward & outward man."

The Westminster Confession of Faith XXVI.1

"But we do good because Christ by his Spirit is also renewing us to be like himself, so that in all our living we may show that we are thankful to God for all he has done for us, and so that he may be praised through us. And we do good so that we may be assured of our faith by its fruits, and so that by our godly living our neighbors may be won over to Christ."

The Heidelberg Catechism Q/A 86

Foreword

The process of writing this work is a small part and indeed a metaphor for life as a journey. As much as it was a Goliath-like project for me, it was a humbling and faith-nourishing experience. I learned so many lessons from doing this project and witnessed God's abundant grace in the process. I was able to complete this writing journey only by his ever-sustaining grace and power. Whenever I look back, I can see how God mercifully strengthened and held me up by his Spirit and power, working through many people, surrounding me with a cloud of witnesses to his presence. Accordingly, the completion of this work was marked by the fingerprints of those individuals and institutions that God sent to assist me in this journey.

My first gratitude goes to my wife, Yuli, and children, Jason and Janice, whose support, love, and understanding have made this project more enjoyable. Their smiles never failed to bring comfort and cheers to my weary soul. My family and I are also much indebted to my Mom, whose help and presence with us during the last six months of the project have given my wife and me much breathing room, enabling me to bring it to completion. I am also grateful to our families back home in Indonesia who have faithfully embraced us in prayers.

I greatly thank and appreciate all the professors at Calvin Theological Seminary who have prepared and instructed me in good faith and with outstanding integrity throughout my theological education. I especially thank my advisor and mentor, Professor Lyle D. Bierma, who introduced me to the richness of the Reformed confessions and catechisms.

Great thanks are also due to Calvin Theological Seminary, John Stott Ministries (Langham Partnership International), and Church of the Servant CRC (Grand Rapids, Michigan, USA), which have not only given substantial financial support and scholarships to me and my family, but also warmth and genuine Christ-like love along the way from the beginning to the completion of the whole doctoral program. I am forever grateful to the community of saints at these institutions for providing a spiritual nurturing fellowship and shelter for me and my family during our memorable years at the seminary. Gratitude also extends to Langham Literature for publishing the work.

All friends, colleagues, students, and fellow servants of God in both Calvin Theological Seminary and Reformed Evangelical Seminary Indonesia also deserve my gratitude. Among them, the greatest recognition of thanks goes to Rev. Yakub Susabda and his wife for their relentless care and support. The opportunities to teach several summer courses and have fellowship with them at the seminary have, in a unique way, sharpened and confirmed my calling to return to Indonesia and serve the Lord with them.

Abbreviations

See bibliography for publishing information.

AC	The Augsburg Confession (1560)
BC	The Belgic Confession (1561)
CC37	Calvin's Catechism of 1537; French edition (1537); Latin edition (1538)
CC45	Calvin's Catechism of 1545; French edition (1541); Latin edition (1545)
CD	Karl Barth's *Church Dogmatics*
CECG	The Confession of the English Congregation at Geneva (1536)
CoD	The Canons of Dort (1618-1619)
FC	The French Confession (1559)
FCB	The First Confession of Basel (1534)
FHC	The First Helvetic Confession, or the Second Basel Confession of Faith (1536)
GC	The Geneva Confession (1536)
HC	The Heidelberg Catechism (1563)
IA	The Irish Articles of Religion (1615)
LA	The Lausanne Articles (1536)
PRRD	Richard A. Muller's *Post-Reformation Reformed Dogmatics*
SC	The Scots Confession (1560)
SHC	The Second Helvetic Confession (1566)
TC	The Tetrapolitan Confession (1530)

TNA   The Thirty-Nine Articles (1563)
WCF   The Westminster Confession of Faith (1646)
WLC   The Westminster Larger Catechism (1647)
WSC   The Westminster Shorter Catechism (1647)

Abstract

With the rise of Pentecostalism in the early twentieth century and the charismatic movement from the middle of the century until recently, a resurgence of interest in the Holy Spirit and Christian spirituality in both theology and the church's life has become evident. Along with the increase of interest in the doctrine of the Holy Spirit in the twentieth century, there are criticisms of the treatment of the doctrine in church history, including in the Reformed tradition, for having neglected the Holy Spirit in both theology and the church's life. These criticisms have helped to incite a burgeoning interest in pneumatology within Christendom. Critical studies of the treatments of the doctrine of the Holy Spirit in church history have been laboriously conducted. However, there have not been many studies on the doctrine of the Holy Spirit in Reformed orthodoxy, particularly in its confessional standards. The purpose of this dissertation is to bridge this gap in the history of scholarship.

To achieve that purpose, this dissertation explores and provides a systematic account of the person and some aspects of the work of the Holy Spirit presented in the major Reformed confessions and catechisms of the sixteenth and seventeenth centuries. The first part gives an overview of the themes of the doctrine of the Spirit that have already been commonly identified by scholars, such as the Spirit in relation to Scripture, the Trinity, Christ (chapter 2), and to salvation, the church, and the sacraments (chapter 3). The next three parts deal with the themes of the doctrine that have not received adequate treatment: the Spirit in relation to creation and providence (chapter 4), the church's unity, diversity of spiritual gifts, and mission (chapters 5 and 6), and social responsibility (chapter 7). In each part the dissertation does a critical analysis of some of the major Reformed confessions and catechisms of the sixteenth and seventeenth centuries, both of the structure of the confessional documents and of the content of articles that teach, explicitly or implicitly, the aspect of the work of the Holy Spirit discussed in that chapter.

CHAPTER 1

Introduction

With the rise of Pentecostalism in the early twentieth century and the charismatic movement from the middle of the century until recently, the doctrine of the Holy Spirit has received more attention than it did before. The widespread impact of Pentecostalism and the charismatic movement is such that "literature on the Holy Spirit is now of such proportions that the mastery of the corpus would be beyond the powers of any individual."[1] A resurgence of interest in the Holy Spirit and Christian spirituality in both theology and the life of the church has become indubitably evident.

However, along with the remarkable increase of interest in the doctrine of the Holy Spirit in the twentieth century, there are criticisms of the treatment of the doctrine of the Holy Spirit in church history, including in the Reformed tradition, for having neglected the Holy Spirit in both theology and the life of the church. The formulation of the doctrine of the Holy Spirit has been perceived by some scholars as scarcely improved since the fourth century and has even been described as "slipshod."[2] As a result, many critics say the church today lacks the guidance of ecumenical statements concerning the Holy Spirit, since the creeds and confessions in the past only contained the barest outline of the doctrine, leaving the doctrine

---

1. Sinclair B. Ferguson, *The Holy Spirit* (Downers Grove: InterVarsity Press, 1996), 11.
2. George S. Hendry, *The Holy Spirit in Christian Theology* (Philadelphia: Westminster, 1st ed. 1956, 2nd ed. 1965), 13. Among others who agree with Hendry, Lewis S. Mudge, *One Church: Catholic and Reformed* (Philadelphia: The Westminster Press, 1963), 68; Daniel L. Migliore, *Faith Seeking Understanding: An Introduction to Christian Theology*, 2nd ed. (Grand Rapids: Eerdmans, 2004), 224.

dogmatically undeveloped[3] or lacking adequate expression in thought and action.[4]

As expected, these criticisms have helped to incite a burgeoning interest in pneumatology within Christendom. Within the last few decades a plethora of books on the Holy Spirit has appeared. Reflection on the third person of the Trinity has been a major topic of theological discourse and discussion within and across theological disciplines.[5] Critical studies of the treatments of the doctrine of the Holy Spirit in church history have been laboriously conducted. As careful explorations of the doctrine of the Holy Spirit within diverse Christian traditions have appeared, the negative sentiment of the criticisms of the Christian tradition's treatment of the Holy Spirit has been by and large counterbalanced.

In spite of a growing number of studies conducted to explore the treatment of the doctrine in church history, there have not been many studies on the doctrine of the Holy Spirit in Reformed orthodoxy, particularly in its confessional standards. An adequate study on the doctrine of the Holy Spirit in the Reformed confessions and catechisms of the sixteenth and seventeenth centuries is yet to be done.

Thesis Statement

Recognizing the gap stated above, this dissertation attempts to explore and provide a systematic account of the person and some aspects of the work of the Holy Spirit as presented in the major Reformed confessions and catechisms of the sixteenth and seventeenth centuries, particularly those

---

3. Josiah Royce, quoted in B. H. Streeter, ed., *The Spirit* (New York: The Macmillan Co., 1921), viii; cf. H. Wheeler Robinson, *The Christian Experience of the Holy Spirit* (London: Nisbet & Co., 1928), 1-2.

4. Oliver Chase Quick, *Doctrines of the Creed: Their Basis in Scripture and Their Meaning To-day* (New York: Charles Scribner's Sons, 1938), 299-300.

5. See Ferguson, *The Holy Spirit*, 11; Donald G. Bloesch, *The Holy Spirit: Works and Gifts* (Downers Grove: InterVarsity Press, 2000), 48-50; Michael Welker, ed., *The Work of the Spirit: Pneumatology and Pentecostalism* (Grand Rapids: Eerdmans, 2006), vii-xvii; F. LeRon Shults and Andrea Hollingsworth, *The Holy Spirit* (Grand Rapids: Eerdmans, 2008), 1-2.

aspects of the work of the Holy Spirit that have not been much explored and are pertinent to contemporary discussions. The aspects of the work of the Holy Spirit that will be addressed are: (1) creation and providence, (2) the church's unity, diversity of spiritual gifts, mission, and (3) social responsibility.

While there is considerable diversity of doctrinal emphasis in the presentation of the doctrine in the confessional documents due to their particular historical contexts, carefully observed, the confessional documents demonstrate and uniformly affirm that the doctrine of the Holy Spirit is of paramount importance in the Reformed tradition. The confessional documents present the Spirit as playing an indispensable role not only in the doctrines commonly and closely associated with the Spirit, such as the Trinity, Scripture, sanctification, faith, and sacraments, but also in other doctrines such as creation, providence, the church, and so forth. Moreover, the doctrine of the Spirit in these documents includes social and political dimensions as well as personal dimensions of Christian life.

As evidenced by its confessional standards, the Reformed tradition offers more materials for theological reflection on the doctrine of the Holy Spirit today than has been perceived. As such, the Reformed tradition may well provide valuable doctrinal sources for the development of the doctrine of the Holy Spirit to meet the need of the church in the contemporary world.

Present Status of the Problem

The criticisms of the treatment of the doctrine of the Holy Spirit in church history have been made by a variety of scholars since the late nineteenth century from both the Protestant camp and the non-Protestant camp. As F. LeRon Shults rightly observes, since the 1950s, most treatments of the doctrine of the Holy Spirit "began with a complaint about the inadequacy of the Christian tradition's treatment of the 'third person' of the Trinity."[6] Some of the recent critics have also made contrasts between the surging

---

6. Shults, *The Holy Spirit*, 1.

interest in the doctrine in contemporary theology—usually marked by the rise of Pentecostalism and the charismatic movement of the twentieth century—and the lack of attention, that is, the neglect, which the doctrine has suffered in past centuries.

However, these critics understand the neglect differently. In recent criticisms, the neglect is often associated with (1) the scarcity of materials of the doctrine in church history (quantity); (2) the less significant place given to the doctrine (priority); (3) the less comprehensive treatment of the doctrine (breadth); and (4) the superficiality of the doctrine (depth). In general, they agree that the doctrine of the Holy Spirit has been neglected, but concerning the nature of the neglect and clear criteria for what amounts to the neglect, the critics are ambiguous. As an instance, some critics have looked at a few confessional documents, for example, the Westminster Confession of Faith, which did not have a chapter on the Holy Spirit, and concluded that the Reformed creeds and confessions do not do justice to the biblical emphasis on the work of the Holy Spirit.[7] One might legitimately question this kind of criticism, whether the absence of a chapter is a sign of neglect. Considering the nature of the confessional documents as professions of faith, one might also ask whether one or even a few chapters of any doctrine in a confessional document could ever do justice to the biblical emphasis on the doctrine discussed. Another problem with these criticisms is that

---

7. Henry P. Van Dusen, *Spirit, Son and Father: Christian Faith in the Light of the Holy Spirit* (New York: Charles Scribner's Sons, 1958), 12; Mudge, *One Church: Catholic and Reformed*, 70-71; Thomas F. Torrance, *The School of Faith: The Catechisms of the Reformed Church* (London: J. Clarke, 1959), xcv-xcvi; I. John Hesselink, "The Charismatic Movement and the Reformed Tradition," in *Major Themes in the Reformed Tradition*, ed. Donald K. McKim (Grand Rapids: Eerdmans, 1992), 380; Millard J. Erickson, *Christian Theology*, 2nd ed. (Grand Rapids: Baker Book House, 1983), 870; Myung Yong Kim, "Reformed Pneumatology and Pentecostal Pneumatology," in *Reformed Theology: Ecumenicity and Identity* (Grand Rapids: Eerdmans, 2003), 174.

There have been attempts by the Presbyterian Church U.S.A. to revise the Confession in the early twentieth century. One of the proposed revisions was an additional new chapter "Of the Holy Spirit," responding specifically to observations that the Confession simply contained no chapter on the Holy Spirit. For the history of the controversy, see Lefferts A. Loetscher, *The Broadening Church: A Study of Theological Issues in the Presbyterian Church since 1869* (Philadelphia: University of Pennsylvania, 1957), 85-87. Cf. O. Palmer Robertson, "The Holy Spirit in the Westminster Confession," in *The Westminster Confession into the 21st Century*, vol. 1, ed. J. Ligon Duncan, III (Fearn: Mentor, 2003), 60-63.

they are mostly undocumented, thus creating a historiographical problem. These criticisms are often overgeneralizations.

The criticisms of the neglect of the Holy Spirit naturally drew out waves of responses. Some scholars attempt to respond to the criticisms by pointing out some broader theological contexts within which the person and work of the Holy Spirit have been largely discussed in Christian theology, namely, creation, sabbath glory, sanctification/holiness, beauty, the communal life of the church as God's present Kingdom.[8] Some do general as well as critical studies of the doctrine of the Holy Spirit that include the development of the doctrine in history. The studies of the doctrine have become more and more available,[9] not to mention relatively short articles on the topic found in the books of systematic theology by many authors. Some other scholars attempt to do further studies of the doctrine of the Holy Spirit in church history. The studies span from the early Church Fathers, the medieval, the Reformation, to the modern period. The historical study and survey on the treatment of the doctrine of the Holy Spirit are growing significantly in number since the early twentieth century.[10] These studies prove that the criticisms of the neglect have little substance.

---

8. Herbert W. Richardson, *Toward an American Theology* (New York: Harper & Row, 1967), 108-160; cf. John Bolt, "The Characteristic Work of the Holy Spirit: Sanctification, Sabbath Glory, Beauty," *Stulos Theological Journal* 3/1 (May 1995): 1-11. See also Meredith Kline, *Images of the Spirit* (Grand Rapids: Baker, 1980); Jürgen Moltmann, *God in Creation: A New Theology of Creation and the Spirit of God*, trans. Margaret Kohl (Minneapolis: Fortress Press, 1993); Patrick Sherry, *Spirit and Beauty: An Introduction to Theological Aesthetics* (Oxford: Clarendon, 1992). Richardson argues that the theological teaching of the Holy Spirit and the sanctification, or "spiritualization," of all things, has never been neglected by the Puritans and all theologians before them. Richardson, *Toward an American Theology*, 113.

9. To name but a few, Hendry, *The Holy Spirit in Christian Theology*; John McIntyre, *The Shape of Pneumatology: Studies in the Doctrine of the Holy Spirit* (Edinburgh: T&T Clark, 1997); Yves Congar, *I Believe in the Holy Spirit*, vol. 1 (New York: Crossroad, 1997).

10. Some of the important ones are as follows. The early Church Fathers period: H. B. Swete, *The Holy Spirit in the Ancient Church* (London: Macmillan & Co., 1912); Stanley M. Burgess, *The Spirit and the Church: Antiquity* (Peabody: Hendrickson, 1984). The medieval period: Howard Watkin-Jones, *The Holy Spirit in the Medieval Church* (London: Epworth, 1922); Burgess, *The Holy Spirit: Medieval Roman Catholic and Reformation Traditions* (Peabody: Hendrickson, 1997); Burgess, *The Holy Spirit: Eastern Christian Traditions* (Peabody: Hendrickson, 1989).

Theologians from many Christian traditions have entered the contemporary scene, marking the recent development in theological thought concerning the Holy Spirit. The theologians that will be mentioned here, however, are merely representations of different traditions. From the Eastern Orthodox tradition, the contributions of theologians such as Paul Evdokimov, John Zizioulas, and Sergius Bulgakov to the theological discussions on pneumatology are manifest.[11] From the Catholic tradition, Yves Congar's three-volume work on the Spirit gives a helpful starting point for grasping the complexity of the development of the doctrine of the Spirit, especially from the Roman Catholic perspective.[12] From the Protestant tradition, some prominent theologians who have contributed to the development of the doctrine of the Holy Spirit are, to name but a few, Herman Bavinck, Abraham Kuyper, Karl Barth, Paul Tillich, Rudolf Bultmann, Jürgen Moltmann, Wolfhart Pannenberg, Regin Prenter, Clark Pinnock, and Michael Welker.[13] Among scholars of significant repute who

---

11. Some of their important works are: Paul Evdokimov, *The Struggle with God*, trans. Sister Gertrude (Glen Rock: Paulist, 1966); *Présence de l'Esprit Saint dans la tradition orthodoxe* (Paris: Cerf, 1969; reprint, 1977); *La Nouveaute de l'Esprit* (Bégrolles en Mauges: Abbaye de Bellefountaine, 1977); *The Sacrament of Love*, trans. Anthony P. Gythiel and Victoria Steadman (Crestwood: St. Vladimir's Seminary Press, 1985); H. Cazelles, P. Evdokimov, and A. Greiner, *Le Mystére de l'Esprit-Saint* (Tours: Maison Mame, 1968); John Zizioulas, *Being as Communion* (Crestwood: St. Vladimir's Seminary Press, 1985); *Community and Otherness: Further Studies in Personhood and the Church*, ed. Paul McPartlan (Edinburgh: T&T Clark, 2006); Sergius Bulgakov, *The Comforter*, trans. Boris Jakin (Grand Rapids: Eerdmans, 2004).

12. Yves Congar, *I Believe in the Holy Spirit*, 3 vols, trans. David Smith (New York: Crossroad, 1997). The overarching themes of Congar's work are the believer's life in the Spirit and the role of the Holy Spirit in uniting the church.

13. Some of their works are: Herman Bavinck, *Reformed Dogmatics*, vol. 4, *Holy Spirit, Church, and New Creation*, trans. John Vriend, ed. John Bolt (Grand Rapids: Baker Academic, 2008); Abraham Kuyper, *The Work of the Holy Spirit*, trans. Henri De Vries (Grand Rapids: Eerdmans, 1975); Karl Barth, *Church Dogmatics*, trans. ed. G. W. Bromiley and T. F. Torrance, vols. 1-4 (Edinburgh: T&T Clark, 2004), especially vols. 1 (in the context of the Trinity) & 4 (in the context of the doctrine of reconciliation) (hereinafter *CD*); Paul Tillich, *Systematic Theology*, vol. 3 (Chicago: University of Chicago Press, 1963); Rudolf Bultmann, *Theology of the New Testament*, trans. Kendrick Grobel (New York: Charles Scribner's Sons, 1951); Jürgen Moltmann, *The Church in the Power of the Holy Spirit*, trans. Margaret Kohl (San Francisco: Harper & Row, 1977); *Trinity and the Kingdom*, trans. Margaret Kohl (San Francisco: Harper & Row, 1981); *God in Creation*; *The Spirit of Life: A Universal Affirmation*, trans. Margaret Kohl (Minneapolis: Fortress Press, 1992); *The Coming of God: Christian Eschatology*, trans. Margaret Kohl (Minneapolis: Fortress Press, 1996); Wolfhart Pannenberg, *Theology and the Kingdom of*

are associated with Pentecostalism are J. Rodman Williams, Gordon D. Fee, Velli-Matti Kärkkäinen, and Amos Yong.[14]

What seems to be missing in the history of scholarship of the doctrine of the Holy Spirit is a comprehensive study of the doctrine in both Reformation period and Reformed Orthodoxy. For studies of the doctrine of the Holy Spirit in the Reformation period, John Calvin has become such a major figure that many studies are conducted to discuss his doctrine of the Holy Spirit by setting it against the historical context of the Reformation. Some important studies on Calvin's doctrine of the Holy Spirit have been done in the twentieth century. The studies, for the most part, reaffirm Benjamin B. Warfield's assertion that Calvin is "the theologian of the Holy Spirit" and that the doctrine of the work of the Holy Spirit is "a gift from Calvin to the Church."[15] A few of these studies worth mentioning are Simon van der Linde's *De Leer van den Heiligen Geist* (1943), Werner Krusche's *Das Wirken des Heiligen Geest nach Calvin* (1957), and H. Quistorp's lengthy essay "Calvin's Lehre vom Heiligen Geist."[16] However, besides the stud-

---

God (Philadelphia: Westminster Press, 1969); *Systematic Theology*, 3 vols, trans. Geoffrey W. Bromiley (Grand Rapids: Eerdmans, 1991, 1994, 1998); Regin Prenter, *Spiritus Creator*, trans. John M. Jensen (Philadelphia: Fortress, 1953); Clark H. Pinnock, *Flame of Love: A Theology of the Holy Spirit* (Downers Grove: InterVarsity Press, 1996); Michael Welker, *God the Spirit*, trans. John F. Hoffmeyer (Minneapolis: Fortress, 1994).

14. J. Rodman Williams, *The Era of the Spirit* (Plainfield: Logos International, 1971); *The Pentecostal Reality* (Plainfield: Logos International, 1972); *Renewal Theology* (Grand Rapids: Zondervan, 1990); Gordon D. Fee, *God's Empowering Presence: The Holy Spirit in the Letters of Paul* (Peabody: Hendrickson, 1994); Velli-Matti Kärkkäinen, *Pneumatology: The Holy Spirit in Ecumenical, International, and Contextual Perspective* (Grand Rapids: Baker Academic, 2002); *Toward a Pneumatological Theology: Pentecostal and Ecumenical Perspectives on Ecclesiology, Soteriology, and Theology of Mission*, ed. Amos Yong (Lanham: University Press of America, 2002); Amos Yong, *Beyond the Impasse: Toward a Pneumatological Theology of Religions* (Grand Rapids: Eerdmans, 2001); *Spirit-Word-Community: Theological Hermeneutics in Trinitarian Perspective* (Burlington: Ashgate, 2002); *The Spirit Poured Out on All Flesh: Pentecostalism and the Possibility of Global Theology* (Grand Rapids: Baker Academic, 2005).

15. Benjamin Breckinridge Warfield, "John Calvin the Theologian," in *Calvin and Augustine* (Philadelphia: Presbyterian and Reformed Publishing, 1956), 484-485. A similar assertion can already be found in Warfield's introduction to Abraham Kuyper's *The Work of the Holy Spirit*, xxxiii-xxxv.

16. Simon van der Linde, *De Leer van den Heiligen Geest bij Calvijn* (Wageningen: Veenman, 1943); Werner Krusche, Das Wirken des Heiligen Geistes nach Calvin (Göttingen: Vandenhoeck & Ruprecht, 1957); H. Quistorp, "Calvin's Lehre vom Heiligen Geist," in De Spiritu Sancto, ed. J. de Graf (Utrecht: Drukkerij V/H Hemink & Zoon,

ies cited above, as I. John Hesselink remarks, "so little has been written concerning Calvin's doctrine of the Holy Spirit" and "we have had only a few essays on isolated themes."[17] Responding to this lacuna, Hesselink has also published some articles in which he deals with some themes in Calvin's doctrine of the Holy Spirit.[18]

Interestingly, not much work has been done to study the development of the doctrine of the Holy Spirit in Reformed orthodoxy, including some major Reformed orthodox figures, such as John Owen, whose *Pneumatologia* has been an evident contribution of Reformed orthodoxy to the doctrine of the Holy Spirit.[19] Abraham Kuyper lists some works done on the doctrine of the Holy Spirit by some theologians from the late sixteenth to the first half of the eighteenth century besides Owen's *Pneumatologia*, including the works by Voetius, Maresius, and Vitringa.[20] Warfield also mentions some works on the doctrine of the Holy Spirit written by some Puritan contemporaries of Owen, such as Godwin, Charnock, and Swinnerton, and some others in later generations.[21] Despite the fact that both Kuyper and Warfield mentioned works on the doctrine of the Holy Spirit by various Reformed orthodox theologians, these works remain uncultivated.

In the fourth volume of Richard A. Muller's *Post-Reformation Reformed Dogmatics*, one can find an apt and brief summary of the Reformed

---

1964), 109-150. Another recent and important work to be noted is that of Paul (Seung Hoon) Chung, *Spirituality and Social Ethics in John Calvin: A Pneumatological Perspective* (Lanham: University Press of America, 2000).

17. Hesselink, "Calvin, Theologian of the Holy Spirit," in *Calvin's First Catechism: A Commentary* (Louisville: Westminster John Knox, 1997), 177.

18. Hesselink, "Calvin, Theologian of the Holy Spirit;" "Governed and Guided by the Spirit: A Key Issue in Calvin's Doctrine of the Holy Spirit," in *Reformiertes Erbe: Festschrift für Gottfried W. Locher zu seinem 80 Geburtstag, Band 2*, ed. Heiko A. Oberman (Zurich: Theologischer Verlag, 1993), 161-171. In "Calvin, Theologian of the Holy Spirit," Hesselink offers a brief discussion on some of the distinctive aspects of Calvin's treatment of themes such as the Spirit and the Trinity, the Spirit and the Word, and the Spirit and the Christian Life. See also "Appendix: Calvin, Theologian of the Holy Spirit," in *Calvin's First Catechism*; "Pneumatology," in *Calvin Handbook*, ed. Herman J. Selderhuis (Grand Rapids: Eerdmans, 2009), 299-312.

19. John Owen, *PNEUMATOLOGIA* (Chancery Lane: J. Darby, 1674).

20. For a complete list, see Kuyper, *The Work of the Holy Spirit*, ix-x.

21. See "Introductory Note," in Kuyper, *The Work of the Holy Spirit*, xxviii-xxix.

orthodox doctrine of the deity and the personhood of the Spirit.[22] Muller does present some brief discussions on the Reformed orthodox teaching of divine works of the Spirit and the *ad intra-ad extra* distinction of the operations of the Spirit. However, his discussions in that particular chapter are more focused on the divinity and the personhood of the Holy Spirit than on the work of the Spirit. The theology of the confessions concerning the Spirit is not discussed.

As to the studies of the confessional documents in Reformed orthodoxy, only in a comparatively few pages can one find the discussions of pneumatological issues.[23] One can certainly find the discussion of the Holy Spirit at various points in the commentaries on the confessions. However, only a few short articles were written, and a few studies conducted, to explore the doctrine of the Holy Spirit in the Reformed confessions and catechisms of the sixteenth and seventeenth centuries, even in Reformed circles.[24] This means that the doctrine of the Holy Spirit in the Reformed confessions and catechisms of the sixteenth and seventeenth centuries still needs to be further studied to see whether the Reformed tradition can in some ways contribute to the contemporary discussions of the Holy Spirit, and whether Reformed orthodoxy, or perhaps Reformed tradition, is appreciative toward the Holy Spirit and pneumatology.

---

22. Richard A. Muller, *Post-Reformation Reformed Dogmatics*, 4 vols. (Grand Rapids: Baker Academic, 2003), IV, 7 (hereinafter *PRRD*).

23. See Karl Barth, *Theology of the Reformed Confessions*, trans. Darrel L. Guder and Judith J. Guder (Louisville: Westminster John Knox Press, 2005); Jan Rohls, *Reformed Confessions: Theology from Zurich to Barmen*, trans. John Hoffmeyer (Louisville: Westminster John Knox Press, 1998).

24. For example: Robertson, "The Holy Spirit in the Westminster Confession of Faith," 57-100; Eugene P. Heideman, "God the Holy Spirit," in *Guilt, Grace, and Gratitude: A Commentary on the Heidelberg Cactechism,* ed. Donald J. Bruggink (New York: Half Moon Press, 1963), 111-135; Torrance, *The School of Faith*, xcv-cxxvi. A committee of CRCNA was assigned to study "Neo-Pentecostalism" and submitted their reports (Report 34) in 1973 that include a very good, albeit very brief, study on the Holy Spirit in a few of Reformed Confessions, focussing particularly on the issues related to Neo-Pentecostalism. "Report 34: Neo Pentecostalism," in *Acts of Synod 1973* (Grand Rapids: CRC, 1973), 398-493. Hesselink gave a lecture at the International Calvin Conference in Emden in the year of 2006, in which he presents with considerable clarity, albeit brief, Calvin's doctrine of the Holy Spirit in both of his catechisms (CC37 and CC45). "Calvin's Use of *Doctrina* in His Catechisms," in *Calvinus sacrarum literarum interpres*, ed. Herman J. Selderhuis (Göttingen: Vandenhoeck & Ruprecht, 2008), 70-87.

The Studies of the Confessional Documents in Reformed Orthodoxy

As mentioned briefly above, the studies that focused on exploring the various confessional documents in Reformed orthodoxy are very few. Two of the studies that remain as valuable sources and are widely used as scholarly guides to the riches of the Reformed confessions are those of Barth and Jan Rohls.[25] Hence their contributions to the studies of the Reformed confes-

---

25. Among many, some other studies of the confessions in Reformed orthodoxy are: Johann Adam Möhler, *Symbolism: Exposition of the Doctrinal Differences between Catholics and Protestants as Evidenced by Their Symbolic Writings*, trans. James Burton Robertson (New York: The Crossroad Herder Book, 1997); Wilhelm Niesel, *Reformed Symbolics: A Comparison of Catholicism, Orthodoxy, and Protestantism*, trans. David Lewis (Edinburgh: Oliver and Boyd, 1962); Milton J. Coalter et al., eds., *The Confessional Mosaic: Presbyterians and Twentieth-Century Theology* (Louisville: Westminster John Knox Press, 1990); Joel R. Beeke and Sinclair B. Ferguson, eds., *Reformed Confessions Harmonized* (Grand Rapids: Baker Books, 1999); Jaroslav Pelikan, *Credo: Historical and Theological Guide to Creeds and Confessions of Faith in the Christian Tradition* (New Haven: Yale University Press, 2003). Even though these studies will not contribute directly to the project of this dissertation, they are valuable for their own worth. *Symbolism* offers exposition of (only) some major doctrinal differences between Catholicism and Protestantism as attested in their confessional documents. *Reformed Symbolics* critically compares the three major Christian traditions, Catholicism, Eastern Orthodoxy, and Protestantism, by utilizing the confessional documents in each tradition to draw doctrinal differences among the traditions. Nielsen, however, centers his attention on how the differing traditions respect the Gospel and communicate it. *The Confessional Mosaic* deals specifically with issues regarding the function of confessions, while *Reformed Confessions Harmonized*, as the title indicates, attempts to demonstrate the harmony of seven major confessions of the sixteenth and seventeenth centuries (the Three Forms of Unity, the Second Helvetic Confessions, and the Wetsminster Standards), by lying out side-by-side doctrine by doctrine each of the creeds/confessions. *Credo* addresses the essential questions about the role of creeds and confessions in the Christian tradition, such as definition of creed and confession, their origins, their authority, and their history; in its fourth chapter, the history of the Reformed confessions is discussed. The valuable source for the collection of texts of the Reformed confessional documents in sixteenth and seventeenth centuries are: Jean François Salvard, *Harmonia confessionum fidei, orthodoxarum et reformatarum ecclesiarum* (Geneva: Apud Petrum Santandreanum, 1581); H. A. Niemeyer, *Collectio confessionum in ecclesiis reformatis publicatarum* (Leipzig: Klinkhardt, 1840); Phillip Schaff, ed., *The Creeds of Christendom with a History and Critical Notes*, vol. 3, *The Evangelical Protestant Creeds with Translations* (New York: Harper & Row, 1931; reprint, Grand Rapids: Baker Books, 1984). Salvard's *Harmonia* has been translated into English and most recently edited by Peter Hall, *The Harmony of Protestant Confessions: Exhibiting the Faith of the Churches of Christ Reformed after the Pure and Holy Doctrine of the Gospel, throughout Europe*, New Ed. (London, J. F. Shaw, 1844). Some other collections of texts of the Reformed confessions available in English translation are: Arthur C. Cochrane, ed., *Reformed Confessions of the Sixteenth Century* (Louisville: Westminster John Knox Press,

sions are not to be overlooked. However, regarding the doctrine of the Holy Spirit in the Reformed confessions, neither has displayed a comprehensive treatment of the doctrine. Considering the different approaches employed in their studies of the confessional documents, it is necessary to give a brief summary in the following paragraphs of how both studies deal with the doctrine of the Holy Spirit contained in the confessional documents.

Barth's *The Theology of the Reformed Confessions* is a series of lectures he gave at Göttingen University during the summer of 1923. The lectures took place between his two important publications, *The Epistle to the Romans* in 1919 and *Church Dogmatics* in 1932-1968. Prior to his series of lectures on the theology of the Reformed confessions, Barth offered lectures on the Heidelberg Catechism (1921-1922), the theology of Calvin (1922), and the theology of Zwingli (1922-1923). Two years after the lectures, Barth also gave a lecture at the twentieth General Assembly of the Reformed Federation on June 3, 1925, in Duisburg-Meiderich, entitled "The Desirability and Possibility of a Universal Reformed Creed." This lecture serves well as a summary of his 1923 lectures.[26]

The Theology of the Reformed Confessions lectures are divided into three parts. The first part discusses, as the chapter is entitled, the significance of the confession in the Reformed church, in contrast to that in the most immediate counterpart to the Reformed church, the Lutheran church. Here Barth contrasts Lutheran and Reformed confessional attitudes. He maintains that in the Reformed church there is no authority given to any confession parallel to that given to the Augsburg Confession by the Lutheran church. The Reformed confessions are always human, thus occasional, historical, provisional, fallible, and, above all, subservient to Scripture. In Barth's words, the Reformed confessions were "fundamentally intended as merely *provisional*, improvable and replaceable *offerings*, never

---

2003); Jaroslav Pelikan and Valerie Hotchkiss, eds., *Creeds and Confessions of Faith in the Christian Tradition*, vol. 2, *Creeds and Confessions in the Reformation Era* (New Haven: Yale University Press, 2003); James T. Dennison, Jr., comp., *Reformed Confessions of the 16th and 17th Centuries in English Translation: Volume 1, 1523-1552* (Grand Rapids: Reformation Heritage Books, 2008).

26. Eberhard Busch, preface to *The Theology of the Reformed Confessions*, by Barth, viii-ix. As Busch also stated, the 1925 lecture was later incorporated in Barth's discussion of the concept of the church's confession in his *Church Dogmatics*. See Barth, *CD*, I/2, 620-660.

as an authority, as the 'form and rule' ['forma et regula'] that the Formula of Concord found in the Augsburg Confession."[27] "The significance of the confession in the Reformed church," Barth asserts, "consists in its essential *non*significance, its obvious relativity, humanity, multiplicity, mutability, and transitoriness."[28]

In the second part, Barth takes up the theme of Scripture principle. In the Reformed church, confession points beyond itself to Scripture; in its entirety, confession is testimony, a pointing toward. The Reformed confession, as Barth remarks, stresses that it is "*only* form and vessel of this content, and does *not* claim as its own the content itself."[29] The content—the Word of God or divine revelation—is that to which the confession witnesses or testifies, is written, written by God's finger on the paper of the Bible and by God's finger in our hearts, "truly and inviolably, completely and sufficiently, neither to be repeated nor to be continued."[30]

In the third part, the longest section of the work, Barth specifically deals with the question of the intention of the authors in the composition of their confessions, in an attempt to gain an overview of the positive doctrine of the confessions. Barth explores and elucidates particular theological themes and issues with attention being given to the historical context of the confession.

Concerning the doctrine of the Holy Spirit in the confessions, Barth does not treat the doctrine exclusively. Barth discusses the personhood and the work of the Holy Spirit insofar as they are discussed in the articles of the confessions that Barth is treating. Barth's approach to find one unifying and overarching theme in every confession in order to present *the* positive doctrine, or the central theme, of each confession not only limits his discussion to a few major theological themes in each confession, but also in some ways tends to overlook the importance and the development of other *secondary* themes in the history of thought, and to bias the understanding of other themes. Even though the central theme of each confession

---

27. Barth, *The Theology of the Reformed Confessions*, 24 (italics his).
28. Barth, *The Theology of the Reformed Confessions*, 38 (italics his).
29. Barth, *The Theology of the Reformed Confessions*, 39 (italics his).
30. Barth, *The Theology of the Reformed Confessions*, 39.

identified by Barth is not necessarily wrong, Barth often uses it as a lens through which one ought to read through a confession. For example, the Heidelberg Catechism, for Barth, is focussed on the question of comfort as its central theme. The way the catechism answers the question, "What is your only comfort?," reflects, for Barth, the typical Calvinist duality of salvation certainty and readiness, of justification and sanctification.[31] While it may be true that comfort, or assurance of salvation, is the overarching theme of the Heidelberg Catechism, setting up the discussion of the Heidelberg Catechism to demonstrate the single unifying theme certainly hinders one from exploring the richness of the catechism. As a result of this approach, when talking about the Holy Spirit, Barth only discusses, often merely in passing, some themes of the doctrine of the Holy Spirit that support the central theme that he proposes, such as being assured of salvation by the Holy Spirit, being raised by the power of the Holy Spirit to a new life, baptism, communion of the saints, the use of spiritual gifts, and the life renewal of individuals through the Holy Spirit. Barth clearly dismisses some important themes of the doctrine of the Holy Spirit one can find in the catechism, such as the personhood of the Holy Spirit, the agency of the Holy Spirit in creation, faith as a gift of the Spirit, the role of the Holy Spirit in Christ's incarnation, and so forth.

Rohls' *Reformed Confessions* is of a different nature and approach from Barth's *The Theology of the Reformed Confessions*. Rohls' *Reformed Confessions* is not a lecture, but a dogmatic work. It is an attempt to present a systematic treatment of the contents of the Reformed confessions. As such, in its second chapter it presents and discusses in a classic topical order the theological contents of the Reformed confessions, ranging from revelation, Trinity, creation, human beings and sin, covenant, justification, and sanctification, to church, sacraments, ministry, and church and state.

Reformed Confessions precedes the dogmatic chapter with a chapter that offers a concise, yet insightful, history of the Old Reformed confessions. It begins with Zwingli, Calvin, and Bullinger and moves on to the spread of Calvinism in Western and Eastern Europe, Philippism and

---

31. Barth, *The Theology of the Reformed Confessions*, 108-109.

German Reformed Theology, the Dordrecht Synod and the theology of the Netherlands, English Puritanism, and the School of Saumur and the Helvetic Consensus Formula. Rohls agrees with Barth in pointing out that the Reformed tradition holds an "open" rather than a "closed" confessional tradition. He affirms that the Reformed church does not have a common confession or a universally binding collection of confessional writings, as does the Book of Concord with its Augsburg Confession in the Lutheran church.[32]

Corresponding with the first chapter, the final chapter discusses the development of the later Reformed confessions in Europe and North America, touching on conciliatory theology, confessionalism and the idea of toleration, the French Revolution, the European revival movement or Awakening, the Development of the Free Churches, the German union movement and church struggle, and finally the Barmen Theological Declaration.

Concerning the doctrine of the Holy Spirit, Rohls does not treat the doctrine exclusively. Employing a classic topical order in arranging his discussion of the theological contents of the Reformed confessions, Rohls does not discuss the Holy Spirit under a separate heading. The doctrine of the Holy Spirit was commonly integrated and discussed in relation to other doctrines. The Reformed confessions and catechisms of the sixteenth and seventeenth centuries, with very few exceptions, are the best examples. Therefore, one might expect to find that the Holy Spirit is discussed in some doctrines closely related to the personhood and the work of the Holy Spirit, such as the revelation, Trinity, Christology, justification by faith, sanctification, sacraments, and the church. However, Rohls does not discuss the Holy Spirit in the same depth in those *loci*. Neither does he adequately present what the confessions teach regarding the Holy Spirit when discussing doctrines in which the Holy Spirit plays a big role, such as the incarnation of Christ, faith, sanctification, and the church and its ministry.

Another study of the confessions is worth mentioning. The Christian Reformed Church (CRC) Synod of 1971 appointed a committee to study the teachings and practices associated with that which is popularly called

---

32. Rohls, *Reformed Confessions*, 9.

"Neo-Pentecostalism," in the light of the biblical teachings on the Holy Spirit and the urgent need of the church for guidance. The fruits of the committee study were not reported until the Synod of 1973.[33] This report, Report 34, not only discusses the Neo-Pentecostalism movement, its definition, and the contemporary cultural context in North America where the movement is growing, but also provides a brief and apt summary of the doctrine of the Holy Spirit both in Scripture and the Reformed confessions.

Report 34 attempts to demonstrate that the Reformed confessions give no less emphasis on the Holy Spirit than the Neo-Pentecostalism movement does. The report begins by pointing out Calvin's legacy to the Reformed churches, that is, his elaboration of the doctrine of the work of the Holy Spirit contained in Book III of the *Institutes*.[34] The subsequent confessional documents handed down from the early days of the Reformation, the report maintains, bearing Calvin's imprint, "manifest Calvin's deep interest to give all glory to God's Holy Spirit in the area of man's benefitting from the salvation accomplished by Christ."[35]

The report then surveys the doctrine of the Holy Spirit as taught by the Belgic Confession, the French Confession (known also as the Gallican Confession or the Confession of La Rochelle), the Heidelberg Catechism, the Catechism of Geneva, and the Canons of Dort. The study committee clearly made choices regarding what facets of the doctrine of the Holy Spirit needed to be presented in the report to serve the purpose of the study. The goal of the committee is not to present a comprehensive account of the doctrine of the Holy Spirit in the Reformed confessions, but to demonstrate that the Reformed confessions, following Calvin, have emphasized the crucial role of the Holy Spirit in the application of the redemptive work of Christ. The report maintains that the important work of the Holy Spirit is emphasized in the Reformed confessions. The Holy Spirit creates faith in the hearts of believers, regenerates, sanctifies, nurtures faith with the Word through sacraments, illumines the minds of believers, and assures them

---

33. "Report 34," 398.
34. John Calvin, *Institutes of the Christian Religion*, 2 vols., ed. John T. McNeill, tran. Ford Lewis Battles (Philadelphia: Westminster Press, 1960).
35. "Report 34," 430.

of salvation. The report contends that the role of the Holy Spirit in the salvation and life of the elect is indispensable. The committee concluded that in the Reformed confessions one can find "a wonderful balance and genuine sensitivity to the work of the Holy Spirit in the hearts of believers," and that the confessions continue to provide the church today "necessary guidelines for elaboration of the biblical doctrine of the Holy Spirit within a milieu which has known the rise of neo-Pentecostalism."[36]

Report 34 has served well its purpose to demonstrate that the Reformed confessions, as represented by the five confessions discussed in the report, emphasize the indispensable role that the Holy Spirit plays in the salvation and life of believers. However, the discussion of the doctrine of the Holy Spirit in the report is very brief and far from comprehensive. Moreover, it merely focuses on the work of the Holy Spirit in the application of redemption done by Christ. It limits the discussion to the topics that commonly fall under the rubric of the order of salvation, with the addition of sacraments and prayer. In the same report one will not find discussions of the personhood of the Holy Spirit and the role of the Holy Spirit in creation and providence, the church, the spiritual gifts, and so forth.

All these studies considered, one cannot help but come to the conclusion that none of them presents a comprehensive treatment of the doctrine of the Holy Spirit in the Reformed confessional documents. An adequate and comprehensive treatment of the doctrine of the Holy Spirit in the Reformed confessions is yet to be done to fill the gap in the history of scholarship regarding the doctrine of the Holy Spirit.

The Importance of Confessional Documents

The Reformed confessions and catechisms, in this regard, are of great significance for several reasons, that is, their nature as standards of orthodoxy, their function as a unifying tool among churches of the same tradition, and their teaching of piety (or spirituality of the church). First, given

---

36. "Report 34," 434.

their nature as standards of orthodoxy, confessional documents consist of statements that express what the church, within the Reformed tradition, believes. For this reason, confessional statements are also understood as articles of faith. Therefore, to explore the standard teaching of the Holy Spirit in the Reformed tradition, one needs to study what the Reformed confessions and catechisms profess and teach about the Holy Spirit.

Second, confessional statements are agreed professions of faith meant to secure a proper unity within a tradition. They were confessions of the church, rather than of individual theologians.[37] The Reformed confessions are thus a series of markers that set boundaries to a diversity of expressions of a broad consensus within the Reformed tradition. Therefore, to understand the doctrine of the Holy Spirit in the Reformed *tradition*, it is necessary to seek the unity of the Reformed faith in the confessions, as well as the thought of single theologians (for examples, Bucer, Zwingli, Bullinger, Calvin, and others).

Third, Reformed confessions and catechisms are as much concerned with the piety of the church as with the precision of doctrinal statements. Confessions provide guidelines for belief and piety that shape the thought and actions of the members of the communion; in fact, piety and doctrine are inseparable. The study of the Reformed confessions and catechisms is of paramount importance for understanding the doctrine of the Holy Spirit in the Reformed tradition, as the study will reveal how the doctrine of the Holy Spirit is integrated with Christian life in the Reformed tradition. Some critics who have lamented over the paucity of materials of the doctrine of the Holy Spirit in the Reformed confessional documents have obviously overlooked the inseparability of doctrine and piety in the Reformed orthodoxy tradition. The doctrine of the Holy Spirit, as laid out in the Reformed confessional documents, permeates almost all other Christian doctrines, from the Trinity to social ethics.

---

37. Muller aptly explains, "In their fundamental intention, confessions transcend individuals and provide ecclesial statement. From the earliest stages of the Reformation, therefore, the confessions provide a source of more objectively stated doctrinal principles and a source of churchly, standardized norms (*norma normata*) within the bounds and under the guidance of which orthodox theological system could develop." Muller, *PRRD*, II, 2.1 (B.1).

The Major Reformed Confessions of the Sixteenth and Seventeenth Centuries

As the Reformed churches of the sixteenth century began to mature, the need for a comprehensive statement of faith began to appear. The earliest confessions of the Protestant churches were quite specifically intended to "reform both Christian life and teaching," by attacking doctrinal abuses and striving to purge the church's teaching of non-biblical elements of late medieval religion and theology, thus only presenting particular points of doctrine "where a return to right teaching was needed."[38] In contrast, the confessional documents of the fourth and fifth decades of the sixteenth century marked the rise of the new need for another form of Protestant confession, that is, the need for a comprehensive statement of faith that belonged to and defined the confessing church.

Having a confession that proclaims the faith of the confessing church was a need commonly shared by the Reformed churches in the sixteenth century. As Muller remarks, "Right statement of a whole body of doctrine, of all the basic articles of faith, is characteristic of institutionally established Protestantism."[39] At least fifty confessions were produced in the first fifty years since the Reformation began. In contrast to Lutheranism, the process of confessional development in the Reformed tradition has not yet come to a conclusion. From time to time, a new confession or statement of faith is born.[40] No one can provide an official list of Reformed confessions.

To study all the confessional documents is indeed a daunting and probably also an impossible task. These Reformed confessions not only differ from each other in their historical contexts, but also in style. They are extraordinarily important for a church's integrity, identity, and faithfulness, but they are also to be acknowledged as "occasional" in nature, relative to

---

38. Muller, *PRRD*, I, 1.1 (B.1).

39. Muller, *PRRD*, I, 1.1 (B.1).

40. As Rohls points out, "In Lutheranism the process of confessional development came to a conclusion with the Formula of Concord (1577) and the Book of Concord (1580). On the Reformed side there is nothing that corresponds to this conclusion." *Reformed Confessions*, 9.

"particular times and places."[41] Recognizing that fact, therefore, this dissertation inevitably has to limit its scope of study to the major confessions and catechisms of the sixteenth and seventeenth centuries.

By the major confessions and catechisms of the sixteenth and seventeenth centuries, I mean the great national confessions and catechisms of the mid-sixteenth century, with the addition of the Geneva Confession and Calvin's Catechisms of the early sixteenth century, and the Canons of Dort and the Westminster Standards of the seventeenth century. Thus, they are: the Geneva Confession (1536; hereinafter GC),[42] Calvin's two Catechisms (1537, 1545; hereinafter CC37 and CC45),[43] the French Confession (1559; hereinafter FC),[44] the Scots Confession (1560; hereinafter SC),[45] the Belgic Confession (1561; hereinafter BC),[46] the Thirty-Nine Articles of the Church of England (1563; hereinafter TNA),[47] the Heidelberg Catechism (1563; hereinafter HC),[48] the Second Helvetic Confession (1566; hereinafter SHC),[49] the Canons of Dort (1618-1619; hereinafter

---

41. Jack L. Stotts, "Introduction: Confessing after Barmen," in Rohls, *Reformed Confessions*, xi.
42. The Geneva Confession, in Cochrane, *Reformed Confessions of the Sixteenth Century*, 120-126.
43. Calvin's Catechism (1537), in Dennison, *Reformed Confessions of the 16th and 17th Centuries in English Translation: Volume 1, 1523-1552*, 354-401 (hereinafter CC37); Calvin's Catechism (1545), in Dennison, *Reformed Confessions of the 16th and 17th Centuries in English Translation: Volume 1, 1523-1552*, 468-519.
44. The French Confession of Faith (1559), in Cochrane, *Reformed Confessions of the Sixteenth Century*, 144-158.
45. The Scottish Confession of Faith (1560), in Cochrane, *Reformed Confessions of the Sixteenth Century*, 163-184.
46. The Belgic Confession, in *Ecumenical Creeds and Reformed Confessions* (Grand Rapids: CRC Publications, 1988), 78-120.
47. The Thirty Nine Articles of the Church of England, in Schaff, *The Creeds of Christendom with a History and Critical Notes*, vol. 3 (Grand Rapids: Baker, 1984), 486-516.
48. The Heidelberg Catechism, in *Ecumenical Creeds and Reformed Confessions* (Grand Rapids: CRC Publications, 1988), 12-77.
49. The Second Helvetic Confession (1566), in Cochrane, *Reformed Confessions of the Sixteenth Century*, 224-301. For the SHC articles division, compare to the Latin edition of the SHC (*Confessio Helvetica Posterior*) in Schaff, *The Creeds of Christendom with a History and Critical Notes*, vol. 3 (Grand Rapids: Baker, 1984), 237-306.

CoD),⁵⁰ the Westminster Confession of Faith (1646; hereinafter WCF),⁵¹ the Westminster Larger Catechism (1647; hereinafter WLC),⁵² and the Westminster Shorter Catechism (1647; hereinafter WSC).⁵³

The choosing of these confessional documents is due to both their historical importance and influence. The great national confessions and catechisms of the sixteenth century are important historically, as Muller writes, because they provided "clear summaries of the basic doctrines of the Reformed churches" or, in other words, "the churchly right doctrine or 'orthodoxy' in the light of which larger structures of theological system could be developed and taught."⁵⁴ The confessional documents chosen in this dissertation are recognized as "the major confessions and catechisms" because they represent the faith of the wide-ranging family of Reformed churches. The Swiss family (both German-speaking and French-Speaking) is represented by the GC, CC37, CC45, FC, and SHC. The Scottish-English family is represented by the SC, TNA, WCF, WLC, and WSC. The Dutch-German family is represented by the Three Forms of Unity: the BC, HC, and CoD. The Westminster Standards are included in this study for several additional reasons. First, the Westminster Standards are widely considered as a manifestation of a fully codified and scholastically elaborated English Puritanism, that "stand at the peak of a great development of English Reformed theology."⁵⁵ Second, the critics often cited the Westminster Standards as an obvious evidence of the neglect of (the doctrine of) the Holy Spirit in the Reformed tradition.⁵⁶

---

50. The Canons of Dort, in *Ecumenical Creeds and Reformed Confessions* (Grand Rapids: CRC Publications, 1988), 122-145.

51. The Confession of Faith, in *The Confession of Faith and the Larger and Shorter Catechism* (Edinbourg: George Swintoun and Thomas Brown, 1683), 3-74.

52. The Larger Catechism, in *The Confession of Faith and the Larger and Shorter Catechism* (Edinbourg: George Swintoun and Thomas Brown, 1683), 75-166.

53. The Shorter Catechism, in *The Confession of Faith and the Larger and Shorter Catechism* (Edinbourg: George Swintoun and Thomas Brown, 1683), 167-192.

54. The great national confessions of the mid-sixteenth century are the FC (1559), SC (1560), BC (1561), TNA (1563), HC (1563), and SHC (1566). Muller, "Reformed Confessions and Catechisms," in *The Dictionary of Historical Theology*, ed. Trevor A. Hart (Grand Rapids: Eerdmans, 2000), 471.

55. Muller, "Reformed Confessions and Catechisms," 482-483.

56. For examples, see Van Dusen, *Spirit, Son and Father*, 12; Mudge, *One Church: Catholic*

Considering the historical importance and the faith of national churches represented, the Reformed confessions and catechisms of the sixteenth and seventeenth centuries may well serve as representatives to Reformed orthodoxy and even to the Reformed churches today worldwide. However, the choosing of the great national confessions and catechisms will not necessarily rule out completely the use of other confessions and catechisms as references in this dissertation.

Proposed Method with Outline

In order to address the gap in the history of scholarship of the doctrine of the Holy Spirit, I propose to explore and provide a systematic account of the person and work of the Holy Spirit in the major Reformed confessions and catechisms of the sixteenth and seventeenth centuries.

In this dissertation I will provide a systematic account on the personhood of the Holy Spirit and some aspects of the work of the Holy Spirit in Reformed orthodoxy, particularly in the confessional documents. However, because of the enormous breadth of the doctrine of the Holy Spirit, I will focus particularly on several aspects of the work of the Holy Spirit which are pertinent to contemporary discussions and often perceived by the critics as neglected in the Reformed tradition. Those aspects of the work of the Holy Spirit are (1) creation and providence, (2) the church's unity, diversity of spiritual gifts, mission, and (3) social responsibility. These will be the topics to be explored and discussed in most of the chapters of the dissertation.

To achieve that purpose, I will divide this study into four parts. The first part (chapters 2 and 3) will give an overview on the themes of the doctrine of the Holy Spirit—his person and work—which have already been commonly identified by scholars. In this part I will also give documentary support for those themes from the confessions and catechisms, such as Scripture, the Trinity, Christ, salvation, the church, and sacraments.

---

and Reformed, 68.

Chapter 2 will deal with the first three aforementioned doctrines, and chapter 3 with the rest.

In the next three parts, I will deal with themes of the doctrine that have not received adequate treatment. In each part, I will discuss an aspect of the work of the Holy Spirit and do a critical analysis of some major Reformed confessions and catechisms of the sixteenth and seventeenth centuries, both of the structure of the confessional documents and of the content of articles that teach explicitly or implicitly the aspect of the work of the Holy Spirit being discussed in that chapter. The critical analysis will be done by setting the doctrine in both the historical context of the documents and the context of the scriptural reference that lie behind the doctrine, with the help of ancillary documents such as treatises and sermons mainly written by the framers of the confessional documents or their contemporaries.

Part Two (chapter 4) will explore and discuss the role of the Holy Spirit in creation and providence as treated in the Reformed confessions and catechisms. The Holy Spirit is the life-giver and life-sustainer actively working in creation and providence. All persons of the Trinity, including the Holy Spirit, work together in creation and providence, not only the heavens and the earth and all that is in them, but also invisible spirits, good and evil. The Holy Spirit is thus involved with all three aspects of divine providence, namely, preservation, concurrence, and government, a common distinction applied by the Reformed tradition.

Part Three (chapters 5 and 6) will discuss the role of the Holy Spirit in the building up of the church. Chapter 5 will deal with the role of the Holy Spirit in both the church's unity and diversity of gifts. The Holy Spirit unites and gathers all saints under Jesus Christ as their Head. The Holy Spirit is the Spirit that unites the church and—along with the Word—governs the church, the community of saints, and sanctifies and perfects the saints in this life to the end of the world. This teaching answers the contemporary concern for church unity with the principles of church unity under the headship of Christ. The second part of this chapter will deal with the teaching of the gifts of the Holy Spirit bestowed upon the church, their purpose and use. The Holy Spirit empowers and enables each member of the church to serve God and one another for the common good. The Reformed confessions and catechisms may not give as fully developed a treatment of the topic as we find today in contemporary discussions. However, they give the core principles essential for the development of the doctrine.

Chapter 6 will discuss the role of the Holy Spirit in the church's evangelistic mission. This chapter will explore and demonstrate the importance of the Holy Spirit in the church's evangelistic mission in the confessions and catechisms. The confessions and catechisms clearly teach that the Holy Spirit plays a significant role in the proclamation of the gospel through preaching and in the empowerment of the church, God's people, to be God's witnesses to the world. The preaching of the gospel is a ministry of the Spirit by which sinners are convinced of their sins and converted, built up in holiness and comfort, through faith, unto salvation. The Holy Spirit also works in true believers to produce faith and its fruits, that is, good works, so that by their godly living people may also be won over to Christ. As the confessions teach, the church is the church for a specific end, for a mission, that is, to glorify God and to benefit others, to proclaim the Gospel and to win others over to Christ.

Part Four (chapter 7) will discuss the role of the Holy Spirit in social responsibility. This chapter will explore the teaching of the Reformed confessions regarding good works and demonstrate that the Reformed confessions consistently teach that the Holy Spirit plays an important role in the social dimension of Christian life. The Spirit does so by working continually, renewing the elect that they may live more in obedience to God, doing what God commanded in his commandments. These commandments include the involvement of the elect in the political and social dimensions of life such as honoring parents, princes, rulers, and superior powers, saving the lives of innocent, defending the oppressed, and helping the poor. The confessions teach that, unless the Holy Spirit works in the heart and will of individuals, no one can perform any of those works in a way that pleases God. No one can do good works apart from the empowering and enabling activities of the Spirit. For the elect, social involvement is a responsibility that every believer has, as a part of his or her sanctification process that the Holy Spirit has initiated, empowered, and guided.

The final chapter, chapter 8, will wrap up the presentation of the doctrine of the Holy Spirit in the Reformed confessions by recapitulating all the conclusions of each preceding chapter. It will also provide some theological reflections on the characteristics of the treatment and the content of the doctrine of the Holy Spirit in the Reformed confessions.

PART ONE

CHAPTER 2

Doctrinal Themes Commonly Associated with the Holy Spirit in the Reformed Confessions and Catechisms – Part A

The first part of this dissertation, which comprises this and the next chapter, will deal with the treatment of some doctrinal themes commonly associated with the Holy Spirit in the Reformed confessions, such as Scripture, the Trinity, Christ, salvation, the church, and sacraments. Scholars in the past who have studied the theology of the Reformed confessions, such as Barth and Rohls, have already identified these themes as containing the doctrine of the Holy Spirit. However, they have not done much to document the places in the Reformed confessions where the Holy Spirit appears in relation to these themes. This and the next chapter will give primary source documentation and a more systematic account than what scholars in the past have done for these themes from the Reformed confessions. This chapter will discuss the treatment of the Holy Spirit in the Reformed confessions in relation to the doctrines of Scripture, the Trinity, and Christ, and the next chapter will discuss it in relation to several other doctrines, that is, the doctrines of salvation, the church, and sacraments.

It should be noted first that, with only few exceptions, the Reformed confessions of the sixteenth and seventeenth centuries do not treat the doctrine of the Holy Spirit independently, separated from other doctrines.[1]

---

1. As Muller indicates, "there was little attempt on the part of the various Reformers to present an independent locus on the Holy Spirit." Muller, *PRRD*, IV, 7.1 (333).

Even when some confessional documents have a separate article or chapter on the Holy Spirit, seemingly to treat it as an independent *locus*, they usually only contain the doctrinal statement regarding the deity of the Holy Spirit, or in a few cases also include some major aspects of the work of the Holy Spirit, such as faith, assurance of salvation, sanctification, and regeneration. The SC, BC, and TNA are three among the eight major confessions used in this dissertation that have a separate article or chapter on the Holy Spirit.[2] The catechisms of the sixteenth and seventeenth centuries, on the other hand, commonly discuss the doctrine of the Holy Spirit under the article of faith in the Apostles' Creed ("I believe in the Holy Spirit"), and in the sections pertaining to sacraments. The discussions of the Holy Spirit in those particular articles of faith, considering their nature as confessional statements, are short and not exhaustive.

However, instead of discussing the Holy Spirit in one independent chapter or heading, the confessions and catechisms of the sixteenth and seventeenth centuries discuss the Holy Spirit under several headings, due to the pervasive nature of the role of the Holy Spirit in Christian doctrine. Unlike the typical church dogmatics of the nineteenth and twentieth centuries, which commonly present the doctrine of the Holy Spirit under a separate chapter, or even volume, the Reformed confessions and catechisms of the sixteenth and seventeenth centuries tend to integrate the discussion of the Holy Spirit—his deity and works—into several doctrinal *loci*. Some critics criticize the Reformed confessional standards for having neglected the doctrine of the Holy Spirit, by basing the arguments on the fact that few independent headings are devoted to discuss the Holy Spirit exclusively. In so doing the critics overlook the breadth of the doctrine of the Holy Spirit and anachronistically force the modern theological *loci* into the theological *loci* followed by the Reformed confessional standards of the sixteenth and seventeenth centuries. The arguments are simply untenable.

In the introductory note to Kuyper's *The Work of the Holy Spirit*, Warfield points out that the doctrine of the Holy Spirit "has been preferably presented under its several rubrics or parts, rather than in its entirety."[3] Regarding

---

2. SC XII, BC XI, and TNA V.
3. *The Work of the Holy Spirit*, xxvii.

the fact that the WCF has no chapter on the Holy Spirit, Warfield rightly argues that instead of giving a chapter to the doctrine of the Holy Spirit, the confession prefers to spend nine chapters discussing it.[4] A closer look at the confession will also reveal that plenty more references have been made by the Westminster Assembly Divines in the Confession than Warfield has claimed. Only eleven out of thirty-three chapters of the Confession do not explicitly mention the Holy Spirit in the articles, and only five out of those eleven do not give any reference at all to the Holy Spirit, either in the articles or in the biblical proof texts.[5]

Another good example of the aforementioned method of treating of the doctrine of the Holy Spirit is the HC. The Catechism makes references to the Holy Spirit in as many as thirty-three out of one hundred twenty-nine sets of Questions and Answers. Fred H. Klooster argues that the entire catechism is Holy Spirit-oriented. He reveals that the Holy Spirit plays the key role in interpreting Q/A 53-129. Moreover, as Q/A 53 indicates, "comfort"—the Catechism's overarching theme—is the Spirit's work. Therefore, the catechism is worthy to be called as "a catechism of the Holy Spirit."[6] Whether or not the HC is correctly claimed as Holy Spirit-oriented, Klooster has demonstrated how pervasively the Holy Spirit is discussed in the catechism.

Carefully observed, the Reformed confessions and catechisms of the sixteenth and seventeenth centuries treat the doctrine of the Holy Spirit in a similar fashion, as Warfield and Klooster point out, that is, always in relation to other doctrines. There are some common places or doctrines in the confessional documents where the Holy Spirit is explicitly discussed that scholars in the past have identified and discussed. But there are also

---

4. *The Work of the Holy Spirit*, xxvii.
5. See WCF VI, XXII, XXIV, XXX, and XXXI. WCF V, IX, XV, XXIII, XXIX, and XXXIII do not mention the Holy Spirit in the articles, but clearly presuppose or assume the activity of the Holy Spirit, as indicated by the corresponding biblical proof texts that accompany the articles.
6. Fred H. Klooster, *A Mighty Comfort: The Christian Faith according to the Heidelberg Catechism* (Grand Rapids: CRC Publications, 1990), 59-62; Appendices 4a-b, 124-125. See also Appendix 5 in page 126 for Klooster's "Systematic Summary of Heidelberg Catechism References to the Holy Spirit."

other doctrinal themes in which the role of the Holy Spirit has not been adequately explored and exposed in the history of scholarship.

This and the next chapter will focus particularly on those doctrines in the confessional documents that have been commonly identified as associated with the Holy Spirit, both the personhood and the work of the Holy Spirit. The subsequent chapters will deal in turn with the doctrines that have not yet received adequate treatment in the history of scholarship. This chapter in particular will briefly present the teaching of the Reformed confessions concerning the Holy Spirit in the doctrines of Scripture, Trinity, and Christ. The doctrine of Scripture will start this discussion, as Scripture is regarded by the Reformed as the sole foundation of theology (*principium cognoscendi theologiae*), upon which all theology should be founded.

The Holy Spirit and the Doctrine of Scripture

The Reformed confessions share with Lutheran and Roman Catholic theology the assumption of the twofold revelation of God. God reveals himself to humankind through his works and Word. The FC, of which the draft was the joint work of Calvin, Beza, and Viret, begins its second article with the statement that God's self-revelation to humankind is twofold, in his works and Word, and that the Holy Scripture is God's Word which was "committed to writing."[7] The BC, originally a personal confession of faith composed by Guido de Brès and then slightly revised by Francis Junius, affirms that the Holy Scripture is the revealed Word of God put in writing at the command of God by God's servants, the prophets, and apostles "being moved by the Holy Spirit."[8] The SC, of which John Knox was believed to be the chief author, identifies Scripture as "the written Word of God" and the Holy Spirit as the one "by whom the Scriptures were written" and who "uniformly speaks within the body of the Scriptures."[9] It is God the Holy Spirit who wrote and still speaks through Scripture.

---

7. FC II; see also WCF I.1, 4.
8. BC III.
9. SC XVIII; see also BC III.

The Reformed confessions identify Scripture as the Word of God. However, both terms—Scripture and the Word of God—are employed by the confessions without blurring their distinction. The confessions understand the term "Word" as having several referents—the Second Person of the Trinity (the eternal, essential Word), Scripture (the written Word), oracles of God (the unwritten Word), the preaching of the Word or the gospel (the preached Word), and so forth—that correspond to the many ways by which God has revealed himself.[10] Heinrich Bullinger—as well as Calvin, his contemporary—acknowledges that "Word of God" has several referents in the SHC, but he asserts more clearly in his *Decades*:

> For *verbum Dei*, "the word of God," doth signify the virtue and power of God: it is also put for the Son of God, which is the second person in the most reverend Trinity. For that saying of the holy evangelist is evident to all men, "The word was made flesh." But in this treatise of ours, the word of God doth properly signify the speech of God, and the revealing of God's will; first of all uttered in a lively-expressed voice by the mouth of Christ, the prophets and apostles; and after that again registered in writings, which are rightly called "holy and divine scriptures." The word doth shew the mind of him out of whom it cometh: therefore the word of God doth make declaration of God.[11]

---

10. See, for examples, "The First Confession of Basel (1534)," in Cochrane, *Reformed Confessions of the Sixteenth Century* (hereinafter FCB), I, XII; FC II, III, VII, VIII; BC II, III, VIII, X; TNA II, XX; SHC I.1. Rohls also fails to see this when he makes a rigid equation of the Word of God and Christ (in the gospel) and thus asserts that the understanding of the Word of God in the orthodox confessional writings—from the First Helvetic Confession to the Helvetic Consensus Formula—is a departure from the understanding of the Word of God in the earlier confessional writings, such as The Synodical Declaration of Berne and Zwingli's Sixty-seven Articles. He argues that the shift of doctrinal understanding is marked by the strict identification of Scripture as the Word of God, a move from the identification of Christ himself as the only Word of God. Rohls, *Reformed Confessions*, 33-37.

11. Heinrich Bullinger, *The Decades of Henry Bullinger*, trans. H. I., ed. Thomas Harding, 4 vols. (Cambridge: The University Press, 1849-1852), I.i (37); cf. Calvin, *Institutes*, I.vi.2-4, I.xiii.7. The Reformed confessions of the sixteenth and seventeenth centuries, therefore, reflect the continuity between the view of the Reformers and of orthodoxy on

The Reformed confessions use the term "Word of God" to refer to God's revelation, God's speech in particular, and to denote diverse ways by which God reveals himself and his will—his declaration—to human beings, that far exceed in clarity, sufficiency, and efficacy his revelation through his works of creation and preservation throughout the history of revelation.[12] Only in this sense, therefore, is Christ correctly understood as the ultimate revelation of God, in which all revelations culminate, as he is the eternal Word of God who became flesh, made his dwelling among us, and has made God and his will known (Jn. 1:1, 14, 18). Calvin, in CC45, teaches that Christ, as a prophet, "was the sovereign messenger and ambassador of God His Father, to give a full exposition of God's will toward the world, and so put an end to all prophecies and revelations (Heb. 1:2)."[13] On the other hand, even though Scripture is the Word of God written, when discussing it, the confessions by no means regard it as the Word of God only in a derivative sense, or as anything less than the Word of God. Scripture is truly the Word of God for its revelatory character, while its writtenness is taken to denote how it historically came into being, that is, written by holy men inspired by God through the agency of the Holy Spirit. In light of the history of revelation, after the cessation of the direct revelations of God, including the revelation of God through Christ in his incarnate state, God now speaks to us through Scripture, as God's written Word, and the biblical preaching of the gospel, as God's preached Word. As Bullinger maintains in the SHC,

---

the matter of "the Word of God," as both typically hold a multileveled understanding of Word, a thesis convincingly argued by Muller against Heinrich Heppe, Emil Brunner, et al. See Muller, *PRRD*, II, 3.3. Heppe makes a contrast between Calvin, and his immediate successors, and "later dogmaticians," on their views of the Word of God, i.e., "the word spoken by God to individual men" and "the word brought to record by inspiration" respectively. Heinrich Heppe, *Reformed Dogmatics: Set Out and Illustrated from the Sources*, trans. G. T. Thomson (Grand Rapids: Baker Book House, 1978), 15. In making such a contrast, Heppe simply overlooks the fact that both Calvin and "later dogmaticians" typically employ a multileveled understanding of the Word of God and never hesitate to identify Scripture as the Word of God.

12. See FC II; SC IV; BC II, III; SHC I.2; WCF I.1.

13. CC45 Q/A 39. In the same line of thought as Calvin, Zacharias Ursinus calls Christ as "the greatest and chief prophet," and "the Word" because "he is the person that spake to the fathers, and brought forth the living word, or gospel from the bosom of the Father." Zacharias Ursinus, *The Commentary of Dr. Zacharias Ursinus on the Heidelberg Catechism*, trans. G. W. Williard (Phillipsburg: P&R, 1985), 173-174.

originally his personal statement of faith, "neither any other Word of God is to be invented nor is to be expected from heaven."[14]

Scripture is the Word of God, since God speaks through it. Bullinger states in the SHC that the canonical Scripture is "the true Word of God;" it records and contains God's speech once given to "the fathers, prophets, apostles," and "God still speaks" through it.[15] To maintain the divine origin and authority of the Holy Scripture, Bullinger in his *Compendium christianae religionis* of 1556 emphatically states that the Holy Scripture is the true Word of God that needs no human endorsement to become authentic.[16] This identification of Scripture with the Word of God does not establish the doctrine of inspiration and authority of Scripture, but rather, the doctrine of inspiration and authority of Scripture lead to a conviction that Scripture is the Word of God.[17] Scripture is identified as the Word of God simply because the Reformed confessions believe and teach Scripture as God's speech, that is, God's Word, for it records and contains God's speech and God still speaks through it through the Holy Spirit.

The Reformed confessions teach that, with respect to both its content and form, Scripture is the Word of God because of the divine authorship of Scripture, attested by the inspiration of the Holy Spirit.[18] With respect to its content, the Reformed confessions teach that God himself initiated

---

14. SHC I.4.

15. SHC I.1.

16. *Compendium christianae religionis* (Zurich, 1556), trans. as *Commonplaces of Christian Religion* (London: Tho. East and H. Middleton, 1572), 9-10. Cf. Barth, *The Theology of the Reformed Confessions*, 59. Barth disagrees with Bullinger, the BC, the Westminster Standards, and some other Reformed confessions on this particular point. For Barth, the Holy Scripture is "intended to be the witness of revelation," not the revelation in and of itself.

17. Cf. Rohls, *Reformed Confessions*, 36-37. The identification of the Word of God and Scripture, Rohls argues, leads the Reformed confessions to a theological consequence, that "ultimately the word of God is no longer determined with respect to content, but purely with respect to form"—a remark very similar to that of Heppe. Rohls then concludes that the identification of the Word of God with Scripture "entails the assertion of the inspiration of Scripture," which later must be necessarily followed by "the thesis of God's authorship." See also Heppe, *Reformed Dogmatics*, 16-18.

18. Cf. Rohls, *Reformed Confessions, 36-37*. In Rohls' view, the doctrine of inspiration and divine authorship of Scripture in the Reformed confessions are grounded on the identification of the Word of God with the form of Scripture (the canonical books of Scripture), rather than with the content of Scripture (the gospel, or Christ).

and "commanded" to put into writing his speech, and reveals himself through it. It is God, the divine Author, who actually works through the instrumentality of human authors to put his Word into holy writings. The books of Scripture are breathed or inspired by God, through the agency of the Holy Spirit. The BC describes more of how Scriptures came into being, that holy men of God spoke as they were moved by the Holy Spirit, and later God commanded them to commit his revealed Word to writing.[19] The idea of human authorship is never denied, but the divine authorship of Scripture, or its origin, through the agency of the Holy Spirit is clearly highlighted. The SC even asserts plainly that Scriptures were written by the Spirit of God.[20] It is the Holy Spirit that moved and inspired the human authors, the "holy men," to write the Holy Scripture. Since it is God who speaks through Scripture, then the authority of Scripture depends solely on God as its sole and divine author, not on the church, men, or angels.[21] The authority of Scripture is solely derived from the Author of Scripture. Once the divine authorship of Scripture is established, its authority follows.

The Reformed confessions teach that, with respect to the form of Scripture (that is, the canonical books), the books of Scripture receive their canonicity not from human beings, nor from any ecclesiastical decision. They are canonical, or holy, solely by virtue of the Word of God that they contain. Deriving the principle from 2 Tim. 3:15-16 and 2 Ptr. 1:21, the FC asserts that what makes the books of Scripture canonical, or qualitatively different from other books, is the fact that "the Word contained in these books has proceeded from God."[22] The church does not grant the canonical status to the books of Scripture, but only recognizes them as such. The BC states that the books of Scripture are "holy and canonical" and "all things contained in them" are from God, "not so much because the church receives and approves them as such."[23] If Holy Scripture is the written Word of God, then, as Heinrich Heppe correctly states, to

---

19. BC III.
20. SC XVIII.
21. GC I; FC V; SC XIX; BC V; SHC I.1; WCF I.5.
22. FC V; see also BC III.
23. BC V.

Scripture belong only "the books written by prophets and apostles, that is, by those persons whom God illumined in a special way with His Spirit."[24] Bullinger in the SHC states that the Scriptures are canonical because God spoke through the human writers of the Scriptures.[25] In his *Commonplaces* Bullinger explains further that the writings of the Bible are severed from others, including the Apocrypha, and called holy primarily because they are inspired by the Holy Spirit and written by holy men.[26] He also states that all things "which are in the Bible, are the worde of God, and when God speaketh all fleshe must bee still."[27]

Apart from asserting the Holy Spirit as the divine author who inspired the biblical authors to write the canonical books of Scripture, none of the Reformed confessions, not even the Formula Consensus Helvetica (1675),[28] includes a detailed doctrine of inspiration, as none of them "saw fit to draw" it into "the realm of confession."[29] Questions regarding a theory of inspiration, or the mode or manner of inspiration, are thereby left to dogmatic systems or individual theologians to deal with and answer.

Nonetheless, most of the Reformed confessions deal with the question concerning the recognition of Scripture as inspired by the Holy Spirit. How is the canonicity of the books of Scripture grounded? The confessions typically give a twofold answer to these questions. Negatively, one recognizes the books as canonical not by any ecclesiastical decision, nor

---

24. Heppe, *Reformed Dogmatics*, 12.

25. SHC I.1.

26. Bullinger, *Commonplaces*, 1. Bullinger also adds that the holy writings are so dependent on God that they "teach nothing but that which is holy, no prophane thinge, no errors."

27. Bullinger, *Commonplaces*, 10.

28. The *Formula Consensus Helvetica* (1675), the last of the orthodox Reformed confessions, is significantly important on this matter. The *Formula* contains in its first three canons the most rigid of verbal inspiration theories. The second canon of the *Formula* states that even the vowels of the original Hebrew Bible handed down by the Hebrew Church were inspired. For the English translation of the *Formula*, see Martin I. Klauber, "The Helvetic Formula Consensus (1675): An Introduction and Translation," *Trinity Journal* 11, no. 1 (Spring, 1990): 103-123. Muller correctly states that the Formula, "in many of its points, steps beyond the bounds usually assigned to confessional documents and elevates fine points of theological system to the level of fundamental articles of faith." Muller, *PRRD*, II, 2.1 (B.5, 92).

29. Muller, *PRRD*, II, 2.1 (B.5, 94).

"by the common accord and consent of the Church," as the FC states.[30] Positively, the canonicity of the books is recognized subjectively by the inward testimony of the Holy Spirit (*testimonium Spiritus Sancti internum*), and objectively by the divine attributes imprinted in the books of Scripture as the work of the Holy Spirit.

The FC confesses that the testimony and inward illumination of the Holy Spirit "enables us to distinguish [canonical books] from other ecclesiastical books upon which, however useful, we cannot found any articles of faith."[31] The BC teaches that one knows the Scriptures are canonical because above all "the Holy Spirit testifies in our hearts that they are from God."[32] The preeminence of the books of Scripture over other books with regard to content and form, that is, the superior literary qualities of the biblical writings, has never been doubted. The WCF testifies that Scripture is self-authenticating (*autopistos*). However, although the books of Scripture may self-evidently manifest their preeminence, authenticating themselves to be the Word of God, "our full persuasion and assurance of the infallible truth and divine authority thereof, is from the inward work of the Holy Spirit," who bears witness "by, and with the Word" in the hearts of believers.[33]

The "by, and with the Word (*per verbum et cum verbo*)" in the article means that the recognition of Scripture as the Word of God goes both ways simultaneously. On the one hand, the Holy Spirit bears witness that Scripture is the Word of God by speaking through it, and only through it "[t]he whole Counsel of God concerning all things necessary for his own

---

30. FC IV. The BC also gives a similar testimony on this, that the church receives the books as holy and canonical "not so much because the church receives and approves them as such but above all because the Holy Spirit testifies in our hearts that they are from God." BC V.

31. FC IV.

32. BC V.

33. The WCF lists some literary features to argue for the preeminence of the books of Scripture with regard to the content and the form, such as "the heavenliness of the Matter, the efficacy of the Doctrine, the Majesty of the stile, the consent of all the parts, the scope of the whole (which is, to give all glory to God,) the full discovery it makes of the only way of mans salvation, the many other incomparable Excellencies, and the intire perfection thereof." WCF I.5. WLC Q/A 4 also states that, although the Scriptures "manifest themselves to be the Word of God," the Holy Spirit "bearing witness by and with the Scriptures in the heart of man, is alone able fully to persuade it that they are the very Word of God."

Glory, man's Salvation, Faith and Life."[34] No new revelation of the Holy Spirit is to be expected at any time outside of and apart from Scripture. This implies that the Holy Spirit works only mediately through Scripture and with Scripture. On the other hand, the Holy Spirit bears witness with the Word in the hearts of believers, affirming Scripture's identity, and its authority thereof, as the Word of God.[35]

The Reformed confessions, as exemplified by the BC, WCF, and WLC, believe that Scripture, as the Word of God, bears in itself attributes or marks of divinity manifested in both its preeminent literary qualities and content. However, these self-evident qualities of Scripture in and of themselves are not sufficient to effectually persuade and assure human beings that Scripture is the Word of God. Furthermore, the Reformed confessions in no way deny, nor undermine, the arguments from reason based on evidences—both intrinsic and extrinsic—that are set for the affirmation of the inspired holy writings. The confessions regard them as also simply insufficient to bring full persuasion to believers in and of themselves, apart from the inward testimony of the Holy Spirit.[36] The confessions clearly follow Calvin in maintaining the priority of the inward testimony of the Holy Spirit for the recognition of Scripture as the Word of God, without denigrating the marks of divinity of Scripture and arguments from reason based on them.[37] In his *Institutes* Calvin explains that to attain to the certainty of the divinity of Scripture through disputation is to do things "backwards."[38] Unless the certainty established by the Holy Spirit, "higher

---

34. WCF I.6.

35. This teaching of the two-way testimony of the Holy Spirit in the confessions is patterned after Calvin's teaching. Calvin asserts that the same Spirit, "who has spoken through the mouths of the prophets must penetrate into our hearts to persuade us that they faithfully proclaimed what had been divinely commanded;" or, in Barth's words, "the Holy Spirit here (in the reader) connects to the Holy Spirit there (in the Scriptures)." See Calvin, *Institutes*, I.vii.4; Barth, *The Theology of the Reformed Confessions*, 57.

36. Thomas Vincent, a prominent English Puritan of the seventeenth century, in his commentary of the WSC, proposes nine arguments for the divine imprint of Scripture, and concludes that without the testimony and teaching of the Holy Spirit "all other Arguments will be ineffectual to perswade unto a saving Faith." Thomas Vincent, *An Explicatory Catechism* (Glasgow: Robert Sanders, 1692), 9.

37. Muller, *PRRD*, II, 4.3 (C.1).

38. Calvin, *Institutes*, I.vii.4.

and stronger than any human judgment," be present, "it will be vain to fortify the authority of Scripture by arguments, to establish it by common agreement of the church, or to confirm it with other helps."[39] But, Calvin continues, "those arguments—not strong enough before to engraft and fix the certainty of Scripture in our minds—become very useful aids," once that certainty is embraced.[40] For Calvin, the arguments are nevertheless "useful aids" that provide "wonderful confirmation" for believers as they ponder "the economy of the divine wisdom" manifest throughout Scripture.[41]

The significant role of the Holy Spirit as the revealer through and the author of Scripture in establishing the canonicity, the divine authorship, and authority of Scripture leads to the role of the Holy Spirit as the teacher and interpreter of Scripture. In the GC Calvin already indicates the need of divine illumination for the "natural man" to come to the right knowledge of God.[42] Later, in CC37, Calvin explains in more detail that only by the Holy Spirit enlightening "with his light," one may come to that knowledge through Scripture. Calvin adds, "without the Spirit there is in us nothing but darkness of understanding and perversity of heart."[43]

As theological controversies and disputations continued to arise in the second half of the sixteenth century, there was a growing need to make the church's teaching regarding the role of the Holy Spirit in the interpretation

---

39. Calvin, *Institutes*, I.viii.1.

40. Calvin, *Institutes*, I.viii.1. Cf. Barth, *The Theology of the Reformed Confessions*, 57-60. Barth sees all other arguments presented besides the inward testimony of the Holy Spirit (that God speaks) in some Reformed confessions, such as the BC, WCF, & WLC, as evidence of struggle to acknowledge the sole grounding principle for Scripture's authority. For Barth, the inclusion of "other reasons for the authority of Scripture" is a scholastic attempt that eventually overshadows the sufficiency of the inward testimony of the Holy Spirit as the sole ground of Scripture's authority. He claims that "its one truly decisive ground is completely forgotten in the plethora of arguments." Barth then contrasts these attempts of the Reformed confessions with Calvin, who says that "the highest proof of Scripture derives in general from the fact that God in person speaks in it." Here Barth fails to see that Calvin, along with the authors of the BC and the Westminster Standards, maintains that the internal testimony of the Holy Spirit holds priority over all other arguments from reason, but is not exclusive from them. Barth also overlooks the fact that Calvin himself lists thirteen arguments from reason following his discussion of the inward testimony of the Holy Spirit.

41. Calvin, *Institutes*, I.viii.1-13. See Muller, *PRRD*, II, 4.3 (A.2).

42. GC IV.

43. CC37 XX ("I believe in the Holy Spirit").

of Scripture into confessional norms. The confessional statements in this period mark the formalization of the priority and normative character of Scripture as the sole authoritative norm of theology, the sole cognitive foundation of theology (*principium cognoscendi theologiae*), on which all church doctrines should be founded and by which theological controversies should be sorted out;[44] or, in the words of the Irish Articles, "The ground of our religion and the rule of faith and all saving truth is the Word of God, contained in the holy Scripture."[45]

Among the major Reformed confessions, the First Helvetic Confession (hereinafter FHC), SC, SHC, and WCF provide explicit and more detailed discussions regarding the interpretation of Scripture, as Barth also identifies.[46] These confessions teach that, in the face of theological controversies, the church is not to seek new revelation of the Holy Spirit or guidance from theologians or traditions. Nor is the church to establish its own authority to solve the controversies, but first and foremost, the church is to seek the inward illumination of the Holy Spirit to understand things revealed in Scripture regarding the disputed matters. The role of the Holy Spirit as the Divine Author of Scripture is seen by these confessions as that which undergirds the unity of Scripture and its interpretation or interpretive principles.

The Reformed churches were set to establish Scripture as the sole authoritative and normative foundation of theology that holds priority over the church, private theologians, and traditions. Therefore, regarding the interpretation of Scripture, the confessions deem it necessary to provide boundaries for interpreting Scripture, rather than a set of instructive rules or normative exegetical models. As a result, the confessions underscore

---

44. For a detailed discussion concerning the concept of Scripture as foundation of theology in its Protestant development, see Muller, *PRRD*, II, 3.1-3.5. The Protestant confessions unanimously declare Scripture as holding the sole authoritative norm of saving knowledge of God, and tend to place the confessional statements concerning Scripture (as the cognitive foundation or *principium cognoscendi* of revealed theology) adjacent to those of God (the essential foundation of theology or *principium essendi* of all theology). As Muller points out, this placement pattern is manifest in the more systematically ordered Reformed confessions, such as the FHC, SHC, FC, and BC; the pattern was later followed in the seventeenth century by the Irish Articles and WCF.
45. "The Irish Articles of Religion A.D. 1615," in Schaff, *The Creeds of Christendom with a History and Critical Notes* (hereinafter IA), I.
46. Barth, *The Theology of the Reformed Confessions*, 55.

the *sola scriptura* axiom of the Reformation by setting out, among others, two important hermeneutical principles, namely, *analogia Scripturae* and *analogia fidei*, which were founded upon the firm belief that the Holy Spirit is the Divine Author of Scripture.[47]

The FHC, drawn up by Bullinger, Grynaeus, and Myconius, having stated the holy Scripture—the Word of God inspired by the Holy Spirit—as "the most ancient, most perfect and loftiest teaching," asserts that The Holy Scripture is its own interpreter (*sacra Scriptura sui ipsius interpres*) and it is to be explained by the rule of faith and love: "This holy, divine Scripture is to be interpreted in no other way than out of itself and is to be explained by the rule of faith and love."[48] The Confession then continues to make a distinction between the teachings according to the rule set out above and those departed from it, or, between the right tradition of the holy fathers and early teachers and "all other human doctrines and articles."[49] While the former are considered as teachings through which God has spoken and operated, the latter are those which lead believers away from God and true faith.

In the same way, the SC teaches that the interpretation of Scripture belongs not to any man, nor to any church or tradition, but "to the Spirit of God by whom the Scriptures were written." Barth correctly identifies this underlying fundamental presupposition when he states that "the actual expositor of the text can only be its author, that is, the Holy Spirit."[50] The Confession also maintains that the Holy Spirit is the Spirit of unity, who

---

47. The analogy of Scripture is a principle which evaluates the meaning of unclear or ambiguous texts by comparing them with clear and unambiguous texts that refer to the same teaching or event. The analogy of faith is a principle which evaluates the meaning of unclear or ambiguous texts by testing them for consistency against what has been believed by the church, i.e., the rule of faith (and love), *regula fidei* (*et caritatis*), that comprise the whole of Christian life and belief historically throughout the church age. Both principles are distinct but related. The analogy of faith, based on the clear and plain passages of Scripture is "simply an extension" of the analogy of Scripture. For descriptions of both principles and their seventeenth century definitions and uses, see Henry M. Knapp, "Understanding the Mind of God: John Owen and Seventeenth-Century Exegetical Methodology" (Ph.D. diss., Calvin Theological Seminary, 2002), 63-68, 72-76.

48. "The First Helvetic Confession, 1536," in Cochrane, *Reformed Confessions of the Sixteenth Century*, I-II.

49. FHC III-IV.

50. Barth, *The Theology of the Reformed Confessions*, 55.

cannot contradict himself, so that the disputed biblical passage or sentence should be discerned in light of "what the Holy Spirit uniformly speaks within the body of the Scriptures and what Christ Jesus Himself did and commanded."[51] Therefore, if an interpretation or opinion of any theologian, or church, or ecclesiastical council, is contrary to "the plain Word of God written in any other passage of the Scripture, it is most certain that this is not the true understanding and meaning of the Holy Ghost," and thus should not be received and be denied accordingly.[52]

The SHC, while affirming the *analogia Scripturae* and *analogia fidei* principles, moves further by describing how the *analogia Scripturae* should be applied:

> But we hold that interpretation of the Scripture to be orthodox and genuine which is gleaned from the Scriptures themselves (from the nature of the language in which they were written, likewise according to the circumstances in which they were set down, and expounded in the light of like and unlike passages and of many and clearer passages) and which agree with the rule of faith and love, and contributes much to the glory of God and man's salvation.[53]

The SHC maintains the priority of Scripture over the interpretations of the church fathers, councils, and traditions; all derive their authority solely from Scripture as the Word of God insofar as they agree with it, and are to be rejected when they are found contrary to it.[54] God himself is the only Judge, "who proclaims by the Holy Scriptures what is true, what is false, what is to be followed, or what is to be avoided."[55] The unity of the apostolic teaching, thus of Scripture, is assumed and affirmed by the Confession, based on the work of the Holy Spirit in the apostles: "The apostolic men"

---

51. SC XVIII.
52. SC XVIII.
53. SHC II.1.
54. SHC II.2, II.3, II.5.
55. SHC II.4.

did not set forth things contrary to each other, as they "walked in the same way, and jointly by the same Spirit did all things (II Cor. 12:18)."⁵⁶

The WCF asserts the sufficiency of Scripture, meaning that "The whole Counsel of God concerning all things necessary for his own Glory, mans Salvation, Faith and life" can be found in Scripture, either "expressly set down in Scripture, or by good and necessary consequence may be deduced from Scriptures." Therefore, "nothing at any time is to be added" unto that which has been laid out in Scripture, whether by "new Revelation of the Spirit, or traditions of men."⁵⁷ The WSC affirms that Scripture is to be "the only rule to direct us, how we may glorify and enjoy" God.⁵⁸ Thomas Watson, in his commentary on the WSC, states that Scripture is a complete rule, "a full and perfect canon," as it shows "the *Credenda*, what we are to believe," "the Agenda, what we are to practise," and "an exact model of religion" that perfectly instructs us "in the deep things of God."⁵⁹ Barth remarks that "*Holy Scripture is the perfect revelation; or, it is the work of the Holy Spirit.*"⁶⁰

The illumination of the Spirit, not new revelation of the Spirit, is necessary for "the saving understanding" of things revealed in the Word.⁶¹ The Spirit is the Teacher who teaches people of God to know God and his counsel through Scripture. God who speaks in Scripture only can enable one to understand Scripture, the WLC teaches.⁶² WCF uses Jn. 6:45 and 1 Cor. 2:9-12 as references for the Holy Spirit teaching people of God through Scripture. When affirming the *sacra Scriptura sui ipsius interpres* principle, the dynamic picture of the Holy Spirit speaking through Scripture always comes to the fore. Watson asserts,

---

56. SHC II.5, II.6.
57. WCF I.6.
58. WSC Q/A 2.
59. Thomas Watson, *A Body of Practical Divinity* (London: Thomas Parkhurst, 1692), 15.
60. Barth, *The Theology of the Reformed Confessions*, 55; emphasis his.
61. WCF I.6.
62. WLC Q/A 157.

> The Scripture is to be its own interpreter; or rather the Spirit speaking in it: nothing can cut the diamond but the diamond; nothing can interpret Scripture but Scripture; the Sun best discovers its self by its own Beams; the Scripture interprets itself in easie places to the Understanding.[63]

The WCF also confesses that the Holy Spirit is the supreme Judge by which all controversies of religion are to be resolved and all other doctrines are to be examined. There can be no other judge but "the Holy Spirit speaking in the Scripture, in whose sentence we are to rest."[64]

While acknowledging that not all things in Scripture are equally plain in themselves, the WCF also believes in the clarity (or *perspicuitas*) of Scripture in things necessary to be known and believed for salvation.[65] Insofar as salvation of the church is concerned, Scripture is sufficient, clear, and effectual, but never without the work of the Holy Spirit illumining people of God so they could arrive at the proper and true knowledge of the revealed Word of God written in Scripture.[66] Even for things obscurely revealed in Scripture, God the Spirit works in and through his people as his instruments, by giving some of them gifts for interpreting difficult passages in Scripture. God has given his people "so much of the Spirit of Discerning," "such a measure of Wisdom and Discretion" that they can discern "between Truth and Errour, and judge what is sound and what is spurious."[67] Scripture itself is to be the sole infallible rule of interpretation of Scripture (*analogia Scripturae*): "when there is a question about the true and full sense of any Scripture (which is not manifold, but one) it must be searched and known by other places that speak more clearly."[68]

---

63. Watson, *A Body of Practical Divinity*, 16.
64. WCF I.10. See also Muller, *PRRD*, II, 5.5 (C).
65. WCF I.7.
66. WCF I.6, I.7; WLC Q/A 2. For a detailed discussion of the Reformed orthodox understanding of the sufficiency, perspicuity, and efficacy of Scripture, see Muller, *PRRD*, II, 5.3 (B.5), 5.4 (B).
67. Watson, *A Body of Practical Divinity*, 16.
68. WCF I.9.

The Holy Spirit and the Doctrine of the Trinity

Perhaps there is no other theological *locus* in the sixteenth and seventeenth centuries dogmatic works where the divinity and the personhood of the Holy Spirit are extensively discussed and elaborated than the doctrine of God, particularly the doctrine of the Trinity. The discussions or statements of the Holy Spirit—especially of the divinity and personhood of the Holy Spirit—in that *locus* found in the confessional documents are quite extensive, and undoubtedly far from merely being undeveloped as some critics allege.

While decidedly adhering to the Western trinitarian tradition (in contrast to the Greek Orthodox tradition, which holds the single procession view of the Holy Spirit: the Holy Spirit proceeds solely from the Father), particularly on the topic concerning *filioque*, the Reformed confessions did not merely replicate the older formulations of the doctrine. Instead of just making references to the standard formulations of the older trinitarian creeds (such as the Nicene and Athanasian creeds) and the early church doctors (such as St. Hilary, St. Athanasius, St. Ambrose, and St. Cyril), the confessions followed their paths and elaborated the arguments at various points to meet the need of the Reformed churches for a standard of orthodoxy regarding the Trinity, as they dealt with the recurring threats from the antitrinitarian foes of all sects and heresies. Only a few Reformed confessions explicitly identified the heresies and heretics that they took into account, while others did not. Bullinger gives quite an extensive list of the heresies and heretics in SHC, which includes: the Monarchians, Novatians, Praxeas, Patripassians, Sabellius, Paul of Samosata, Aëtius, Macedonius, Anthropomorphites, and Arius, as well as the Jews and Mohammedans who reject the Trinity at all cost.[69] In the late second half of the sixteenth century, the Socinians came publicly to the stage and joined other heretics to renounce the orthodox Christian doctrine of the Trinity. With these antitrinitarian debates serving as the backdrop, the formalization of the

---

69. SHC III.5. BC gives a similar list: Jews, Muslims, Marcion, Mani, Praxeas, Sabellius, Paul of Samosata, and Arius.

refined doctrine of the divinity and personhood of the Holy Spirit made its way to the Reformed confessions of the sixteenth and seventeenth centuries.

In response to heresies and heretics that deny the divinity of the Holy Spirit, the Reformed confessions seamlessly orchestrated their arguments of the equal divinity of the Holy Spirit with the Father and the Son in a number of articles of faith, while presenting what the Reformed churches believe concerning several matters. The arguments set forth in the confessions pertain to the origin, the attributes, the worship, and the work of the Holy Spirit.

The Reformed confessions unanimously hold firm the orthodox belief in one only, true, living and almighty God, "whom we are both to worship and serve, and in whom we are to put all our confidence and hope."[70] This one and only God is, in the words of the FCB, "God the Father, God the Son, God the Holy Spirit, one holy, divine Trinity, three Persons and one single, eternal, almighty God, in essence and substance, and not three gods."[71] "When we name the Father, Son, and Holy Spirit, we do not imagine three gods," Calvin says in CC37.[72] When one talks about the unity of the Godhead, it is not the unity of many distinct essences that is referred to, but is instead the unity of the distinct persons in one simple, undivided essence (one *ousia*), the sole divine essence. God is not divided, although there are three distinct persons in one Godhead.[73] Rohls rightly

---

70. GC II.

71. FCB I. It is acknowledged that the terms *ousia* and *hypostasis* were used interchangeably for the divine unity in the late fourth century, as exemplified in the anathemas of the Nicene Creed and in some works of Athanasius. But as Cornelius Plantinga and Zizioulas rightly point out, the Cappadocian Fathers chose *ousia* (parallel to essence or substance) as the main oneness term, reserving *hypostasis* (subsistence) for what Father, Son, and Spirit are individually. See Cornelius Plantinga, Jr., "Social Trinity and Tritheism," in *Trinity, Incarnation, and Atonement*, eds. Ronald J. Feenstra and Cornelius Plantinga, Jr. (Notre Dame: University of Notre Dame Press, 1989), 21-47; "Gregory of Nyssa and the Social Analogy of the Trinity," *The Thomist* 50 (1986): 325-352; and John D. Zizioulas, "The Doctrine of the Holy Trinity: The Significance of the Cappadocian Contribution," in *Trinitarian Theology Today: Essays on Divine Being and Act*, ed. Christoph Schwöbel (Edinburgh: T&T Clark, 1995), 44-60. As a result, the Latin terms *essentia* (essence) and *substantia* (substance), without any significant difference in meaning are later used interchangeably to translate *ousia*.

72. CC37 XX.

73. CC45 Q/A 19, 20; see also BC VIII; HC Q/A 25; SHC III.3.

points this out when he notes that according to the Reformed Confessions the persons' differentiation implies "no plurality of gods and thus no division of the divine essence."[74]

Since there is only one divine substance, simple and undivided, there is no rank or level of divinity in the Godhead. WSC teaches that the three persons are "one God, the same in substance, equal in power and glory."[75] In commenting on the WSC regarding the three persons in the Godhead, Watson remarks that "one person is not God more then [sic] another."[76] Therefore, all divine persons of the Trinity, although distinct from one another, are equally divine.

The Holy Spirit, as one of the three distinct persons in the "one sole and simple divine essence," is "of the same substance" (or consubstantial), and thereby "equal in eternity and power" with the Father and the Son.[77] The Holy Spirit, the SC confesses, is "God, equal with the Father and with His Son."[78] Perhaps Bullinger's statement of the matter reveals clearly the heart of the argument, when he states in the SHC:

> Thus there are not three gods, but three persons, consubstantial, coeternal, and coequal; distinct with respect to hypostases, and with respect to order, the one preceding the other yet without any inequality. For according to the nature or essence they are so joined together that they are one God, and the divine nature is common to the Father, Son and Holy Spirit.[79]

The Holy Spirit is distinct from the Father and the Son by proceeding eternally from the Father and the Son (*ex patre filioque*)—a standard view

---

74. Rohls, *Reformed Confessions*, 50.
75. WSC Q/A 6.
76. Watson, *A Body of Practical Divinity*, 63
77. FC VI; see also SC I, TNA I; BC XI; WCF II.3; WSC Q/A 6. In arguing for the divinity of Christ, CoD teaches that all three persons of the Trinity are of the same eternal and infinite essence with the Father and the Holy Spirit. CoD II.4.
78. SC XII; see also "The Confession of the English Congregation at Geneva (1556)," in Cochrane, *Reformed Confessions of the Sixteenth Century* (hereinafter CECG), III; WLC Q/A 9.
79. SHC III.3.

of procession inherited from the Western Churches of the Middle Ages, in contrast to the Eastern Churches who hold that the eternal procession of the Holy Spirit is from the Father alone. This procession of the Holy Spirit (and the causal distinctions of both the Father and the Son) in no way implies any sense of subordination insofar as the divine essence is concerned. Nor does it imply the slightest alteration in divine essence as a result of the begetting of the Son and/or the procession of the Holy Spirit.

The Reformers and later the Reformed orthodox, as exemplified in the Reformed confessions, argue that the procession of the Holy Spirit does prove otherwise, that the Holy Spirit is equally divine with the Father and the Son. It is proven by pointing to the fact that the Holy Spirit merely proceeds from both, neither is the Spirit made or created.[80] The causal distinctions of the Trinity distinguish the persons only with respect to the order within the Godhead, but not their divinity. "In regard of the order," the BC confesses, "[the Holy Spirit] is the third person of the Trinity," but in regard to his divinity, he is "of one and the same essence" with the Father and the Son.[81]

The divinity of the Holy Spirit is next displayed by ascribing unto the Holy Spirit "such names, attributes, works, worship, as are proper to God only."[82] The Holy Spirit is called true God not because he is identical with the Father (or the Son), but because he is, with the Father and the Son, true and eternal God.[83] The confessions commonly use the term "God the Holy Spirit" to highlight his divinity.[84] The third person of the Trinity, besides being commonly called "the Holy Spirit," is also often called God's virtue and power, the Sanctifier, the Lord of Hosts, the Power of the Most High, the Counselor, the Spirit of truth, and many other names only proper to

---

80. BC XI; see also FC VI; TNA V. Calvin does not deal with this matter in the GC, CC37, and CC45. However, in his *Institutes*, one may find that for Calvin the distinction of the Holy Spirit from the Father (and the Son) is not "a distinction of essence, which it is unlawful to make manifold," but rather a distinction of "subsistence." Calvin, *Institutes*, I.xiii.2.

81. BC XI.

82. WLC Q/A 11.

83. TNA V; BC XI; HC Q/A 53.

84. For examples, HC Q/A 24; WCF II.3.

God, to denote his divinity.[85] The Holy Spirit is coeternal, coessential (or consubstantial), one in truth, in power, goodness, mercy, majesty, glory with the Father and Son.[86] These names and attributes would not have been ascribed to the Holy Spirit if he were an intermediary being or any being less than God. Assuming the Holy Spirit as God, Bullinger also asserts that all sins, whether mortal, venial or other kind of sin, are "the sin against the Holy Spirit which is never forgiven (Mark 3:29; I John 5:16)."[87]

The Reformed confessions follow the Athanasian and Nicene Creeds in testifying that the Holy Spirit is worthy of receiving the same honor and glory with the Father and the Son. Generally the confessions follow the Athanasian Creed in using the general term "God" or "God the Trinity" when affirming the worship of one God, in which the Father, Son, and Holy Spirit are simply assumed either explicitly or implicitly.[88] However, some confessions follow the Nicene Creed to give a more explicit expression of the equality of the Holy Spirit in receiving the same worship, honor, and glory as the Father and the Son do receive. The SC, in its doxology near the end of the last article, gives "all honour and glory" to the Father "with the Son and the Holy Ghost."[89] The WCF makes the similar assertion that religious worship, which includes the sacraments, prayers, preaching and hearing of the Word, and other religious observances, is to be done in and given to God, the Father, Son, and Holy Spirit only, not to any other creature, indicating a clear Creator-creature distinction between the persons of the Trinity and created beings.[90] The use of Matt. 28:19 as the standard orthodox formula for baptism and in Christian prayer is a clear testimony of the church's historic acknowledgement of the divinity of the Holy Spirit.

The Reformed confessions also testify to the divinity of the Holy Spirit by ascribing to him the works of God. Some of the works are attributed

---

85. CC37 20; CC45 Q/A 19; FC VI; BC VIII; SHC III; WLC Q/A 11 (see biblical references).
86. BC VIII; TNA I; CoD II.4; WCF II.3; WLC Q/A 8-9; WSC Q/A 6.
87. SHC VIII.
88. GC II; SC I; SHC V.
89. SC XXV.
90. WCF XXI.2; see also WCF II.2.

to God in general, the Father, Son, and Holy Spirit, while some others are exclusively attributed to the Holy Spirit. In the former group of confessions, some explicitly mention the Holy Spirit, while others simply use the general term "God" to refer to the three co-working persons of the Trinity. The FC, along with some other Reformed Confessions, explicitly teaches that, with the Father and the Son, the Holy Spirit created all things, preserves, governs, and directs all created things, visible and invisible, including disposing and ordaining by his sovereign will all that happens in the world and restraining "the devils and all our enemies, so that they cannot harm us without his leave."[91] The works of God that are exclusively attributed to the Holy Spirit are, to name but a few, the inspiration and inward illumination of Scripture, the personal application of redemption (including the calling of believers, regeneration, justification, sanctification), and the building of the church, all of which this dissertation is about to explore in this and following chapters.

Concerning the personhood of the Holy Spirit, the Reformed confessions assembled some arguments developed by the Reformers and later by the orthodox to affirm that the Holy Spirit is a distinct subsistence or a distinct Divine Person in the Godhead. As Muller summarizes,

> the Reformed defended the doctrine in four sets of arguments—from the personal properties attributed to the Spirit, from personal appearances or theophanies of the Spirit, from personal 'operations' of the Spirit, and from biblical references to the Spirit in conjunction with but also distinct from the Father and the Son.[92]

The arguments found in the confessions mainly draw on the use of the biblical notion "spirit" and the personal or the role distinction of the Holy Spirit in divine operations *ad intra* and *ad extra*.[93]

---

91. FC VII, VIII; see also SC I; SHC VII.
92. Muller, *PRRD*, IV, 7.2 (B.1).
93. Drawing upon several articles of faith, Robertson offers another set of arguments for the personhood of the Holy Spirit found particularly in WCF. He argues that the Holy

Although not discussing exclusively the term "spirit," the Reformed confessions cautiously and carefully use and never ambiguously employ the term, when referring to the created spirits (of humans or angels), the divine essence, and the third Person of the Trinity. When applying the term to God, the confessions clearly distinguish between "spirit" as a substance, that is, the being of God ("God is spirit") as opposed to the corporeal nature of all creatures, and "Spirit" as a subsistence or person, that is, the third Person of the Trinity ("God the Holy Spirit"). The Reformers and the orthodox were aware of the multifold meanings of the biblical term "spirit" and the potential of theological confusion that a misuse of such term may cause.[94]

The Reformed confessions followed the view of "Spirit" outlined by the Reformers, and later by the orthodox, in attesting to the personal distinction of the Holy Spirit. The confessions affirm the biblical notion of "the Holy Spirit" not only as a distinct subsistence from the Father and the Son, but also as a distinct yet equal person with the Father and the Son. The Holy Spirit is not a less-than-God substance, as the term "spirit" may refer to when applied to anything other than God. Nor is he identical with the Godhead or a divine property as some heretics contend. The Holy "Spirit" is God, equally divine in rank and essential order, but not identical with either the Father or the Son. He is none other than the third person of the Godhead. Or, in the words of SC, he is "whom we confess to be God, equal with the Father and with His Son."[95] The WLC stresses the personal distinction of the Holy Spirit when it states that, along with the Son, the Scriptures manifest that the Holy Spirit is "God equal with the Father," ascribing unto him "such names, attributes, works, and worship, as are

---

Spirit is a person because he has a will (capable of being grieved, WCF XVII.3; XVIII.4), moral standards (he sanctifies the elect, WCF XIII.1, 3; XIX.7), and he communes with people (he speaks, WCF I.1; he persuades sinners to believe and obey, WCF VIII.8; he governs the human heart, WCF VIII.8; he testifies to the human spirit about salvation, WCF XVIII.2; he makes possible personal communion with God through prayer, WCF XXI.3). Robertson, "The Holy Spirit in the Westminster Confession of Faith," 68-70.

94. For a detailed discussion, see Muller, *PRRD*, IV, 7.1 (B and C). See also Robertson, "The Holy Spirit in the Westminster Confession of Faith," 64-66.

95. SC XII; see also BC XI; TNA V.

proper to God only."⁹⁶ In other words, were the Holy Spirit not God nor a true person, ascribing all the aforementioned things to him would be an utter blasphemy and idolatry.

The next two affirmations for the personal distinction of the Holy Spirit are derived from the distinction of the Holy Spirit in the divine operations *ad intra* and *ad extra*. The former pertains to the inward work or operation of the Holy Spirit in the Godhead, that is his procession, while the latter to the distinct role of the Holy Spirit in divine works towards the creatures, in them, and by them.

The Holy Spirit as the third hypostasis in the Godhead is distinguished from the Father and the Son by his incommunicable property, that is, his procession.⁹⁷ Whereas the incommunicable property of the Father as the origin of all things is his ingenerability, his unbegottenness, and that of the Son is his begottenness, so the personal property of the Holy Spirit is his procession or emanation. This personal distinction, the distinction according to which they exist, is what lies beneath the order of the persons, as found in some passages of Scripture (for examples, Matt. 18:19; 1 Jn. 5:7). The Reformed confessions unanimously affirm the Western tradition view of the *filioque*, that the Holy Spirit is proceeded from the Father and the Son with reference to John 15:26.⁹⁸ In commenting on the persons distinction in the Godhead in the HC, Ursinus aptly explicates,

> The Father is the first person, and, as it were, the fountain of the divinity of the Son and Holy Spirit, because the Deity is communicated to him of no one; but he communicates the Deity to the Son and Holy Spirit. The Son is the second person, because the Deity is communicated to him of the Father, by eternal generation. The Holy Ghost is the third

---

96. WLC Q/A 11.
97. A property that cannot be communicated, nothing analogous is found in another. Ursinus, *The Commentary*, 130.
98. FC VI; BC XI; TNA V; WCF II.3; WLC Q/A 10.

person, because the Deity is communicated to him from the Father and the Son, by an eternal inspiration or procession.[99]

The Reformed Confessions do not go into detail and leave it to the various Reformed theological systems to give explanations concerning what the Holy Spirit's "proceeding" means, how the Spirit's "proceeding" should be differentiated from the Son's "begetting," and why the double procession.[100] However, the confessions state firmly what the doctrine ought to demonstrate, that is, the *ad intra* distinction among the persons of the Holy Trinity. The FC states, "The Son begotten from eternity by the Father. The Holy Spirit proceeding eternally from them both; the three persons not confused, but distinct, and yet not separate, but of the same essence, equal in eternity and power."[101] BC emphatically maintains that the three persons of the Trinity are "really, truly, and eternally distinct according to their incommunicable properties" and enumerates the personal distinctions of the three persons, stating the Holy Spirit as "the eternal power and might, proceeding from the Father and the Son."[102] The WCF succinctly attests to the doctrine: "The Father is of none, neither begotten, nor proceeding: The Son is eternally begotten of the Father: The Holy Ghost eternally proceeding from the Father and the Son."[103]

While the *ad intra* distinction demonstrates the personal distinction of the Holy Spirit from the inner operations of the persons in the Godhead, and thus from their incommunicable properties, the *ad extra* distinction of the Holy Spirit does the same by setting forth the office, or distinct role, of the Holy Spirit in the unity of divine operations.[104] Even though

---

99. Ursinus, *The Commentary*, 135.
100. For a detailed discussion of the Reformed view of the Spirit's procession, see Muller, *PRRD*, IV, 7.4 (A.1-A.3).
101. FC VI.
102. BC XI.
103. WCF II.3; see also WLC Q/A 10.
104. Regarding the *ad extra* distinction of the Trinity, Calvin states in his *Institutes*, "It is this: to the Father is attributed the beginning of activity, and the fountain and wellspring of all things; to the Son, wisdom, counsel, and the ordered disposition of all things; but to the Spirit is assigned the power and efficacy of that activity." *Institutes*, I.xiii.18; see also CC37 XX; CC45 Q/A 19. Calvin's *ad extra* distinction within the Godhead exemplifies

Doctrinal Themes Commonly Associated with the Holy Spirit - Part A

the Reformed confessions had no intention of providing exhaustive enumeration of the distinct role of the Holy Spirit, they gave more than sufficient testimonies of the Spirit's distinct role in the *ad extra* activity of the Trinity. For example, in creation and providence, the Holy Spirit is typically depicted as the agent of Creation and Providence. He is God's virtue, power, and efficacy, whereas the Son is God's "Word and eternal wisdom," by which God the Father created the world.[105] The Holy Spirit is actively involved in creation. The HC only asserts that the Father out of nothing created heaven and earth and everything in them, but in his commentary, Ursinus expounds,

> God, the Father, created the world through the Son and Holy Ghost. Of the Son, it is said, "All things were made by him." (John 1:3.) Of the Holy Ghost, it is said, "The Spirit of the Lord moved upon the face of the waters." "The Spirit of God hath made me." (Gen. 1:2. Job 33:4.)[106]

In his commentary on the HC, Olevianus also offers a similar remark, stating that the work of creation and providence is not the work of God the Father alone, but the Father works "through His eternal Son together with the Holy Spirit."[107] The Holy Spirit is also called the preserver who preserves and rules all created things, while the Father is called the Creator who created all things by his Word and Wisdom, that is his Son. In the words of the FCB,

---

a typical formulation operating within the Reformed tradition. The similar formulation can also be found in FC VI; BC VIII. Also in Herman Bavinck, one may find a succinct formulation expressing this line of tradition, "All things proceed from the Father, are accomplished by the Son, and are completed in the Holy Spirit." Herman Bavinck, *Reformed Dogmatics*, trans. John Vriend, 4 vols. (Grand Rapids: Baker Academics, 2003-2008), II, 319.

105. FC VI; VII.

106. HC Q/A 26; Ursinus, *The Commentary*, 143.

107. Caspar Olevianus, *A Firm Foundation: An Aid to Interpreting the Heidelberg Catechism*, trans. Lyle D. Bierma (Grand Rapids: Baker Books, 1995), Q/A 26.

We also believe that God has created all things by His eternal Word, that is, by His only-begotten Son, and preserves and strengthens all things by His Spirit, that is, by His power; and therefore, God sustains and governs all things as He created them.[108]

The FHC even identifies the Holy Spirit as God's Providence when it states that God "has created all things out of nothing by His Word, that is, by His Son, and by His providence justly, truly and wisely rules, governs and preserves all things."[109]

In revelation, as discussed in the preceding section, the Father reveals himself through his works and Word, the Son is the Word incarnate, the ultimate revealer of the Father, and the Holy Spirit is the inspirer of Scripture, who wrote Scripture, reveals and bears testimony for the Word in the hearts of believers.

In salvation, the Father is considered to be the fount of salvation, who calls those whom he has chosen in Christ from eternity to display in them the riches of his mercy; the Son is the redeemer and mediator whom the Father sent to reconcile sinners to God by his perfect obedience and sacrifice; and the Holy Spirit is the Sanctifier who regenerates and sanctifies the elect, by whom all the benefits of redemption are applied to all believers.[110] The HC teaches that the Holy Spirit, "as well as the Father and the Son, is eternal God" and that he has been given to believers personally, "so that, by true faith, he makes me share in Christ and all his blessings, comforts me, and remains with me forever."[111] In his commentary on the HC, Olevianus explains further the office of the Holy Spirit by enumerating seven titles or names that Scripture ascribes to the Holy Spirit pertaining to the Spirit's role in human salvation—as the "Holy Spirit," "Spirit of Adoption," "seal and deposit," "water," "fire," "anointing," and "Comforter." He then sum-

---

108. FCB I; SHC VII.1.
109. FHC VI.
110. See among many, "The Tetrapolitan Confession (1530)," in Cochrane, *Reformed Confessions of the Sixteenth Century* (hereinafter TC), IV; FHC X, XI, XIII; GC VI, VII, VIII; CECG III; FC XII, XIV, XVII, XIX, XXI, XXII; SC III, VI, VIII, IX, X, XI, XII.
111. HC Q/A 53.

marizes well the distinct role of the Holy Spirit as the Applier of Christ's redemption, that is, as "that bond of union by which Christ abides in us and we in Him . . . For there is no other means whereby we can share in Christ and all His benefits than the Holy Spirit, who incorporates us into Christ."[112] Commenting on the article of faith, "I believe in the Holy Spirit," in his *An Exposition of the Apostles' Creed*, Olevianus also states that the Holy Spirit engrafts believers into Christ through faith and makes them partakers of Christ and all his benefits. The Holy Spirit brings about in believers the union with Christ and his benefits as he "sprinkles us with the blood of Christ (1 Peter 1[:2]), makes us 'members of Christ' (1 Cor. 6[:15]), feeds us with Christ (John 6[:50-58]), gives us Christ to drink (1 Cor. 10[:4, 16]; 12), and builds us on Christ (Eph. 2[:20])."[113]

The Reformed confessions, while recognizing the role distinction of the three persons of the Trinity, do not perceive it as a division within the Godhead. God is of the one same, simple, undivided essence. The distinction is in no way suggesting the inferiority of the Son and the Holy Spirit as compared to the Father. Rather, every person is working his particular task, playing his peculiar role together with the other two, without diminishing the equal dignity that each person in the Trinity has. In their operations *ad intra* and *ad extra*, the unity of the three persons and their equal divinity are fully exhibited. One may not find a lengthy discussion on this in the Reformed Confessions, although it is clearly presupposed by the Reformed.[114] This theological presupposition explains why in the

---

112. Olevianus, *A Firm Foundation*, Q/A 128-129.

113. Olevianus, *An Exposition of the Apostles' Creed*, trans. Lyle D. Bierma (Grand Rapids: Reformation Heritage Books, 2009), 124.

114. For Ursinus, the *ad extra* distinction arises from the *ad intra* distinction. Ursinus, *The Commentary*, 137. Muller similarly points out the Reformed stance on this, that in the case of the Holy Spirit, "The *ad intra* procession of the Spirit is mirrored and followed by the *ad extra* procession or 'mission' of the Spirit," as Muller states. Muller, *PRRD*, IV, 7.4 (B.1, 378). See also John Owen's account on the same doctrine, "And the reason hereof is, because the several Persons are *individed* in their Operations, acting all by the same Will, the same Wisdom, the same Power. Every Person therefore is the Author of every Work of God, because each Person is God, and the Divine Nature is the same *individed* Principle of all Divine Operations. And this ariseth from the Unity of the Persons in the same Essence. . . . The Reason therefore why the Works of God are thus distinctly ascribed unto each Person, is because in the *individed* Operation of the Divine Nature, each Person doth the same Work in the Order of their Subsistence; not one as the Instrument of the other

Reformed confessions one can find the notion of "co-working" persons and that all divine operations are commonly ascribed unto God, in spite of the *ad intra* and *ad extra* distinctions among the three person of the Trinity, as also recognized by Rohls.[115] In any case, the divinity and the personhood of the Holy Spirit are well affirmed by the establishment of the personal distinction and the unity of operations of the Trinity.

The Holy Spirit and the Doctrine of Christ

As discussed above, all three persons of the Trinity work together in every divine work and are undivided in their operations, so that all divine works are justly ascribed to God. In the incarnation of Christ, the three divine persons also jointly worked together. The role of the Holy Spirit in the incarnation of Christ did not go unnoticed in the Reformed confessions. The Holy Spirit played a very significant role in the earthly ministry of Christ, as shown in the conception of Christ, his anointing, and his resurrection.

The Reformed confessions, especially the catechisms, typically cited and offered a brief exposition of the words of the Apostles' Creed, and in it an article that confesses the orthodox belief in the holy conception of Christ wrought in the womb of virgin Mary by the Holy Spirit: "I believe . . . in Jesus Christ, his Only Son, Our Lord, who was conceived by the Holy Spirit, born of the virgin Mary." The virgin conception of Christ by the Holy Spirit is necessary, so that the Mediator between God and human beings, the Word made flesh, Jesus Christ himself, would be born perfect, untainted by sin from his very conception. "Christ's sinlessness is necessary for the sake of reconciliation," states Rohls.[116] Calvin wrote in CC37 that

---

or meerly employed by the other, but as one common Principle of Authority, Wisdom, Love, and Power." Owen, *PNEUMATOLOGIA*, I.iv.1-2 (68-69). Bavinck states similarly: "All the works of God *ad extra* have one single Author (*principium*), namely, God. But they come into being through the cooperation of the three persons, each of whom plays a special role and fulfills a special task, both in the works of creation and in those of redemption and sanctification." Bavinck, *Reformed Dogmatics*, II, 319.

115. Rohls, *Reformed Confessions*, 49-50.
116. Rohls, *Reformed Confessions*, 113.

Christ himself "has been conceived in the bosom of the virgin through the virtue of the Holy Spirit (marvelous and unspeakable for us), so that he would not be born stained by any carnal corruption, but sanctified by sovereign purity."[117] Calvin in his *Institutes* stresses the sanctifying role of the Holy Spirit in the process of conception; Christ was free of all stain "not just because he was begotten of his mother without copulation with man, but because he was sanctified by the Spirit that the generation might be pure and undefiled."[118] In the words of CC45, as the seed of man is corrupt, "it was necessary that the power of the Holy Spirit should intervene in this conception, in order to preserve our Lord from all corruption, and to fill him with holiness," to consecrate Christ to God in purity from the very beginning, "in order that He may not be subject to the universal corruption of the human race."[119]

The HC says that the holy conception and birth of Christ prove his innocence and perfect holiness.[120] Commenting on this in his commentary, Ursinus explains further that the holy conception of Christ by the Holy Spirit sanctified Christ, "so that original sin did not attach itself to that which was thus formed" in the hypostatical union of the two natures, the divine and the human.[121] Being sanctified from his mother's womb by the Holy Spirit, Christ might then "make satisfaction for sin," "by his purity, sanctify others," and be found truthful, that "whatever the Son says is truth, and in him there is no falsehood."[122] In the same line of thought, Olevianus states that through the miraculous work of the conception of Christ, the Holy Spirit could "keep free and pure of any stain the one who was going

---

117. CC37 XX ("Who was conceived by the holy Spirit, born of the virgin Mary"); see also CC45 Q/A 50. FC XIV states, "he was conceived by the secret power of the Holy Spirit."

118. Calvin, *Institutes*, II.xiii.4.

119. CC45 Q/A 53-54. Commenting on WSC Q/A 27 regarding in which Christ's humiliation consist, Watson argues further that "Had he been born after the ordinary course of nature, he had been defiled; (all that spring out of *Adam's* Loins have a tincture of sin) but that *Christ's substance might remain pure and immaculate*, he was born of a Virgin." Watson, *A Body of Practical Divinity*, 112.

120. HC Q/A 36.

121. Ursinus, *The Commentary*, 206.

122. Ursinus, *The Commentary*, 206-207.

to sanctify all of us" and fill Christ "with true holiness while still in the womb, so that the Son might be sanctified unto God the Father and have in himself all perfect holiness to sanctify us unto His Father."[123] The virgin birth of Christ expounded in the confessions, therefore, not only affirms that the whole conception is strictly a work of God, and that God the Father alone is the true Initiator of the incarnation, without the will and instrumentality of man, but the statement also highlights the role of the Holy Spirit in sanctifying the whole enterprise of incarnation. However, this emphasis is somehow overlooked by some modern commentators.[124]

The holy conception of Christ by the Holy Spirit is also understood by several confessions as a safeguard for the doctrine of Christ's hypostatical union of the two natures, and thus his Mediatorship in divine redemption.[125] SC contends that God sent His Son, "the substance of his glory, into this world, who took the nature of humanity from the substance of a woman, a virgin, by means of the Holy Ghost," so that there are "two perfect natures united and joined in one person," thereby ruling out the teachings of heresies—for examples, Arius, Marcion, Eutyches, Nestorius, and others—that either denied "the eternity of His (Christ's) Godhead, or

---

123. Olevianus, *A Firm Foundation*, Q/A 68-69.

124. For examples, Herman Hoeksema, *The Triple Knowledge of God: An Exposition of the Heidelberg Catechism*, 3 vols. (Grand Rapids: Reformed Free Publishing Association, 1970-72), I, 603-611; Hesselink, *Calvin's First Catechism*, 119-121. Similarly, Andrew Kuyvenhoven is content to simply state that the conception of Christ by the Holy Spirit is an immediate act of interference that made Jesus "holy, set apart, sinless, and guarantees his divinity," without further elaboration. Andrew Kuyvenhoven, *Comfort & Joy: A Study of the Heidelberg* Catechism (Grand Rapids: Faith Alive, 1988), 89-93. Robertson rightly points out that "the specific role of the Holy Spirit in [Christ's] conception may not have been given due attention." Robertson also states that "Apart from the preserving work of the Holy Spirit in keeping Christ from all sin, he could not have been the Holy One who died substitutionally for others." Having highlighted the significant role of the Holy Spirit in the conception of Christ, he maintains that WCF develops quite fully "The essential role of the Spirit in the accomplishment of the great mystery of the incarnation." Robertson, "The Holy Spirit in the Westminster Confession of Faith," 77-78. A quite comprehensive treatment on the role of the Holy Spirit in the virgin birth and incarnation of Christ can be found in Klooster's commentary of HC. *Our Only Comfort: A Comprehensive Commentary on the Heidelberg Catechism, 2 vols. (Grand Rapids: Faith Alive, 2001)*, I, 416-445.

125. This very important notion, however, is interestingly missing in Rohl's *Reformed Confessions* and Barth's *The Theology of the Reformed Confessions*.

the truth of His humanity, or confounded them, or else divided them."[126] The BC adds that by being thus conceived, the two natures are so "united in a single person, with each nature retaining its own distinct properties," that "they are not even separated by [Christ's] death."[127] The WCF also teaches clearly that Christ was conceived by the power of the Holy Spirit in order that the two perfect, distinct natures, "the Godhead and the Man-hood, were inseparably joyned together in one person, without Conversion, Composition, or Confusion," that is in one *theanthropic* person, one Christ, who is very God and very man, "the only Mediator between God and man."[128] In the words of Watson, the conception of Christ in the womb is the work of the Holy Spirit in a wonderful manner uniting "Christ's *Humane Nature* to his *Divine*, and so of both made *one person*."[129] The Mediator has to be true God and true man to be able to save and reconcile sinners to God, or as de Brès succinctly states in the BC: "true God in order to conquer death by his power, and true man that he might die for us in the weakness of his flesh."[130] Therefore, as the two natures of Christ are the key answer to the *Cur Deus homo* question in divine redemption, the role of the Holy Spirit in the conception of Christ, which is right at the heart of the scheme of divine redemption, is undoubtedly an indispensable one.

The co-working of the Holy Spirit in the incarnation of Christ is even more pervasively displayed in Christ's earthly ministry. The Holy Spirit anointed the second person of the Trinity to be Christ, the Anointed One, to undertake his offices as Prophet, Priest, and King throughout his life, death, and resurrection. There is no single work that Christ carried out on earth in which the Holy Spirit was not upon and empowering him.[131]

---

126. SC VI; see also BC XVIII; HC Q/A 23, 35; SHC XI.4, 6.
127. BC XIX.
128. WCF VIII.2; see also WLC Q/A 37; WSC Q/A 22.
129. Watson, *A Body of Practical Divinity*, 112.
130. BC XIX.
131. Robertson correctly remarks that the work of redemption is accomplished only in the unity of the Godhead and that the Holy Spirit "must not be perceived as playing a part in man's salvation only after Christ had completed his work. Instead, he embodied the enabling power by which the Son fulfilled his commission." Robertson, "The Holy Spirit in the Westminster Confession of Faith," 78-79.

Following the schema of the threefold office of Christ (*munus triplex Christi*) to describe the work of Christ as the Mediator outlined by Calvin as early as the second edition of his *Institutes* (1539),[132] the Reformed confessions elucidate the inextricable involvement of the Holy Spirit in Christ' earthly ministry. Calvin asserts in CC45 that by the very name of Christ "His office is still better expressed," for the name "signifies that He was anointed by the Father to be ordained King, Priest, and Prophet."[133] As according to Scripture kings, priests, and prophets in the past were anointed with visible oil, the Son of God was anointed by the Father with the Holy Spirit, "who is the reality signified by that outward anointing made in time past (Isa. 61:1; Ps. 45:7)," Calvin asserts.[134]

Calvin teaches that Christ is the King of his Kingdom—a kingdom which is spiritual in nature—and that his reigning consists in the Word and Spirit of God.[135] Or, in the words of the HC, Christ has been anointed by the Holy Spirit to be our eternal king "who governs us by his Word and Spirit, and who guards us and keeps us in the freedom he has won for us."[136] With this anointing at the outset of Christ's office, it is just to infer that the Holy Spirit empowers Christ in executing all the tasks given to him as King by the Father.[137] The WSC uses Matt. 12:28 as biblical reference to maintain this Spirit's empowering character: "But if I cast out devils by the Spirit of God, then the kingdom of God is come unto you."[138]

As Priest, Christ was sanctified by the Holy Spirit since he was in the womb of the virgin Mary in order to present himself before God as a pure, undefiled sacrifice acceptable to him.[139] Christ is "the only high priest who

---

132. Hesselink, *Calvin's First Catechism*, 119. See also Rohls, *Reformed Confessions*, 100-102. On the development of the schema of the threefold office of Christ, see John F. Jansen, *Calvin's Doctrine of the Work of Christ* (London: James Clarke, 1956), chapter 2; Barth, *CD*, IV/3, 13ff.; Otto Weber, *Foundations of Dogmatics*, trans. Darrell L. Guder, vol. 2 (Grand Rapids: Eerdmans, 1981-83), 172ff.
133. CC45 Q/A34.
134. CC45 Q/A 36.
135. CC45 Q/A 37.
136. HC Q/A 31.
137. WLC Q/A 45; WSC Q/A 25
138. WSC Q/A 26.
139. CC45 Q/A 38; WCF VIII.5.

has set us free by the one sacrifice of his body, and who continually pleads our cause with the Father," the HC explains.[140] The WLC elucidates that, only by the virtue of the Holy Spirit that fills and sanctifies him, Christ might offer himself without spot to God, as a perfect sacrifice that satisfies God's justice (Heb. 9:14), to be a reconciliation for the sins of his people, to be the perfect Mediator between God and sinful human beings.[141]

To be anointed with the Holy Spirit as Prophet, as Calvin indicates, Christ was empowered to be the "sovereign messenger and ambassador of God His Father, to give a full exposition of God's will toward the world and so put an end to all prophecies and revelations (Heb. 1:2)."[142] Based on texts such as Lk. 4:14-19 and Isa. 61:1, the HC points out that the Holy Spirit is upon Christ, anointing him to preach the gospel, to perfectly reveal to us "the secret counsel and will of God for our deliverance."[143] The SHC states that the apostle Paul calls the preaching of the Gospel "the spirit" and "the ministry of the spirit" (2 Cor. 3:6).[144]

With the Word, the Holy Spirit is considered the means by which Christ executes his prophetic office—the same means used by Christ to perform his kingly office.[145] The HC teaches that Christ "has been ordained by God the Father and has been anointed with the Holy Spirit to be our chief prophet and teacher."[146] In his commentary of the HC, Ursinus explains further that the prophetic office of Christ also includes the duty to teach believers "internally by his Spirit, to illuminate their minds, and move their hearts to faith and obedience by the gospel."[147] In the same line of thought, the WLC states clearly that "Christ executeth the office of a Prophet, in his revealing to the church, in all ages, by his Spirit and Word, in divers wayes

---

140. HC Q/A 31.
141. WLC Q/A 38, 40, 44.
142. CC45 Q/A 39.
143. HC Q/A 31.
144. SHC XIII.4.
145. See WCF VIII.8.
146. HC Q/A 31.
147. Ursinus, *The Commentary*, 173.

of administration, the whole will of God, in all things concerning their edification and salvation."[148]

The pneumatological character of the anointing of Christ is undoubtedly clear. The Holy Spirit is the sole agent who anointed Christ. Moreover, the act of anointing itself implies the ever present accompaniment or the dwelling of the Holy Spirit. The Holy Spirit is upon Christ, as signified by the event recorded in Matt. 3:17, Lk. 3:22, Jn. 1:33, prophesied by Isaiah (Isa. 11:1-5; 42:1-4), and fulfilled throughout Christ's ministry (Matt. 12:17-21). As Ursinus explains, the anointing signifies both an ordination, or calling to the office for which the anointed person is set apart, and the promise and bestowment of the gifts necessary to sustain the anointed person. Through the anointing by the Holy Spirit, Christ has received all the gifts of the Spirit in the highest number and degree necessary for the accomplishment of the offices for which Christ was sent.[149] In executing his offices as the One anointed by the Holy Spirit, therefore, Christ has been thoroughly furnished, as God has given him all treasures of wisdom and knowledge, put all power and judgment in his hand, and given him commandment to execute his office.[150]

However, as explicitly stated by Calvin in his catechisms and the Westminster Assembly Divines in the Westminster Standards, the anointing not only denotes the Holy Spirit equipping and empowering Christ in his earthly ministry, but also the bestowal of all the graces of the Holy Spirit upon Christ so Christ may distribute the graces of the Holy Spirit to all believers beyond his earthly ministry. Calvin teaches that, after the accomplishment of his earthly ministry, having experienced the cross, death, and resurrection, Christ is now seated at the right hand of the Father. And from there, Calvin continues, Christ is now executing his lordship over all things by his power, and dispensing all the graces of the Holy Spirit that he has fully received to believers, enriching them with the graces of the Holy Spirit.[151] In CC45, Calvin adds that Christ receiving the Holy Spirit in

---

148. WLC Q/A 43; see also WSC Q/A 24.
149. Ursinus, *The Commentary*, 170-171.
150. WCF VIII.3; see also WLC 42.
151. CC37 XX; see Acts 2:33; Calvin, *Institutes*, II.xvi.16; Hesselink, *Calvin's First*

full perfection with all his graces is such that "He may lavish them upon us and distribute them, each according to the measure and portion which the Father knows to be expedient (Eph. 4:7). Thus we may draw from Him as from a fountain all the spiritual blessings we possess."[152] Therefore, on the one hand, from God's perspective we may see that the Father, through Christ his Son, sent the Holy Spirit with all his graces to us, so that we may receive all the spiritual blessings according to the measure and portion as God pleases. But on the other hand, from a human perspective, we may also see that we receive the Holy Spirit and his spiritual blessings because the Father through Christ, the Mediator, sent the Holy Spirit and his blessings to us.[153]

The purpose of the bestowal of the Holy Spirit upon believers is none other than the continuation of the execution of Christ's offices and of his presence; as Christ himself promised: "And surely I am with you always, to the very end of the age" (Matt. 28:20).[154] The outpouring of the Holy Spirit upon believers begun at Pentecost is never understood by the Reformed confessions as either the cessation of Christ's or the beginning of the Holy Spirit's epochs. On the contrary, the outpouring of the Holy Spirit upon believers merely marks the beginning of a new administration, or dispensation, of the execution of the same Christ's offices as King, Priest, and Prophet beyond Christ's ascension and before his second coming. The WCF clearly indicates this understanding when it states:

> To all those for whom Christ hath purchased redemption, he doth certainly and effectually apply and communicate the same; making intercession for them, and revealing unto them, in and by the word, the Mysteries of Salvation; effectually perswading them by his Spirit to believe, and obey, and governing their hearts by his Word and Spirit; overcoming all

---

Catechism, 127.
152. CC45 Q/A 41.
153. See WLC Q/A 38.
154. Unless otherwise indicated, all Scripture quotations are from the New International Version (NIV) Bible.

their enemies by his Almighty Power and Wisdom, in such manner, and ways, as are most consonant to his wonderful and unsearchable dispensation.[155]

The Holy Spirit is, therefore, the invisible agent of Christ, or as he is often called "the Spirit of Christ," whose presence and activities represent Christ's presence and activities in ruling and protecting us, interceding for us, and revealing to us God and his holy counsel. With respect to his Spirit, Christ "is not absent from us for a moment."[156]

The role of the Holy Spirit in the incarnation of Christ is also clearly displayed in Christ's resurrection, in which he is attributed with the power to raise Christ from the dead. Scripture in various passages, especially the Pauline letters, ascribes the resurrection of Christ not only to one person of the Trinity. For example, Paul teaches in 2 Cor. 13:4, as Calvin cites, that Christ was raised by the power of the Holy Spirit: "He suffered in weakness of the flesh, but rose again by the power of the Spirit."[157] In Eph. 1:19-20, Paul also states that it was God the Father who raised Christ from the dead: "That power is like the working of his mighty strength, which he exerted in Christ when he raised him from the dead and seated him at his right hand in the heavenly realms." In Jn. 10:18 Jesus states, "I have authority to lay it down and authority to take it up again." By whose power, then, was Christ raised?

The HC indicates that the power of Christ, which resurrected him from the dead is now resurrecting believers to a new life.[158] The WLC uses Jn. 10:18 as reference to indicate that Christ was raised from the dead by his own power.[159] However, there is no intention in either catechism to strictly

---

155. WCF VIII.8; see also WLC Q/A 54-55; WSC Q/A 23-26.
156. HC Q/A 47.
157. Calvin, *Institutes*, II.xvi.13; see also Rm. 8:11 and 1 Pet. 3:18.
158. HC Q/A 45.
159. WLC Q/A 52. Cf. Robertson, "The Holy Spirit in the Westminster Confession," 80-81, 97-98. Robertson attributes the power that raised Christ from the dead to the Holy Spirit, without specifying the articles of WCF from which he derives his conclusion. He seems to draw his conclusion by looking at the passage in Rm. 8:11 and the fact that WCF XXXII.3 interchangeably uses the terms "by the power of Christ" and "by his Spirit."

distinguish between the power of the Father, of Christ, and of the Holy Spirit. Instead, the catechisms seem to understand the power by which Christ was raised as the power of the Holy Spirit. In his commentary of the HC, Olevianus affirms this, identifying the power of Christ as the power of the Holy Spirit. On the benefit of Christ's resurrection, he states that "By the power of our Head, Jesus Christ, through the Spirit of faith, we rise in this life to a new life," and that "It was necessary, therefore, that Christ raise us with Him by the power of His Spirit in order that we might begin to glorify and praise God here, until we reach the goal of perfection after this life (2 Cor. 4; Phil. 2; Col. 3; Rom. 6, 8)."[160] Vincent, in his commentary of the WSC, leans in the same direction. Having cited both Jn. 10:17-18 and Rm. 1:4, Vincent maintains that Christ was raised from the dead by his own power and Spirit.[161]

However, it is Ursinus who offers a clearer presentation of the doctrine and a better solution for this matter. The HC teaches that "by his power we too are already now resurrected to a new life."[162] Commenting on this article, Ursinus expounds further Christ's power of resurrection and how he was raised. In his reply to an objection about whether Christ raised himself, Ursinus remarks that in Christ's resurrection the three persons of the Trinity work together as they ordinarily work. The Father raised the Son through the Son himself, and "through another person of the same essence of himself, and of infinite power, through whom the Father ordinarily works," that is, the Holy Spirit. Ursinus adds, "The Son was raised by the Father through himself; he himself raised himself by his Spirit."[163] The resurrection of Christ, therefore, is not to be understood as the work of merely

---

160. Olevianus, *A Firm Foundation*, 73.
161. Vincent, *An Explicatory Catechism*, 85. Cf. William Ames, *The Marrow of Theology*, ed. John D Eusden (Grand Rapids: Baker Books, 1968), I.xxiii.14; *A Sketch of the Christian's Catechism*, trans. Todd M. Rester (Grand Rapids: Reformation Heritage Books, 2008), 89. Ames argues that the power by which Christ was raised from the dead is attributed to Christ's own power, because the power can only pertain to his divine nature. When Christ is said to be revived by God or by the Spirit of God, it properly pertains to Christ's human nature. However, Ames' argument is not purported to defend the divinity of Christ to the exclusion of the Father's and the Holy Spirit's roles in the resurrection.
162. HC Q/A 45.
163. Ursinus, *The Commentary*, 234.

one divine person of the Trinity, but as the work of all persons in unity, inseparable yet distinguishable in each of their distinct roles. It is certainly true that the resurrection of Christ is the work of the Trinity: the Father, Son, and Holy Spirit. However, considering each role of the persons of the Trinity and their unity in divine operations, it is just to say that as Christ was conceived by the Holy Spirit, empowered and led by the Holy Spirit, he was also made alive, raised from the dead by the power of the Holy Spirit, who is also known as the Spirit of God and the Spirit of Christ. It is through the agency of the Holy Spirit, by his power, that the work of God in Christ's resurrection has been accomplished.

As this chapter has already demonstrated, the Holy Spirit is not treated in the Reformed confessions exclusively in an independent chapter or section. Even those confessions which have a section on the Holy Spirit do not compartmentalize their discussion of the Holy Spirit in that particular section. Instead, the Reformed confessions discuss the Holy Spirit always in relation to other doctrines, such as the doctrines of Scripture, Trinity, and Christ. The next chapter will continue to present the treatment of the Holy Spirit in the Reformed confessions in relation to several other doctrines, those that pertain to the application of the work of Christ, that is, the doctrines of salvation, the church, and sacraments.

CHAPTER 3

Doctrinal Themes Commonly Associated with the Holy Spirit in the Reformed Confessions and Catechisms – Part B

The previous chapter has discussed the treatment of the Holy Spirit in the Reformed confessions in relation to the doctrines of Scripture, the Trinity, and Christ. As the Reformed confessions move into the application of the work of Christ, the work of the Holy Spirit becomes more apparent. Personal salvation is not the only topic that the application of the work of Christ covers. The fingerprints of the Holy Spirit are also evident in the gathering of all believers—that is, the church—and the administration of sacraments. Many scholars in the past, such as Barth and Rohls, have already identified these *loci* as common places where some aspects of the work of the Holy Spirit are noted and discussed, in addition to those discussed in the preceding chapter. However, in their works they did not provide much primary source documentation for their claims and oftentimes discussed the Holy Spirit in relation to the aforementioned doctrines only in passing.

This chapter will attempt to discuss and provide a more thorough account of the Holy Spirit in relation to the doctrines of salvation, the church, and sacraments, by offering more documentary support for these themes from the Reformed confessions. It will explore particularly how the work of the Holy Spirit permeates every aspect of Christian life, gives identity and marks to the true church, and invigorates the church through sacraments.

The Holy Spirit and the Doctrine of Salvation

The primary role of the Holy Spirit in the divine work of redemption is to apply Christ's redemption to the people of God. Whereas the Father has planned redemption from eternity and the Son has accomplished the redemption objectively in history, the Holy Spirit applies the redemption fully and subjectively in the hearts and lives of believers. This application of redemption by the Holy Spirit is nonetheless multifaceted.

The aspects included in the application of redemption range from calling, regeneration, faith, repentance, justification, sanctification, and perseverance. The discussions of these aspects in the Reformed confessions are never intended to present a chronological "order of salvation" (*ordo salutis*).[1] The WCF exemplifies this clearly. In the WCF, while a certain logical order is clearly assumed, the aspects of the application of redemption are not discussed chronologically, nor exclusively from each other. Contrary to the order many scholars commonly perceive or expect, such as Andrew Murray, Louis Berkhof, and Anthony Hoekema, the chapters that discuss saving faith and repentance are not presented before but appear after the chapters concerning justification, adoption, and sanctification.[2]

However, regardless of the difference in the orders of salvation that one finds in the writings of the Reformed or in the Reformed confessions, as Herman Kuiper correctly observes, a distinguishing mark of Reformed theologians is that "they always champion the glory of God over against all tendencies to exalt man. And it is especially in its doctrine of the Ordo Salutis that Reformed theology magnifies God as the Sole Author of our salvation."[3] To be precise, the Reformed confessions unequivocally affirm

---

1. The term *ordo salutis* was coined by a Lutheran, Jakob Carpov, in the year 1737. For the history of the doctrine of the order of salvation, see Herman Kuiper, *By Grace Alone: A Study in Soteriology* (Grand Rapids: Eerdmans, 1955), 17-37. See also Anthony Hoekema's discussion on the question of the order of salvation. Anthony A. Hoekema, *Saved by Grace* (Grand Rapids: Eerdmans, 1989), 11-28.

2. See for examples, Andrew Murray, *Redemption, Accomplished and Applied* (Grand Rapids: Eerdmans, 1955), 102-104; Louis Berkhof, *Systematic Theology*, new edition (Grand Rapids: Eerdmans, 1996), 418-420; Hoekema, *Saved by Grace*, 14-17.

3. Kuiper, *By Grace Alone*, 36. See also "Report 34," 430-435.

the sole agency of the Holy Spirit in the application of the blessings of salvation to the people of God.

The agency of the Holy Spirit in the calling of believers is manifest despite the use of the ministry of men in the propagation of the Word. The external call to salvation through the preaching of the Word comes to both believers and unbelievers. However, without the inward work of the Holy Spirit, the preaching of the Word or the Gospel can never be effectual. The Word and Spirit in the effectual calling of the elect are inseparably bound together in the Reformed confessions.

In the SHC, Bullinger maintains that the preaching of the Gospel is called by Paul the apostle "the ministry of the Spirit" because the Holy Spirit makes the external preaching of the Gospel, or the Word, effectual internally through his illumination and by faith (2 Cor. 3:6).[4] The Dort Fathers, drawing from Rm. 8:30, hold that before the foundation of the world God decided "to give the chosen ones to Christ to be saved, and to call and draw them effectively into Christ's fellowship through his Word and Spirit."[5]

In a similar fashion, the Westminster Standards emphatically assert that the effectual call is of God's free and special grace alone; the elect, and they alone, are effectually called.[6] The Westminster Standards teach that effectual calling is an act that comprises all the work of the Holy Spirit in God's appointed time, without which sinful human beings are unable to positively respond to the call of salvation out of their miserable sinful condition by their own powers.[7] The WCF descriptively elucidates effectual call as the act of the Holy Spirit

> inlightening [the elect's] minds spiritually and savingly to understand the things of God, taking away their heart of stone, and giving unto them an heart of flesh, renewing their wills,

---

4. SHC XIII.4.
5. CoD I.7.
6. WLC Q/A 68. WCF X.3 teaches that the elect includes infants dying in infancy and others who are incapable of being outwardly called by the ministry of the Word.
7. WCF III.6; VIII.8; X.1; WLC Q/A 155; WSC Q/A 89.

and by his Almighty power, determining them to that which is good, and effectually drawing them to Jesus Christ: yet so, as they come most freely, being made willing by his grace.[8]

In his answer to the question, "What is effectual calling?," Watson in his commentary on the WSC, acknowledges a distinction between external and internal calling and illustrates, "The Ministry of the Word is the Pipe or Organ, the Spirit of God blowing in it, doth effectually change Men's hearts."[9] In this effectual calling, out of God's free and special grace alone, the Holy Spirit works in such a way that human freedom is not overruled. The Holy Spirit restores, by quickening and renewing the sinful human heart, convinces, and humbles sinners by the preaching of the Word.[10] Once restored, sinners are hereby made willing and able freely to answer God's call and to accept and embrace the grace offered and conveyed in it.[11]

Another aspect of redemption is regeneration. Regeneration is the act of the Holy Spirit that brings a spiritual renewal into the hearts and lives of sinners. Through regeneration by the Holy Spirit, God makes a person anew, a new creature, and brings her into an estate of salvation by the covenant of grace.[12] Being by nature subject to sin, by faith "we are regenerated in newness of life," the FC teaches.[13]

---

8. WCF X.1; see also WLC Q/A 67; WSC Q/A 31. Vincent states that the work of the Holy Spirit in effectual calling of the elect is twofold: upon their minds (convincing the elect of their sin and misery and enlightening them in the knowledge of Christ) and upon their wills (renewing their wills by putting new inclinations and dispositions in them). *An Explicatory Catechism*, 91-92.

9. Watson, *A Body of Practical Divinity*, 128, 404-408. Heppe correctly points out that the inward work of the Holy Spirit distinguishes "the calling of the elect" (*vocatio specialis, supranaturalis* and *evangelica*) from "the calling of all men" (*vocatio universalis* and *naturalis*). Heppe, *Reformed Dogmatics*, 510-511.

10. Despite his disagreement (or perhaps disappointment) with the dogmatic framing of WCF, which he alleges to be centered around the doctrine of predestination, Barth correctly identifies the role of the Holy Spirit in quickening and renewing the otherwise passive sinful human heart. Barth, *The Theology of the Reformed Confessions*, 140.

11. WCF X.2; WLC Q/A 67, 155; WSC Q/A 89. Believers actively receive the offer and this active receiving is "an elicited act of faith" that depends "partly upon an inborn principle or attitude toward grace and partly upon the action of God moving before and stirring up." Ames, *The Marrow of Theology*, I.xxvi.25-27.

12. BC XXIV; CC45 Q/A 326; WLC Q/A 30; WSC Q/A 20.

13. FC XXII.

As noted by Kuiper, Calvin understood regeneration in a very wide sense as denoting the entire life renewal of the elect, including repentance and sanctification.[14] In CC37, Calvin teaches that, while repentance means conversion, namely, the turning over to the way of the Lord, regeneration is the inner change which is manifest in repentance. This inner change, for Calvin, consists of two aspects: "the mortification of our flesh, that is, a killing of our inborn corruption; and the spiritual vivification through which man's nature is restored into integrity."[15] As such, regeneration is thought of as a lifetime process; the "regeneration is never accomplished as long as we are in the prison of this mortal body," says Calvin.[16]

However, regeneration can also be understood in a narrow sense, as the later generation of Reformed theologians generally used the term, that is, to denote a gracious action of God through the Holy Spirit, of which repentance and faith are the fruit.[17] Regeneration is here viewed as a starting point of a new life, of being born again (or rebirth), rather than a lifetime process of renewal.[18] The SC employs the term regeneration to denote the born again experience wrought by the Holy Spirit, without which no one can be freed from the power and dominion of everlasting death.[19] Through regeneration, the Holy Spirit creates "in the hearts of chosen ones an assured faith" by which they "grasp Christ Jesus with the graces and blessings promised in Him."[20] The HC, CoD, and Westminster Standards resonate

---

14. Kuiper, *By Grace Alone*, 36.
15. CC37 XVIII; GC VIII.
16. CC37 XVIII.
17. See for example Francis Turretin, *Institutes of Elenctic Theology*, trans. George Musgrave Giger, ed. James T. Dennison, Jr., 3 vols. (Philipsburg: P&R, 1992-1997), XII.i.8; XV.iv-vi. Turretin sees the spiritual regeneration as a similitude of the physical generation of human beings. Cf. Gulielmus Bucanus, a French Reformed theologian of the late sixteenth century, who seemingly followed Calvin in viewing regeneration as a process of "transformation or renewing of the soul," which "shall be perfected in the life to come." *Institutions of Christian Religion*, trans. Robert Hill (London: 1659), 349. Rohls seems to hold this narrow view of regeneration. *Reformed Confessions*, 159.
18. Regeneration as "the very beginning of a new life, a new creation, a new creature." Ames, *The Marrow of Theology*, I.xxvi.19.
19. See Barth, *The Theology of the Reformed Confessions*, 130.
20. SC III. The SC XII indicates that there are moments before and after regeneration, meaning that regeneration is understood as an event rather than a process.

with the SC on this. Drawing from Jesus' discourse with Nicodemus (Jn. 3:3-5), the HC teaches regeneration as the beginning point of a new life, the overcoming of the dominion of original sin; "unless we are born again," we are "totally unable to do any good and inclined toward all evil."[21] Defining the regeneration of the Holy Spirit as "the new creation, the raising from the dead, and the making alive," the CoD similarly points out that this regeneration initiates the radical change in human will, a reform of the "distorted nature" of human beings that sets the elect free from the reign and slavery of sin.[22] The WCF views regeneration as integrated with effectual calling. It takes place prior to and is followed further by sanctification.[23]

True faith (or saving faith) is unequivocally attributed by the Reformed confessions solely to the Holy Spirit. Acknowledging that faith is a human act of believing, the Reformed unwaveringly aver the nature of true faith as God's gift.[24] Calvin emphatically states, "we shall not doubt that faith greatly surpasses all the power of our nature and that faith is a unique and

---

21. HC Q/A 8. Ursinus is indecisive about this as he uses the term regeneration equivocally. On the one hand he seems to suggest that regeneration is God's initial act of renovating the nature of man through the Word of God by his Spirit. On the other hand, he also suggests that regeneration will only be perfectly accomplished in the state of glorification. Ursinus, *Commentary*, 64-65. Klooster leans more to the former interpretation than to the latter. For Klooster, regeneration is a radical change, a root change, that takes place in believers, a moment in which they are brought from death to life. Regeneration is the beginning point of a lifelong process of sanctification, whereby a born-again believer is renewed in holiness by the Spirit until she reaches the goal of perfection (HC Q/A 115). Klooster, *Our Only Comfort*, 110-120.

22. CoD III/IV.3, 12; V.1.

23. WCF X.1-3; XIII.1-3. William Perkins, one of the foremost leaders of the Puritan movement in the Church of England, also known as the father of pietism, holds that regeneration (or being born again) is the initial point of a new life; it is the starting point where sanctification begins. It is putting on of the new self, which radically changes the inclination of the soul. Perkins refers to Ef. 4:24. William Perkins, "A Treatise of God's Free Grace and Man's Free-Will," in *The Whole Works of That Famous and Worthy Minister of Christ in the Vniversitie of Cambridge* (London: John Legatt, 1631), 1:729-730; "Golden Chaine," in *The Whole Works*, 1:85. Being regenerated is necessary for beginning the mortification of sin and the vivification of a renewed life, as the union with Christ brings forth spiritual blessings. Regeneration is the gift of the Holy Spirit, whereby "a childe of Satan . . . is made the child of God." Perkins, "An Exposition of the Symbole," in *The Whole Works*, 1:271.

24. Bullinger in SHC XVI.1 defines faith as threefold, consisting of "a most firm trust" (*fiducia*), "assent of the mind" (*assensus*), and "a most certain apprehension of the truth of God" (*notitia*). See Ursinus, *The Commentary*, 108; Turretin, *Institutes of Elenctic Theology*, XV.viii; Rohls, *Reformed Confessions*, 129-130.

precious gift of God."²⁵ The Holy Spirit is the sole agent behind the creation of faith. True faith is, as Calvin succinctly states, "the singular gift of the Holy Spirit."²⁶ The Holy Spirit creates faith in the hearts of believers by enlightening their minds and making them capable of understanding what would otherwise be incomprehensible to them, and fortifying in them in certitude, sealing and imprinting the promises of salvation on their hearts.²⁷

Faith, as the sole instrument of justification given only to the elect, is the only means pleasing and acceptable to God by which human beings can be partakers of the divine redemption in the covenant of grace.²⁸ By this faith, believers may receive all the graces and blessings that Christ has obtained in his redemption as promised in the Gospel. This saving faith is irresistible and effectual as it is given by the power of the Holy Spirit along with other saving graces.²⁹ Therefore, having true faith, and consequently bearing fruit of repentance, is a sign of being a true member of Jesus Christ, of election.³⁰ True faith and its fruit provide the elect with the proper assurance of election, and since both faith and its fruit evidently flow from the work of the Holy Spirit, the elect "have no cause to glory, but are bound to be doubly thankful" that they have been chosen by God.³¹ There is no room for the so-called "works righteousness" in the Reformed faith. Even good works are stained by sin. It is by God's grace through the Holy Spirit that the elect are enabled to do good works, arising out of true faith.³² Moreover, faith is given not only to introduce the elect into the way of salvation but also to persevere in it to the end.³³ Only through true faith in Jesus Christ

---

25. CC37 XV. FC XXI states that faith is "a gratuitous and special gift which God grants to whom he will." See Barth, *The Theology of the Reformed Confessions*, 98.
26. CC45 Q/A 112; see also SC XII; SHC XVI.2; CoD II.7-8; WCF VII.3; XIV.1; WLC Q/A 32, 59; WSC Q/A 30; Rohls, *Reformed Confessions*, 128-129.
27. CC37 XV; CC45 Q/A 113; SC III. See Rohls, *Reformed Confessions*, 129.
28. WCF VII.3, 5; XI.2; see WSC Q/A 85, 88. See Rohls, *Reformed Confessions*, 128.
29. CoD III/IV.14; WLC Q/A 32.
30. CC45 Q/A 359; BC XXIX; HC Q/A 32; WCF VII.3; see WLC Q/A 59; WSC Q/A 30.
31. FC XX-XXII; BC XXII; XXIV; CoD III/IV.15; V.10-11; see CoD I.12.
32. See for examples, CC45 Q/A 127; FC XXII; SHC XVI; HC Q/A 91; WCF XVI. See Barth, *The Theology of the Reformed Confessions*, 100.
33. FC XXI; CoD II.8; V.7. HC Q/A 53 teaches that the Holy Spirit is given to make the elect by true faith partakers of Christ and all his benefits, to comfort, and to abide with

produced by the Holy Spirit can the elect stay the course to the end amidst accusations, doubts, and adversities that they may have received.[34] The CoD explicate this by stating that by his Word and Spirit, through faith, God effectively renews the elect to repentance so that, having a heartfelt and godly sorrow for their sins, they may seek and obtain forgiveness in the blood of Christ, and from then on "more eagerly work out their own salvation with fear and trembling."[35]

The tightly knit connection between the Spirit and Word is again exhibited. As true saving faith is based on the promise of God revealed to us in his Word, it can never be independent from the Word. On the one hand, without the Spirit and faith that the Spirit produces in the hearts of the hearers, the preaching of the Word—"the letter," or the law—works wrath and provokes sin (2 Cor. 3:6). But on the other hand, as the BC states, faith is produced by the hearing of the Word and by the work of the Holy Spirit.[36] By God's Word and Spirit through faith, the elect are ever renewed and brought to repentance by God so they may experience again the grace of God and persevere to the end.[37]

Repentance—as conversion to God, that is a sincere turning to God and all good, and earnest turning away from the devil and all evil—always goes together with faith as a result of regeneration.[38] In regeneration God works immediately turning sinners unto himself—giving them new spirits and dispositions—and believers assume a passive role, but in repentance, God works mediately through his outward means of grace and believers assume an active role. Repentance, taking place along with sanctification as a lifelong process of turning one's self from sin to God, is thus twofold. It consists of two parts: the mortification of the old life and the vivification of the new life.[39] Repentance is a manifestation of the spiritual change of

---

them forever.
34. HC Q/A 60.
35. CoD V.7.
36. BC XXIV; HC Q/A 21-22, 65; SHC XIII.4, XVI.2.
37. CoD V.7.
38. CC37 XVIII; CC45 Q/A 127; SHC XIV.2-3.
39. CC37 XVIII; see also Perkins' detailed discussion of these two parts of repentance in "Two Treatises," in *The Whole Works*, 1:457-458.

disposition, or in Calvin's words, "Dissatisfaction with and a hatred of evil and a love of good proceeding from the fear of God, and inducing us to mortify our flesh, so that we may be governed and led by the Holy Spirit, in the service of God."[40]

Without underestimating the active role and responsibility of believers, the Reformed confessions teach that it is the Holy Spirit who works throughout the process by enabling, governing, and empowering believers to repent from a sinful life.[41] Repentance is also a gift from God, an evangelical grace wrought by the Holy Spirit.[42] As the HC states, it is through the Holy Spirit that God assures us of eternal life and makes us sincerely willing and ready to live unto God (2 Cor. 1:20-22; 5:5; Eph. 1:13-14; Rm. 8:16).[43] The only part of repentance in which believers take part, and thus are held responsible, is an active obedience to God's will to live a life of service to God, that is, to walk after the Spirit.[44]

God justifies believers in Christ and makes them right with him, through faith. Believers are justified for the sake of Christ alone because the righteousness of Christ is credited to them. God does not justify believers by the infusion of righteousness, or on the basis of their faith (the act of believing) or obedience, but on the basis of the imputation of the obedience and satisfaction of Christ unto them alone.[45] Faith itself, graciously given by the Holy Spirit to believers, plays a significant role in justification as the sole instrument of justification through which believers receive their justification.[46] Thus, as the WCF well summarizes, "God did from all

---

40. CC45 Q/A 128; see Rohls, *Reformed Confessions*, 140.
41. CC45 Q/A 128; SHC IX.7; WCF X.1. Barth correctly states that faith and repentance are not to be found outside the Holy Spirit. *The Theology of the Reformed Confessions*, 103.
42. SHC XIV.3; WCF XV.1; WLC Q/A 76; WSC Q/A 87.
43. HC Q/A 1.
44. SHC XIV.10. It thus makes sense that, as Bullinger states, all actual sins are fundamentally sins against the Holy Spirit. SHC VIII.5.
45. CC37 XVII; HC Q/A 60-61; see WLC Q/A 70, 77. To be noted, as WCF points out, it is through "the eternal Spirit" that Christ by his perfect obedience and sacrifice of himself once offered up unto God and has fully satisfied the justice of the Father. WCF VIII.5. Barth correctly identifies that "Calvin is an adherent of a strictly imputative doctrine of justification." Barth, *The Theology of the Reformed Confessions*, 99.
46. BC XXIV; WCF XI.2.

eternity, decree to justify the elect; and Christ did, in the fullness of time, die for their sins and rise again for their justification; nevertheless they are not justified until the Holy Spirit doth, in due time, actually apply Christ unto them."[47]

"By the power of the Holy Spirit," Calvin states, "[Christ] justifies, sanctifies and purifies, calls and attracts us to himself in order that we may obtain deliverance."[48] Through the Holy Spirit God makes believers partakers of the redemption by dwelling in their hearts to apply Christ's redemption to them and confirming it in them.[49] The elect, that is, the members of the invisible church, have communion in grace with Christ and been united with Christ by virtue of their justification applied by the Holy Spirit.[50]

Being justified or made right with God, believers are made children of God through adoption, by receiving the Spirit of adoption, the Spirit of the Son.[51] The radical change concerns the believers' lives as much as their status before God and their relationship with him. Believers are now therefore enabled by the Holy Spirit to live before God as children of God, living a righteous, holy life in the fear of God according to the Word, working out what has been worked within.

Inseparable yet distinct from justification is sanctification.[52] Sanctification is a gracious act of the Holy Spirit to renew one's entire nature according to

---

47. WCF XI.4; cf. Barth, *The Theology of the Reformed Confessions*, 141.
48. CC37 XX; see also WCF III.6; WSC Q/A 33-35. WSC does not mention the Holy Spirit when it defines justification, adoption, and sanctification. Instead, it uses the term "an act of God's free grace." But from the nature of the works involved, the works clearly imply the agency of the Holy Spirit.
49. CC45 Q/A 89-91, 95; WLC Q/A 58-59; WSC Q/A 29-30.
50. WLC Q/A 69.
51. TNA XVII; HC Q/A 33; WCF XII; WLC Q/A 74.
52. See Rohls, *Reformed Confessions*, 140. WLC Q/A 77 states the difference between the two very clearly. "Although Sanctification be inseparably joyned with justification, yet they differ, in that God in Justification imputeth the righteousness of Christ; in Sanctification his Spirit infuseth grace, and enableth to the exercise thereof: in the former, sin is pardoned, in the other, it is subdued, the one doth equally free all believers from the revenging wrath of God, & that perfectly in this life, that they never fall into condemnation, the other is neither equal in all, nor in this life perfect in any, but growing up to perfection."

the image of God, the consecration of the holy people by the Holy Spirit.[53] The Reformed confessions treat sanctification always in relation to the other gracious acts of the Holy Spirit, such as regeneration, faith, justification, and perseverance. However, the close connection of justification and sanctification is more noticeable than other connections in the Reformed confessions. For Calvin, believers are considered as righteous and are sanctified not only by the same God, but also through the same operation, which is that of the Holy Spirit in applying to them Christ's righteousness with all the benefits he acquired for his people. Christ provides righteousness, which then serves as the basis for sanctification. "Christ has been made for us not only righteousness but also sanctification. Hence we cannot receive through faith his righteousness without embracing at the same time that sanctification."[54] The WLC defines sanctification as a gracious act of God through the Holy Spirit applying the death and resurrection of Christ unto the elect to renew them wholly after the image of God.[55]

Unlike justification, the Reformed confessions portray sanctification as a progressive process. Justification does not admit of degrees, but sanctification does. A believer cannot be more elected or justified than she is, but she can be more sanctified than she is. As a lifetime process, sanctification consists of two parts: a positive and negative part. Positively, with respect to the virtue of Christ's redemption and God's image, sanctification means drawing from Christ's fulness and receiving grace that Christ has acquired for his people by the help of the Holy Spirit, so the elect may be renewed after the image of God. Negatively, with respect to sins of flesh, sanctification

---

53. The Holy Spirit is usually called the Spirit of sanctification, or the Sanctifier, i.e., the Divine Agent by which God sanctifies his people. CC37 XVII, XX; CC45 Q/A 96, 156, 173 (God governs us by the Holy Spirit, as we mortify our flesh and renounce our own nature), 203; SHC XXVI.1 (the human bodies are the temples of the Holy Spirit); SC XII; BC IX, XXVII; HC Q/A 24; Cf. CC45 Q/A 96; WCF III.6, XIII.1; WLC Q/A 13, 69, 75; WSC Q/A 36. See Barth, *The Theology of the Reformed Confessions*, 99.

54. CC37 XVII. The BC and HC follow Calvin on this, but express it in a different way, by pairing "the blood" and "the Spirit of Christ" together in their discussions concerning sanctification. BC XXVII teaches that the holy catholic church is washed by Christ's blood and sanctified and sealed by the Holy Spirit. HC Q/A 70 similarly teaches that in baptism the church is reminded and reassured of Christ's promise that we are "washed with his blood and Spirit."

55. WLC Q/A 75.

means mortifying the deeds of flesh through the power of the Holy Spirit. In both parts, responsible human participation is definitely involved; but nevertheless, the Holy Spirit plays an indispensable role in the process.[56] In the sanctification process, the elect receive the benefits from the indwelling of the Holy Spirit; they are empowered by the Holy Spirit to "more and more die unto sin, and rise unto newness of life."[57]

In mortifying the old self, the Holy Spirit applies the death and resurrection of Christ unto the elect, removing the guilt of sin from our consciences and affirming God's gracious pardon in them.[58] In Calvin's words, "As the blood of Christ is our cleansing, the Holy Spirit must sprinkle our consciences with it that they may be cleansed."[59] By this Calvin means that the Holy Spirit "makes us feel the virtue" of Christ's redemption, as he "enlightens us to know His benefits; He seals and imprints them in our souls, and makes room for them in us (Eph. 1:13)."[60] Moreover, as Calvin wonderfully illustrates, the Holy Spirit also daily mortifies and consumes "more and more the vices of our desire or greed," such that "without the Spirit there is in us nothing but darkness of understanding and perversity of heart."[61]

In quickening the new self, the Holy Spirit applies all the blessings and gifts offered to believers in Jesus Christ necessary for the new life.[62] In his catechism, Calvin teaches that Christ by his Spirit sets believers at liberty in their conscience and fills them with spiritual riches so that they may live in righteousness and holiness.[63] Without a doubt, spiritual disciplines—such as prayer and fasting—are of paramount importance in the lives of

---

56. Barth seems to overlook the role of human responsibility in sanctification when he regards sanctification—along with calling, justification, adoption—as "the things that mainly happen to man," in which human beings are considered to assume a passive role. *The Theology of the Reformed Confessions*, 141-142.
57. WLC Q/A 75.
58. WLC Q/A 75.
59. CC45 Q/A 90.
60. CC45 Q/A 91.
61. CC37 XX ("I believe in the holy Spirit").
62. CC45 Q/A 91.
63. CC45 Q/A 42. In BC XXIX, the distinguishing marks of Christians include the desires to follow after righteousness and to love the true God and neighbor.

believers, as some of the Reformed confessions teach.⁶⁴ However, it is the Spirit that works through them and makes spiritual disciplines effectual. As Calvin asserts, the Spirit helps believers pray, induces and urges them to approach God, governs them by the Word, and creates in them new spirits and new hearts, "so that we may will nothing of ourselves, but rather that His Spirit may will in us, and bring us into full agreement with Him."⁶⁵ By his Word and Spirit dwelling in the elect, as the WCF also asserts, God quickens and strengthens them, in all saving graces, to the practice of true holiness, so that they may grow in grace and press on in holiness in the fear of God.⁶⁶ The Reformed confessions also assert that besides working inwardly through his Spirit in the hearts and lives of believers, God also gives outward means through which the Holy Spirit operates in the process. God bestows upon believers the law to guide, the sacraments to nourish, and the church to nurture them as they walk in the path of righteousness, cultivating holiness, employing spiritual gifts, and doing good works all the rest of their lives. These outward means will be discussed in detail in following sections.

God preserves; the elect persevere. The Reformed confessions teach that true believers, or the elect, will eventually persevere to the end.⁶⁷ They may lose temporarily in spiritual warfare against their spiritual enemies and thus "depart from the grace given and fall into sin," but then by the grace of God they may arise again and amend their lives.⁶⁸

In the Reformed theology, the decisive role in the perseverance of the elect is God, who works through the Holy Spirit to preserve and sustain, and is never human beings in themselves. The thorough explication of the doctrine of perseverance in the CoD (that is, "The Fifth Head of the Doctrine") is definitely a helpful summary of the doctrine developed in the Reformed tradition. The fifth Canon witnesses the attribution of the

---

64. See for example SHC XXIV. Bullinger regards fasting as a spiritual discipline by which we are humbled before God, and we deprive the flesh of its fuel so that it may the more willingly and easily obey the Spirit.
65. CC45 Q/A 244, 250, 268, 273; see also HC Q/A 116, 117, 120, 123.
66. WCF XIII.2-3; see also WLC Q/A 77.
67. For examples, SC XII; XIII; SHC IX.10; CoD V.3; WCF XVII.1.
68. TNA XVI.

perseverance of the elect to the Holy Spirit. Almost every article in the section acknowledges the work of the Holy Spirit as the comforting reality that assures and secures the salvation of the elect. Salvation of believers rests on God, who works through the Holy Spirit according to his perfect and immutable will: "So it is not by their own merits or strength but by God's undeserved mercy that they neither forfeit faith and grace totally nor remain in their downfalls to the end and are lost."[69]

The indwelling of the Holy Spirit in believers is "the sealing" that "can neither be invalidated nor wiped out," and "God, who is rich in mercy, according to his unchangeable purpose of election does not take his Holy Spirit from his own completely, even when they fall grievously."[70] In other words, it is the Holy Spirit, given once-for-all as promised, that effectually and unfailingly helps believers to persevere. The work of the Holy Spirit in the lives of believers, therefore, brings consolation and assurance of salvation that will give them hope and true faith necessary to stay the course and be faithful to the end.[71]

The Holy Spirit and the Doctrine of the Church

The Reformed confessions testify to the manifold work of the Holy Spirit in the life of the church. However, only some aspects of the work of the Holy Spirit in the teaching of the Reformed confessions pertaining to the church have been commonly identified by some scholars such as Barth and Rohls. These aspects of the Spirit's work in the church pertain to the

---

69. CoD V.8.
70. CoD V.6, 8; WCF XVII.2; XVIII.4; WLC Q/A 79, 81.
71. HC Q/A 1; CoD V.8-11; WCF XVIII.1-4; XXXIII.3. Cf. *The Theology of the Reformed Confessions*, 108-109 (on HC), 143-144 (on WCF). Barth seems to overlook the WCF's (and also HC's) emphasis on this point. By assuming the assurance of salvation to be probably the sole purpose of the doctrinal elaboration in the WCF, Barth overlooks the fact that even though the assurance of salvation in the WCF as in other Reformed confessions is something to be sought or to make sure of, it is not purported to be the end in and of itself. Instead, the assurance given is to be grace that accompanies believers and encourages them to be diligent in the duties of obedience. See Watson, *A Body of Practical Divinity*, 221-223 (the three uses of perseverance).

identity and the marks of the true church. Other aspects, which pertain to the preservation of the church, the unity of the church, the diversity of spiritual gifts, and the evangelistic mission of the church remain inadequately treated. This section will discuss briefly those aspects that have already been identified and leave the other aspects for more detailed discussions in the following chapters.

The church is not in any sense an appendix to the application of redemption upon individual believers, in spite of the common placement of the doctrine of the church following the doctrine of salvation in the Reformed confessions.[72] Rather, the church is the necessary and anticipated result of, and inseparable from, the divine work of redemption.[73] The salvation of individual believers is definitely not the terminal point of redemption, as the Holy Spirit continues to gather the elect, unite them into the one body of Christ, his church, and equip and empower them—as one body—to do God's mission. The work of the Holy Spirit is as inseparable from the life of the church as it is from the lives of believers.

The Reformed confessions teach that the presence and work of the Holy Spirit distinguish the church from other social entities. The whole existence of the church and its continuation—its being and *raison d'être*, its identity and action—come from God, who works through his Spirit.

The Holy Spirit is involved in the church from its inception, even before the constitution of the world. Rohls correctly identifies the close connection between the doctrine of the church and of election in the Reformed confessions. "The church is no longer defined as a *community* elected by Christ, to which individuals belong, but as a communion of elect *individuals*."[74] Calvin sees God the Trinity as "the fountain from which the Church springs."[75] He then defines the catholic church as the assembly of

---

72. As Barth points out, in the Tarczal-Torda Confession, which is basically the adaptation to the Hungarian situation of a confession written by Theodorus Beza in 1560, the Holy Spirit (chapter 4) and the church (chapter 5) are even posited as the actual center of the confession. Barth, *The Theology of the Reformed Confessions*, 116-117.
73. Calvin, for example, asserts that the church is the fruit that proceeds from the death of Christ. CC45 Q/A 94.
74. Rohls, *Reformed Confessions*, 167; emphasis his.
75. CC37 XX ("I believe the holy Church universal, the communion of saints").

the people of God, the community of the faithful, "of which Christ our Lord is the leader and prince and head, as of one body, so that in him they have been elected before the constitution of the world, to the end that they may be all assembled in the kingdom of God."[76] The SC defines the church as "one company and multitude of men chosen by God, who rightly worship and embrace Him by true faith in Christ Jesus."[77] In a similar tone, the BC states that the holy catholic church is "a holy congregation and gathering of true Christian believers," who are "being washed by [Christ's] blood, and sanctified and sealed by the Holy Spirit."[78] The HC also asserts that Christ, through his Spirit and Word, gathers, protects, and preserves for himself from the beginning of the world to its end "a community chosen for eternal life," out of the entire human race.[79]

Identifying the holy catholic church as a communion of the elect leads the Reformed to make a distinction between the invisible and visible church. The distinguishing point between the two is made with pneumatological awareness. It is the inward work of the Holy Spirit that differentiates the membership compositions of both churches. While the invisible church consists of none but the elect, thereby only visible to God, the visible church consists of both the elect and the non-elect mingling together for a time. As Calvin elucidates, without the work of the Holy Spirit applying divine redemption, "no persons are received" into the invisible church.[80] Ursinus similarly states that the visible church consists of those who are regenerated and unregenerated, while the invisible church consists only of those who are regenerated by the Holy Spirit.[81] In other words, without the inward work of the Holy Spirit applying divine redemption, one can only

---

76. CC37 XX ("I believe the holy Church universal, the communion of saints"); CC45 Q/A 93; see SHC XVII.1.

77. SC XVI.

78. BC XXVII.

79. HC Q/A 132; see also Olevianus, *A Firm Foundation*, Q/A 54; Ursinus, *The Commentary*, 286. Cf. Rohls, *Reformed Confessions*, 174. Rohls asserts that as faith arises from the hearing of God's word, the church as the communion of the faithful is itself a creature of the word (*creatura verbi*) and lives from the word of God. The reference to the Holy Spirit, as evident in the Reformed confessions, is curiously missing here.

80. Calvin, *Institutes*, IV.i.7.

81. Ursinus, *The Commentary*, 287; see also Bullinger, *Decades*, V.1 (7).

become a member of the visible church, but never of the invisible church. The non-elect may outwardly confess Christ, profess the true religion, and even enjoy the outward work of the Holy Spirit together with the elect in the preservation and government of the visible church, but only the elect, the members of the invisible church, can truly experience the inward work of the Holy Spirit, spiritually nurturing, nourishing, and sanctifying them through the outward means of church ministry.[82]

Are there signs that mark the true visible church? Rohls rightly identifies "the pure teaching of the gospel (*pura doctrina evangelii*) and the right administration of the sacraments (*recta administratio sacramentorum*)" as the two most necessary signs of the true visible church according to most of the Reformed confessions.[83] Some Reformed confessions include a few other things as marks of the true church. The SC, for example, adds ecclesiastical discipline as the third mark of the true church and qualifies it by asserting that it is so "as God's Word prescribes, whereby vice is repressed and virtue nourished."[84] Similarly, for the BC, besides "the pure preaching of the gospel" and "the use of the pure administration of the sacraments," the true church can be recognized by its practice of "church discipline for correcting faults." The BC then adds, "In short, [the true church] governs itself according to the pure Word of God."[85] Bullinger in his *Decades* teaches that there are "two special and principal marks"—namely, "the sincere preaching of the word of God" and "the lawful partaking of the sacraments of Christ"—and states further that some add unto the two principal marks things that are included in them.[86] Later in the SHC, Bullinger declares that the true church should be characterized especially by its "lawful and sincere preaching of the Word of God" and then adds that its members should bear marks such as right worship ("worship but one God"), perseverance in "the bond of peace and holy unity," and participation in "the sacraments

---

82. SHC XVII.16; WCF XXV.3; see also SC XXV; WLC Q/A 63, 65-66, 68, 83.
83. Rohls, *Reformed Confessions*, 174-177. See also TC XV; FHC XIV; GC XVIII; FC XXVIII; TNA XIX; Calvin, *Institutes*, IV.x.10-11.
84. SC XVIII; see also CECG IV; CoD III/IV.17.
85. BC XXIX. See also Ursinus, *The Commentary*, 288-289.
86. Bullinger, *Decades*, V.i (17).

instituted by Christ."[87] The WCF adds the purity of public worship to "the doctrine of the gospel" and "ordinances" as one of the marks of the true church.[88]

However, regardless of the slightly diverse formulations of the true marks of the true church in the Reformed confessions, the Word and sacraments are undoubtedly considered by the Reformed as the two principal marks of the true church, as Bullinger states. In both marks and other additional marks, although often not explicitly stated, the role of the Holy Spirit is nevertheless definitely presupposed and prominent.[89]

On the one hand, there is no church where the Word of God is not preached, taught, kept, and lived out. Nor is there any faithful ministry of the Word without the presence and work of the Holy Spirit. The Holy Spirit cannot be separated from the Word. There can be no church "where the Word of God is not received, nor profession made of subjection to it, nor use of sacraments," the FC states.[90] It is through the work of the Holy Spirit that one recognizes, receives, and believes in the Word of God—and along with it its authority—as it is written, preached, taught, expounded, and enlivened.[91] The Holy Spirit quickens the dead souls of the elect, removes the darkness from their minds, and bows their stubborn hearts to the obedience of the will of God, when it is revealed through the propagation of the Word by the church.[92] In the SHC Bullinger warns against attributing too much to ministers and the ministry and asserts that "God teaches

---

87. SHC XVII.

88. WCF XXV.4.

89. Beza states that the preaching of the Word and sacraments are the ordinary and common means that the Holy Spirit uses for the benefit of God's children. Theodorus Beza, *A Briefe and Piththie [sic] Sum of the Christian Faith, Made in Forme of a Confession, with a Confutation of All Such Superstitious Errours, as are Contrarie Thereunto*, trans. R. F. (London: William How, 1572), IV.4; *A Little Catechisme* (London: Hugh Sngleton, 1579), VII.1; see also Barth, *The Theology of the Reformed Confessions*, 116, 119. Beza's *Sum of the Christian Faith* is also known as *Confession de la Foy Chrétienne*, which was probably published in French in 1559, the same year when twenty delegates representing seventy-two churches met secretly in a private house in Paris to adopt the Genevan draft, written by Calvin, Beza, & Viret, with a few alterations. See Cochrane, *Reformed Confessions of the Sixteenth Century*, 138.

90. FC XXVIII.

91. See chapter 2, "The Holy Spirit and the Doctrine of Scripture."

92. SC XII; see also CC45 Q/A 113.

us by his word, outwardly through his ministers, and inwardly moves the hearts of the elect to faith by the Holy Spirit; and that therefore we ought to render all glory unto God for this whole favor."[93] The WCF asserts that by the power of the Spirit the ministry of the church becomes effectual for the gathering and perfecting of the saints, for the upbuilding of the church.[94] It is the power and authority of the Holy Spirit that accompanies the faithful ministry of the Word and makes it vital and effectual for the church.[95]

On the other hand, the sacraments are also ordained by God to be added to the Word as means by which God nourishes and strengthens the faith of believers. This being said, a discussion of the work of the Holy Spirit in the sacraments is in order.

The Holy Spirit and the Doctrine of Sacraments

In the midst of the theological controversy of the sixteenth and seventeenth centuries concerning the sacraments, the Reformed theologians felt the need to formulate their view of the sacraments. The incorporating of the doctrine of sacraments into confessional norms reveals how important the issue of the sacraments is to the Reformed. The teaching of the sacraments in the Reformed confessions discloses what the Reformed communities confessionally believe and teach about sacraments. At the same time, the Reformed confessions also point out the different views of sacraments held by churches of different traditions, that is, the Roman Catholic and Lutheran traditions.

On the one hand, as the historical context of the confessions shows, the Reformed, along with the Lutherans, took a stand against the Roman Catholic *ex opere operato* understanding of sacraments as declared in the Council of Trent (1545-1563), that the efficacy of the sacramental rites

---

93. SHC XVIII.2.
94. WCF XXV.3; see also Watson, *A Body of Divinity*, 128, 404-408.
95. Rohls, *Reformed Confessions*, 177-181. Barth identifies this teaching in the third article of the Frankfurt Confession that deals with the Holy Spirit. Barth, *The Theology of the Reformed Confessions*, 107-108.

rests on the work performed.⁹⁶ On the other hand, the Reformed and the Lutherans were also faced with the teaching of various Enthusiasts (*Schwärmer*) and Anabaptists. The former claim the immediacy of the Spirit, namely, that the Spirit works without the use of the means of grace—the preaching of the Word or the Gospel and sacraments.⁹⁷ As David Dickson points out, the latter, with the Socinians, maintain that the sacraments are not seals of the covenant of grace, but only "bare tokens" and "[t]ests of our Christian profession."⁹⁸

In their objection to these views of sacrament, the Reformed offer a high view of sacrament, that sacraments are divinely ordained visible signs and not bare or empty signs.⁹⁹ Sacraments play a significant role in the life

---

96. The Council of Trent, *The Canons and Decrees of the Sacred and Oecumenical Council of Trent*, trans. J. Waterworth (Chicago: The Christian Symbolic Publication Society, 1848), VII.6-8. Ludwig Ott maintains that the *ex opere operato* formula of the Council of Trent asserts, "positively, that the sacramental grace is caused by the validly operated sacramental sign" to the extent that any identification of the sacramental language *ex opere operato* with *ex opere a Christo operato* is "historically false; for the scholastic term does not purport to indicate the source (causa meritoria) of the sacramental grace, but the nature and manner of the sacramental operation of grace." Ludwig Ott, *Fundamentals of Catholic Dogma*, trans. Patrick Lynch (Rockford: Tan Books and Publishers, 1974), 329-330. See also Richard P. McBrien, *Catholicism*, 2 vols. (Minneapolis: Winston Press, 1980), II, 4.21 (734-735). However, the contemporary Catholic Church leans toward a different *ex opere operato* understanding from the one expounded by Ott, attributing the efficacy of the sacraments to Christ's merit—the sacraments act *ex opere operato* "by virtue of the saving work of Christ, accomplished once for all"—and giving less emphasis on the sacramental rite in its objective accomplishment. See Catholic Church, *Catechism of the Catholic Church*, 2nd ed. (Vatican City: Libreria Editrice Vatican, 2000), II.1127-1128; Peter J. Kreeft, *Catholic Christianity: A Complete Catechism of Catholic Beliefs* (San Francisco: Ignatius Press, 2001), 296-298.

97. Rohls, *Reformed Confessions*, 177. As Muller also notes, the Enthusiasts "claim spiritual gifts for themselves and who claim to be infused with a spiritual form of salvation that is distinct from and perhaps higher than the salvation of the baptized hearer of the Word who participates regularly in the sacrament of the Lord's Supper." Muller, "The Holy Spirit in the Augsburg Confession: A Reformed Definition," *Concordia Theological Quarterly* 61, no. 1-2 (January-April 1997): 62-63. See also FC XXXVIII; Calvin, *Institutes*, I.ix.1-3. Calvin defends the unity of the Word and Spirit against the Enthusiasts (or the fanatics), who insist that the Holy Spirit may work in the life of believers apart from the instrumentality of the Word.

98. David Dickson, *Truths Victory over Error* (Edinburgh: John Reid, 1684), XXVII.1 (264).

99. FHC XX states, "Consequently we confess that the sacraments are not simply outward signs of Christian fellowship. On the contrary, we confess them to be signs of divine grace by which the ministers of the church work with the Lord for the purpose and to the end which He himself promises, offers and efficaciously provides. We confess, however, that all

of the church because at the heart of sacraments is the presence and work of God through the Holy Spirit. Alongside the Lutherans, the Reformed insist that sacraments do not hold their significance primarily because of the work performed by the church at the command of God. Nor do the administrators of sacraments in and of themselves—the church and her lawfully called ministers—add to the vitality and importance of sacraments. In their definition and description of sacraments, especially in relation to faith, the efficacy and corresponding uses of sacraments, the key role of the Holy Spirit in sacraments is declared and highlighted.

The Reformed confessions define sacraments as visible signs and seals ordained and instituted by God to be the means by which he nourishes faith in the hearts of believers.[100] In their expositions of sacraments, the Reformed confessions not only maintain that the past reception of the invisible grace of God is signified by the sacraments, but also that God actually works through sacraments by his Spirit.[101] Sacraments can become expedient to the faith of God's people only by the operation of the Holy Spirit.

---

sanctifying and saving power is to be ascribed to God, the Lord, alone. . . ." SC XXI even states, "And so we utterly condemn the vanity of those who affirm the sacraments to be nothing else than naked and bare signs." See also TNA XXV; WCF XXVII.3; WLC Q/A 161; WSC Q/A 91.

100. See GC XIV; CC37 XXVI; CC45 Q/A 310; TNA XXV; WCF XXVII.1; WLC Q/A 162; WSC Q/A 92. As Muller indicates, the Reformed Confessions and catechisms "tend to indicate that the Word is the primary and necessary means of grace, while the sacraments are subordinate to the Word and are to be understood as means, certainly, but as means that 'confirm' or 'seal' the grace given in and through the Word." Muller, "The Holy Spirit in the Augsburg Confession," 65. Also to be noted, the Reformed and the Lutherans only admit two sacraments (baptism and the Lord's Supper), while the Roman Catholics also include confirmation, confession, holy orders, matrimony, and the anointing of the sick. For further discussion regarding type and number of sacraments, see Rohls, *Reformed Confessions*, 189-193.

101. Despite differences among the Reformed confessions in their ways to explicate the relationship between the administration of the sacraments and the work of the Holy Spirit, the Reformed confessions fully agree that when a sacrament is administered, the Holy Spirit actually works. As Muller points out, the Reformed confessions "affirm either that sacraments are means of grace or that grace is certainly made available through the work of the Spirit as signified by the sacramental elements." The former view is associated with Calvin; it maintains "a clear sacramental instrumentality." Calvin holds for the operation of the Holy Spirit in and through the administration of the sacraments, the ordained signs. The latter, associated with Bullinger, contends for "a covenantal parallelism between the outward administration of the signs and the inward work of the Spirit." In any case, the work of the Holy Spirit is never in question. Muller, "The Holy Spirit in the Augsburg

The significance of the Holy Spirit and his operation for understanding the role of faith in the sacraments cannot be overstressed when seen from the larger context of the doctrine of faith. The Reformed confessions give evidence of the crucial role of faith—and thus of the Holy Spirit—in sacraments, that faith is prerequisite for and the purpose of receiving the sacraments. Rohls correctly identifies in the Reformed confessions, that faith is a necessary subjective disposition for the sacrament to be efficacious—the spiritual benefits of the sacraments can only be received in and by faith.[102] The GC confesses that faith—proceeding from the Holy Spirit alone—is "the entrance which we have to the great treasures and riches of the goodness of God that is vouchsafed to us" and God has ordained the sacraments to be "exercises of faith."[103] Or, as Calvin firmly and clearly asserts, the sacraments can only give assurance of grace when one "receive them in faith, seeking Jesus Christ alone and His grace in them."[104] Bullinger maintains that the sacraments were given to the peoples of both the Old and New Testaments. The sacraments "should be received spiritually by faith, and should bind the receivers to the church, and admonish them of their duty."[105]

The role of the Holy Spirit as the giver and creator of faith has been discussed in the previous section. The role of the Holy Spirit in the growth of faith by the right use of sacraments is now in order. As Rohls notes, the Reformed confessions teach that sacraments are ordained by God to be outward signs of God's grace by means of which God, through his

---

Confession," 69. For further discussion of both Calvin's and Bullinger's positions on sacraments (especially the Lord's Supper), of their negotiations, and of the final agreement, see Paul Rorem, *Calvin and Bullinger on the Lord's Supper* (Bramcotte: Grove Books Limited, 1989); Rohls, *Reformed Confessions*, 181-185.

102. Rohls, *Reformed Confessions*, 185-189.

103. GC X; XI; XIV. CC37 XXVI also teaches sacraments as "exercises of our faith both before God and before men."

104. CC45 Q/A 316-317. FC XXXVI calls baptism "a sacrament of faith and penitence" and the Lord's Supper "a witness of the union which we have in Christ, so heavenly that "it can only be apprehended by faith." Beza, one of the framers of the FC, in his *A Confession of Faith*, contends that those who receive sacraments without a true faith will not enjoy the things signified. Beza, *A Confession of Faith, Made by Common Consent of Diuers Reformed Churches beyond the Seas* (London: Henry Bynneman, 1571), XIX. SC XXIII similarly holds that both sacraments are only for the faithful.

105. SHC XIX.5.

Spirit, sustains and nourishes the faith of believers through the sealing of the divine promises offered in the Word of God.[106] In CC45 Calvin defines a sacrament as "An outward attestation of the grace of God," which represents "spiritual things to imprint the promises of God more firmly in our hearts, and to make us more sure of them," which is divinely ordained for "the alleviation of our weakness."[107] Following this definition, Calvin immediately makes a distinction between the power of the Holy Spirit and that of the sacraments in bringing assurance to the conscience of believers. For Calvin, the power to touch and move hearts, enlighten minds, and assure consciences belongs entirely to the Spirit of God so that praise may be ascribed to God alone, not to the visible signs or sacraments of themselves.[108] God uses sacraments as "inferior instruments according as it seems good to Him, without in any way detracting from the power of His Spirit."[109] The power and instrumentality of sacraments in the life of the church is fully dependent on and tied to the work of the Holy Spirit. In his *Institutes,* Calvin states,

> But the sacraments properly fulfill their office only when the Spirit, that inward teacher, comes to [the participants], by whose power alone hearts are penetrated and affections moved and our souls opened for the sacraments to enter in. If the Spirit be lacking, the sacraments can accomplish nothing more in our minds than the splendor of the sun shining upon blind eyes, or a voice sounding in deaf ears.[110]

---

106. Rohls, *Reformed Confessions,* 183-185; see also "Report 34," 431-432.
107. CC45 Q/A 310, 314; see also CC37 XXVI.
108. CC45 Q/A 311-312.
109. CC45 Q/A 312-313. The FC makes a similar emphasis, that sacraments are added to the Word that "they may be to us pledges and seals of the grace of God," as means "to aid and comfort our faith." The FC then goes on to say that they are "outward signs through which God operates by his Spirit, so that he may not signify any thing to us in vain" and that without "their substance and truth," which is in Jesus Christ, sacraments of themselves are "only smoke and shadow." FC XXXIV. Beza also states that by means of the sacraments God strengthens and increases one's faith by the Holy Spirit working in his/her heart. Beza, *A Confession of Faith,* XIX.
110. Calvin, *Institutes,* IV.xiv.9.

Calvin even strongly warns against diminishing sacraments and their use. In CC45 Calvin contends that since God is pleased to use the sacraments to meet the needs of his people, one who rejects the use of them "condemns Jesus Christ, rejects His grace, and quenches His Holy Spirit."[111]

In the words of the BC, sacraments are "not empty and hollow signs" because they are means by which "God works in us through the power of the Holy Spirit," nourishing, sustaining, and grounding faith in Jesus Christ, and because "their truth is Jesus Christ, without whom they would be nothing."[112] The HC teaches a similar definition of sacraments to that of the BC, highlighting the role of the Holy Spirit in sacraments at the beginning of its discussion of the sacraments. "In the gospel the Holy Spirit teaches us and through the holy sacraments he assures us that our entire salvation rests on Christ's one sacrifice for us on the cross," the HC teaches.[113] In his commentary on the HC, Ursinus in a somewhat scholastic form makes a distinction between the role of the Holy Spirit and the Word and sacraments in producing faith, similar to the distinction that Calvin makes between the Holy Spirit and sacraments. He contends that the Holy Spirit works and confirms faith in believers as "the efficient cause," while the Word and sacraments do the same as "instrumental causes." The Holy Spirit "can also work faith in us independent of the word and the sacraments," while these instruments, on the other hand, "can affect nothing independent" of the Holy Spirit.[114]

Bullinger in the SHC highlights the role of the Holy Spirit in the sacraments, stating that through the sacraments God reminds the church of "the great benefits he has shown to men," "seals his promises," "outwardly represents," and "offers unto our sight those things which inwardly he performs for us, and so strengthens and increases our faith through the working of God's Spirit in our hearts."[115] God, the author of the sacraments, continu-

---

111. CC45 Q/A 315.
112. BC XXXIII.
113. HC Q/A 67. HC Q/A 65 states, "The Holy Spirit produces it in our hearts by the preaching of the holy gospel, and confirms it through our use of the holy sacraments."
114. Ursinus, *The Commentary*, 340. See also Muller, "The Holy Spirit in the Augsburg Confession," 71-72.
115. SHC XIX.1.

ally works in the church in which the sacraments are rightly carried out, so that the church receives the sacraments as from the hand of God.[116] While Christ the Savior is "the principal thing which God promises in all sacraments and to which all the godly in all ages direct their attention," the Holy Spirit is the one through whom Christ circumcises the hearts of the elect, washes them from all their sins, and nourishes them with the very body and blood of Christ unto eternal life.[117] Compared to the sacraments of the Old Testament, that is, circumcision and the Paschal Lamb, the sacraments of the New Testament are more excellent, primarily because they testify that both the substance and the promise have been fulfilled and perfected in Christ. Moreover, Bullinger also adds that the sacraments of the New testament excel because "by the Holy Spirit [these sacraments] kindle greater faith, a greater abundance of the Spirit also ensues."[118]

The SC incorporates both the idea of covenant between God and his people and the concept of *unio mystica* into its definition of sacraments. Sacraments, both of the Old Testament (circumcision and the passover) and of the New (baptism and the Lord's Supper), are ordinances instituted by God and intended to confirm in the hearts of the partakers "that most blessed conjunction, union, and society, which the chosen have with their Head, Christ Jesus." The SC then remarks that "this union and conjunction which we have with the body and blood of Christ Jesus in the right use of sacraments is wrought by means of the Holy Ghost."[119] In line with this thought, the WCF defines sacraments as "holy signs and seals of the covenant of grace, immediately instituted by God, to represent Christ and his benefits, and to confirm our interest in him." The WCF also points to the work of the Holy Spirit as the link that ties together the outward, visible sign and the inward, spiritual grace signified. "The grace which is exhibited in or by sacraments," the WCF confesses, "is not conferred by any power in them," but by "the work of the Holy Spirit, and the word of institution."[120]

---

116. SHC XIX.3.
117. SHC XIX.4.
118. SHC XIX.6.
119. SC XXI.
120. WCF XXVII.3; see also WLC Q/A 161; WSC Q/A 91; Dickson, *Truths Victory over*

Still in relation to faith, two crucial issues of the concept of sacraments which the Reformed Confessions deal with demand special attention. They are the controversies of infant baptism and the participation in the Lord's Supper by the unworthy (the *manducatio impiorum* or *indignorum*). In both cases, the Reformed, as exemplified by the Reformed confessions, maintain the primacy of the work of the Holy Spirit over human works and administrations.

In the case of infant baptism, the Reformed condemn the error of the Anabaptists who deny that children should be baptized before they have faith and understanding, or, in other words, before human preparations or works. The Reformed confessions teach that baptism ought to be received by the children of believers as well as adult believers, since God, through his Spirit, works faith with no regard to age, and the grace of redemption is promised to children as well as to adults. The children born of believers are in God's covenant and thus are his people.[121] The HC adds that infants should be baptized because they, "no less than adults, are promised the forgiveness of sin through Christ's blood and the Holy Spirit who produces faith."[122] In his commentary on the HC, Ursinus explicates further that infants of believers "are included in the covenant, and church of God, unless they exclude themselves." They are "also disciples of Christ, because they are born in the church, or school of Christ; and hence the Holy Spirit teaches them in a manner adapted to their capacity and age."[123]

Error, XXVII.3. Barth identifies this and states that faith is the work of the Holy Spirit, accomplished by the effect of Word and sacrament. Barth, *The Theology of the Reformed Confessions*, 142.

121. FHC XXI; CC45 Q/A 333-339; SC XXIII; BC XXXIV; HC Q/A 74; WCF XXVIII.4; WLC Q/A 166; WSC Q/A 95; see also Heppe, *Reformed Dogmatics*, 620-624.

122. HC Q/A 74; see also BC XXXV; CoD I.17.

123. Ursinus, *The Commentary*, 366-367. In his *Commentary*, Ursinus offers four arguments based on his assertion that children of believers are included in the covenant and that the Holy Spirit works faith regardless of age: (1) all that belong to the covenant and church of God are to be baptized; (2) those to whom the benefit of the remission of sins, and of regeneration belongs are not to be excluded from baptism; (3) God has instituted the sacrament of baptism to distinguish the church from all the various sects and therefore it ought to be extended to all, regardless their age; (4) baptism occupies the place of circumcision in the New Testament, and has the same use that circumcision had in the Old Testament. Against the objection of the Anabaptists that infants are incapable of faith and cannot understand preaching, Calvin argues that Christ is able to sanctify in

In the case of the participation in the Lord's Supper by the unworthy, the Reformed deny a genuine reception of Christ's body and blood by unworthy recipients, namely, the faithless. The faithless do indeed eat and drink the elements, but they do not spiritually eat and drink Christ's body and blood. For the sacrament to be efficacious, the signs ought to be received bodily and the substance—which the signs signify, that is, the communion of the body and blood of Christ, the salvation acquired on the Cross, and forgiveness of sins—ought to be received in faith. The sacraments, the FHC maintains, are not "mere empty signs, but consist of the sign and substance," and "the entire power, efficacy and fruit of the sacraments lies in these spiritual and substantial things" which can only be received in faith.[124] For the same reason, the GC teaches that according to God's ordinance, the Lord's Supper "ought to be distributed in the company of the faithful, in order that all those who wish to have Jesus for their life be partakers of it," and also that Christ feeds and strengthens the believing participants with the substance of his body and blood by the secret and incomprehensible power of his Spirit.[125] Therefore, the sacrament is "heavenly, it can only be apprehended by faith."[126] Or, in other words, Christ is communicated only to believers.[127] Those who come to the Lord's Table lacking the required faith can in no way receive and enjoy the spiritual substance offered in the sacrament, but instead, they bring condemnation upon themselves for their unbelief (1 Cor. 11:26-29).[128]

---

himself his elect from every age without distinction through the power of the Holy Spirit, regenerating and granting faith to them. Calvin, *Institutes*, IV.xvi.17-22. See also Dickson, *Truths Victory over Error*, XXVIII.3.

124. FHC XX; Heppe, *Reformed Dogmatics*, 600; 650-652.

125. GC XVI.

126. FC XXXVI; see also SC XXIII. In *Institutes*, Calvin asserts that the sacraments have effectiveness to foster, confirm, and increase the true knowledge of Christ in ourselves "when we receive in true faith what is offered" in the sacraments and the sacraments are "of no further benefit unless the Holy Spirit accompanies them." Calvin, *Institutes*, IV.xiv.16-17.

127. BC XXXV.

128. See for examples TNA XXV; HC Q/A 81; SHC XXI.9; WCF XXIX.7-8; Calvin, *Institutes*, IV.xiv.16; Ursinus, *The Commentary*, 350-351; Dickson, *Truths Victory over Error*, XXVII.2.

In summary, all Reformed Confessions teach that the sacraments are divinely ordained to be expedient for the faith of the godly, the people of God. Therefore, the sacraments, duly observed, are efficacious and profitable only to the faithful, not to the unfaithful, because at the very nature of the sacraments lies faith and the work of the Holy Spirit confirming faith. Or, in other words, when faith is not present, no benefit or growth of faith might be derived from the observance of the sacraments.[129] Both the requisite faith for sacraments and the growth of faith resulted from the observance of the sacraments are the fruits of the work of the Holy Spirit.

The Reformed confessions highlight even more the crucial importance of the Holy Spirit in the sacraments when describing each of the two sacraments—baptism and the Lord's Supper. In describing each sacrament, the Reformed confessions often reiterate the distinction between the visible signs and the things signified in each sacrament, and then go on to declare the Holy Spirit as the one who works through the sacraments and whose operation or power makes each sacrament effectual.

Baptism has to be administered in the name of the Father, of the Son, and of the Holy Spirit (Matt. 28:19). Not all Reformed confessions explicitly mention the baptism formula in their discussions of the sacrament of baptism.[130] However, none of the Reformed confessions doubt that the holy baptism is the divine work of the Holy Trinity in spite of its administration by human beings. As the FCB asserts, in baptism "the washing away of sins is offered to us by the ministers of the church but can only be effected by the Father, Son, and Holy Spirit."[131]

With regard to the role of the Holy Spirit in baptism, the Reformed confessions also emphasize some aspects of the work of the Holy Spirit that baptism signifies and how the Holy Spirit actively works in the sacramental

---

129. In Heppe's words, "For the unbeliever [sacraments] are completely meaningless, because the unbeliever has no connection with the covenant of grace. . . . The sacraments bring their blessing not *ex opere operato*, i.e., by a saving power dwelling objectively in them, but purely because of the promise, which Christ fulfills directly and personally in believing reception of the sacrament by the power of the H. Spirit." Heppe, *Reformed Dogmatics*, 603-604.

130. For examples, are the GC, CC37, CC45, FC, etc.

131. FCB VI; see also GC XV; FC XXXV; BC XXXIV; HC Q/A 70.

act of baptism. Despite different accents in their presentation, all Reformed confessions agree that the presentation of baptism generally signifies God's grace of adoption, forgiveness of sins, and regeneration or spiritual renewal through Christ's redemption by the Holy Spirit. Baptism denotes an entrance into the church of God, an ingrafting into Christ, or God's adoption, and as such, baptism also represents all benefits inseparable to adoption, namely the forgiveness of sins and regeneration or spiritual renewal.[132]

In Calvin's words, baptism for believers means the entrance into the church of God, that "God receives us as members of His family."[133] Baptism represents particularly two things: forgiveness of sins and regeneration, or spiritual renewal.[134] Calvin's subsequent discussions expound the role of the Holy Spirit in both, that is, that the Holy Spirit regenerates and sprinkles the consciences of believers.[135] Furthermore, as Calvin maintains in CC45, the proper use of baptism consists in faith and repentance, both fruits of the work of the Spirit, by which believers are compelled to receive the sacrament and grow in faith and the renewal of life. By partaking in the sacrament of baptism in faith, Christians voluntarily and publicly give a solemn testimony, or a public profession of faith, to the fact that "we are clothed with Jesus Christ, and receive His Spirit," and that "His Spirit dwells in us to mortify our natural desires and bring us to follow the Will of God."[136] The FC similarly confesses that baptism is "given as a pledge of our adoption; for by it we are grafted into the body of Christ, so as to be washed and cleansed by his blood, and then renewed in purity of life by his Holy Spirit."[137] The BC declares that by baptism "we are received into God's church and set apart from all other people and alien religions." Baptism also witnesses to believers that God "will be our God forever."[138] Bullinger similarly states in the SHC that to be baptized is "to be enrolled, entered,

---

132. CC37 XXVIII; CC45 Q/A 323; FC XXXV; SC XXI; BC XXXIV; TNA XXVII; HC Q/A 69-73; SHC XX.3; WCF XXVIII.1; WLC Q/A 165, 177; WSC Q/A 95.
133. CC45 Q/A 323; see also Q/A 365.
134. CC45 Q/A 324; see also CC37 XXVIII.
135. CC45 Q/A 326-327.
136. CC45 Q/A 331-332.
137. FC XXXV; see also SC XXI.
138. BC XXXIV.

and received into the covenant and family, and so into the inheritance of the sons of God," namely, "to be called a son of God; to be cleansed also from the filthiness of sins, and to be granted the manifold grace of God, in order to lead a new and innocent life."[139]

The strong emphasis that the Reformed confessions put on the ingrafting of the believers into Christ and the offering of all benefits of Christ in baptism conveyed through the agency of the Holy Spirit is not to be confused with arguing for the necessity of baptism to salvation, so as to say that without receiving baptism one cannot be saved, as the Council of Trent and the Augsburg Confession argue.[140] Nonetheless, as Muller rightly points out, "many of the major [Reformed] Confessions contain the teaching that Baptism belongs so intimately to the divinely ordained order or means of salvation that it dare not be set aside."[141] Calvin asserts in CC37 that baptism has been given to us by God to help our faith in him and our profession of faith before men. In baptism, the visible sign of water is not the cause, nor even instrument, of purgation and regeneration, "but only that the knowledge of such gifts is received in the sacrament."[142] However, for Calvin, belittling the use of sacraments as God has ordained them is condemning Jesus Christ, rejecting His grace, and quenching the Holy Spirit.[143] The BC affirms that God has "commanded that all those who belong to him be baptized with pure water," signifying to us that "just as water washes away the dirt of the body . . . so too the blood of Christ does the same thing internally, in the soul, by the Holy Spirit."[144] The HC similarly teaches that the outward washing with water itself does not wash away sins. Only the blood of Christ and the Holy Spirit cleanse the people of God from all sins.[145] So it is not the physical water, nor the

---

139. SHC XX.2.
140. The Council of Trent, *The Canons and Decrees of the Sacred and Oecumenical Council of Trent*, VII.4; "The Augsburg Confession A.D. 1530," in Schaff, *The Creeds of Christendom with a History and Critical Notes*, vol. 3 (Grand Rapids: Baker, 1984) (hereinafter AC), I.9.
141. Muller, "The Holy Spirit in the Augsburg Confession," 68.
142. CC37 XXVIII.
143. CC45 Q/A 315.
144. BC XXXIV.
145. HC Q/A 72.

sacramental act *per se,* that cleanses souls from sins, but "the sprinkling of the precious blood of the Son of God" that does it.[146] The WCF explains that although "it be a great sin to contemn or neglect this ordinance, yet Grace and Salvation are not so inseparably annexed unto it, as that no person can be regenerated or saved without it, or that all that are baptized are undoubtedly regenerated."[147]

Through baptism, as the BC also confesses, the Holy Spirit brings into actuality in the life of God's people the power of the blood of Christ that "washes and cleanses" their souls from their sins and "transforms" them "from being the children of wrath into the children of God."[148] Whereas ministers give "the sacrament and what is visible," God through his Spirit "gives what the sacrament signifies." Moreover, baptism is profitable not only "when the water is on us and when we receive it but throughout our entire lives."[149] The HC teaches that by means of the visible water as the element of baptism the Holy Spirit actually represents to believers and assures them of the promised grace of Christ's redemption, which itself is conveyed to believers by the incomprehensible inward work of the Holy Spirit. This assurance comes from the spiritual relation between the sign and the things signified: "the blood and Spirit of Christ wash away our sins just as water washes away dirt from our bodies." The HC even emphatically states that "the washing away of our sins spiritually is as real as physical washing with water."[150] In the words of Bullinger, "For inwardly we are regenerated, purified, and renewed by God through the Holy Spirit, and outwardly we receive the assurance of the greatest gifts in the water, by which also those great benefits are represented."[151] In a more explicit manner, the WCF states that by the right use of baptism, "the grace promised is not only offered, but really exhibited, and confer'd, by the Holy Ghost, to such (whether of

---

146. BC XXXIV; see also FHC XX.
147. WCF XXVIII.5; Dickson, *Truths Victory over Error*, XXVIII.4.
148. BC XXXIV.
149. BC XXXIV; see also WLC Q/A 167.
150. HC Q/A 73.
151. SHC XX.2.

age or infants), as that grace belongeth unto."[152] Through the right and lawful administration of baptism, the Holy Spirit works, actually edifying the faith of believers by assuring them of salvation as promised in the gospel.

Whereas baptism points to the adoption of believers into God's church and thus it is to be received only once, the Lord's Supper testifies to the continuing spiritual communion with Christ in which Christ spiritually nourishes and feeds believers. Christ, who instituted the Lord's Supper, also promised to present and proffer himself, his flesh and blood, for the nourishment of believers. Christ—particularly his presence—was definitely the focus of the prolonged polemics over this sacrament in the sixteenth and seventeenth centuries. However, the role that the Holy Spirit plays in the sacrament is by no means insignificant. The Holy Spirit gives faith required of the participants to participate in the Lord's Supper, makes possible the sacramental union between Christ and God's people through the sacrament, and fosters unity among the members of the same body of Christ through the observance of the sacrament.

The Reformed confessions testify to the link that the Reformed theologians made to the work of the Holy Spirit in the sacrament in order to explain the union of believers with Christ, as already identified by some scholars.[153] The Reformed confessions condemn the identification of the elements—the bread and wine—with the carnal flesh and blood of Christ. The GC regards this view of the sacramental elements as a blasphemy, superstition, and abuse of the Word of God, without specifying the reasons

---

152. WCF XXVIII.6; see also CC45 Q/A 328.

153. Some scholars have identified that the work of the Spirit in the sacraments plays a key role in the Reformed doctrine of the Lord's Supper, particularly as found in Calvin's presentation of the doctrine. In his *Institutes*, Calvin enunciates his concept of a spiritual received substance of Christ by emphasizing the work of the Spirit in the sacrament, as Muller points out, "the work of bringing about a participation in Christ through the union of 'things separated by space.'" Calvin, *Institutes*, IV.xvii.10; Muller, "Calvin on Sacramental Presence, in the Shadow of Marburg and Zurich," *Lutheran Quarterly* 23, no. 2 (Summer 2009): 157. Pruett offers a useful presentation of the similar position as held by Calvin in some other Protestant figures such as Bullinger, Bucer, Peter Martyr Vermigli, Thomas Cranmer, and John Jewel. He also argues that the Protestant doctrine of the real presence is precisely dependent upon the Reformed understanding of faith and the Holy Spirit. Gordon E. Pruett, "Protestant Doctrine of the Eucharistic Presence," *Calvin Theological Journal* 10, no. 2 (November 1975): 142-174.

behind its rejection.¹⁵⁴ In CC37 Calvin specifies the rationale behind the rejection, that is, that Christ's bodily presence is not ubiquitous since he has ascended to heaven, seated at the right hand of God the Father; his ascension has led to a different mode of his presence.¹⁵⁵ Calvin also asserts that "without any doubt we must be assured that Christ with all his riches is there [in the sacrament] presented to us, not less than if he could be put in the presence of our eyes and be touched by our hands."¹⁵⁶ For Calvin, the true and spiritual communication of Christ's body and blood, which God presents to believers under the sacramental signs of bread and wine, is made possible by Christ's own Spirit. Calvin argues,

> This communication is content with the bond of his spirit, and does not require at all a presence of the flesh enclosed under the bread, or of the blood under the wine. For, although Christ, being elevated to heaven, has left his abode on earth in which we are still pilgrims, yet no distance can dissolve his power of nourishing his own with himself.¹⁵⁷

Again in CC45, Calvin maintains that the power of the Holy Spirit makes possible participation in the body of Christ without enclosing the (carnal) body of Christ in the elements. Arguing for the reception of the very substance of Christ, which for Calvin is the substance in a spiritual sense, Calvin asserts, "I do not doubt that He makes us partakers of His very substance, in order to unite us with Himself in one life."¹⁵⁸ Regarding the question of how the body of Christ in heaven can be communicated to believers on earth, Calvin answers that it is made possible by "the comprehensible power of His Spirit, who conjoins things separated by distance."¹⁵⁹

---

154. GC XVI.
155. Therefore, to regard the bread and wine as the very own physical body and blood of Christ is to adore the elements as God, "an idolatry condemned by God himself." GC XVI. See also Hesselink, *Calvin's First Catechism*, 147-149.
156. CC37 XXIX; see also XXIX.7.
157. CC37 XXIX.
158. CC45 Q/A 353.
159. CC45 Q/A 354; see also Calvin, *Institutes*, IV.xvii.10; Barth, *The Theology of the*

To have the reality of the sacraments, Calvin teaches, "we must lift up our hearts on high to heaven, where Jesus Christ is in the glory of His Father . . . and do not seek Him in these corruptible elements."[160]

Similar references to the power of the Holy Spirit, which makes possible the union with Christ in the sacrament, can also be found in several other Reformed Confessions. The FC argues that although Christ is in heaven until he comes to judge all the earth, "still we believe that by the secret and incomprehensible power of his Spirit he feeds and strengthens us with the substance of his body and of his blood."[161] The FC strongly maintains that the spiritual nature of this communication ought not to be regarded as unreal in any sense. The spiritual nature of Christ's own presence never reduces its reality. It is certainly not to be thought of as putting "imagination and fancy in the place of fact and truth." God actually gives "the true possession and enjoyment of that which [the sacraments] present to us," so that all partakers of the sacrament, who by true faith come at "the sacred table of Christ, receive truly that of which it is a sign; for the body and the blood of Jesus Christ give food and drink to the soul, no less than bread and wine nourish the body."[162] The union and conjunction that believing participants have with the body and blood of Christ, as the SC clearly points out, is "wrought by means of the Holy Ghost, who by true faith carries us above all things that are visible, carnal, and earthly, and makes us feed upon the body and blood of Christ Jesus."[163] What the SC means by carrying believers above visible, carnal, and earthly things is the uniting of things separated by distance, as Calvin already pointed out. The SC then asserts,

> Notwithstanding the distance between His glorified body in heaven and mortal men on earth, yet we must assuredly believe that the bread which we break is the communion of Christ's body and the cup which we bless the communion of

---

Reformed Confessions, 177.
160. CC45 Q/A 355.
161. FC XXXVI.
162. FC XXXVII; see also Beza, *A Confession of Faith*, XXI.
163. SC XXI; see also Heppe, *Reformed Dogmatics*, 645.

> His blood. Thus we confess and believe without doubt that the faithful, in the right use of the Lord's Table, do so eat the body and drink the blood of the Lord Jesus that He remains in them and they in Him; they are so made flesh of His flesh and bone of His bone....[164]

In other words, the real feeding and drinking upon the Christ's own body and blood is never in question because of the incomprehensible work of the Holy Spirit.

The BC fully concurs with the SC in affirming that Christ "works in us all he represents by these holy signs" through the hidden and incomprehensible operation of God's Spirit.[165] God does not prescribe the sacrament in vain. Through the work of the Spirit believing participants eat and drink Christ's own natural body and blood. They do so "not by the mouth but by the Spirit, through faith."[166] Through the same operation of the Spirit, Christ, albeit in heaven, "never refrains... to communicate himself to us through faith."[167] The HC affirms the union between Christ and his people through the Holy Spirit despite their separation, that he is in heaven and they are on earth.[168]

---

164. SC XXI.
165. BC XXXV; see also HC Q/A 79-80; SHC XXI.3.
166. BC XXXV. In the same article, the BC also states that "We receive these [i.e., the true body and true blood of Christ] by faith, which is the hand and mouth of our souls." See also HC Q/A 78-79. The eating and drinking of the true body and blood of Christ means that we have a share in Christ's true body and blood through the Holy Spirit's work. The use of terms "natural" and "true" body and blood of Christ never mean that the corporeal body and blood of Christ are eaten in the sacraments for the Reformed. In a response to an "Objection" regarding the body and blood of Christ consisting of that which is material and earthly, Ursinus answers that the body and blood of Christ are the things signified in the Lord's Supper, and therefore they are spiritual. The signs are earthly, visible, and material, while the things signified are always heavenly, invisible, and spiritual. "Spiritual" here, for Ursinus, "signifies an object of the Spirit, or of spiritual influences, which is received by the influence of the Holy Spirit, or which is given to those whom the Holy Spirit dwells." The things signified are received only by believers in faith and in the Spirit. Therefore, they are received by none but believers. Ursinus, *The Commentary*, 347. See also Dickson, *Truths Victory over Error*, XXIX.6.
167. BC XXXV.
168. HC Q/A 76.

In the SHC, Bullinger holds to the true communication of the body and blood of Christ in the sacrament through the work of the Holy Spirit. He makes a clear distinction between corporeal, spiritual, and sacramental eating of Christ—the former is to be refuted, while the latter two are to be accepted by faith. The spiritual eating of Christ's body is different from the sacramental eating. In the latter, a believing participant not only spiritually and internally "participates in the true body and blood of Christ, but also, by coming to the Table of the Lord, outwardly receives the visible sacrament of the body and blood of the Lord."[169] Regarding the communication of the body and blood of Christ that takes place in both the spiritual and sacramental eating of Christ, Bullinger explains that it is wrought by the Holy Spirit, "not in a corporeal but in a spiritual way," as the Holy Spirit "applies and bestows upon us these things which have been prepared for us by the sacrifice of the Lord's body and blood for us, namely, the remission of sins, deliverance, and eternal life; so that Christ lives in us and we live in him."[170] Through the work of the Holy Spirit, the body and blood of Christ "not only refresh and strengthen our souls, but also preserve them alive." Moreover, the efficacy of the sacrament rests not upon the eating and drinking of the elements, but upon the spiritual eating, that is, the spiritual communication of the body and blood of Christ by the Holy Spirit.[171] In the sacramental eating, the faith of believing participants produced by the spiritual eating is continued to be "kindled and grows more and more, and is refreshed by spiritual food."[172]

As this and the preceding chapter have revealed, the Reformed confessions demonstrate the pervasiveness of their doctrine of the Holy Spirit by relating the Holy Spirit—his personhood and work—to several doctrines: Scripture, the Trinity, Christ, salvation, the church, and sacraments. However, this is not the end of their treatment. There are also aspects of the work of the Holy Spirit which the Reformed confessions teach but have not received adequate attention and treatment in the scholarly literature. The following chapters will attempt to extend the discussion of the doctrine of the Holy Spirit in the Reformed confessions as it relates to several other doctrines.

---

169. SHC XXI.8.
170. SHC XXI.5; see also WCF XXIX.1
171. SHC XXI.6.
172. SHC XXI.8.

PART TWO

CHAPTER 4

The Holy Spirit and the Doctrine of Creation And Providence

The preceding chapters in the first part have dealt with six doctrinal themes commonly associated with the Holy Spirit in the Reformed confessions. As noted, scholars of the study of the Reformed confessions, such as Barth and Rohls, have identified and acknowledged these themes as containing the doctrine of the Holy Spirit. Now, in the second part of this dissertation, the focus shifts to doctrinal themes in the Reformed confessions that contain rich teaching regarding the Holy Spirit but nevertheless have not been adequately treated or acknowledged by scholars in the past. The second part of this dissertation, that is, this chapter, will specifically discuss the treatment of the Holy Spirit in the Reformed confessions in relation to the doctrines of creation and providence.

Rohls, in his treatment of the doctrine of creation and providence in the Reformed confessions, has highlighted the indivisibility of the divine works *ad extra*. Using articles of a few Reformed confessions, he pointed out that, since both creation and providence are the work of the whole Trinity, they are thus also of the Spirit. However, with regard to the unique role of the Holy Spirit in creation and providence, Rohls did not give much elaboration.[1] In this chapter, one will find a more throughly documented and systematic account of the role of the Holy Spirit in creation and providence as treated in the Reformed confessions than Rohls did. It will also discuss

---

1. Rohls, *Reformed Confessions*, 54-57.

some facets of both doctrines in the Reformed confessions, such as beauty and order, preservation of believers in salvation, and church government, in which the unique role of the Holy Spirit is discussed but has not been identified and treated by Rohls.

As the preceding chapters have discussed, one underlying belief or principle of the Reformed confessions when discussing the triunity of God and his works is the inseparability of the distinct divine persons of the Trinity in the divine operations *ad intra* and *ad extra*. Once the divinity of God in contrast to the creatureliness of the world is declared, the triunity of God confirmed, and the role distinction of the divine persons in divine operations *ad intra* established, the discussions of the divine works or operations *ad extra* as the execution of God's eternal decree are set to follow. The divine works *ad extra* can be divided into two categories: the *opus naturae* (the divine work through the natural operation of things) and the *opus gratiae* (the divine work of grace conferred on the elect). While the divine works of creation and general providence—providence over all creatures and events in general—fall into the category of the *opus naturae*, the work of special providence—providence over the elect or the church—is duly regarded as of the *opus gratiae*. This chapter will discuss the role of the Holy Spirit in relation to the divine works of both creation and providence, general and special, as treated in the Reformed confessions.

The Reformed confessions usually state the doctrine of creation and providence in several *loci* immediately following the doctrine of God. The Reformed catechisms discuss the doctrine of creation and some part of the doctrine of providence mainly under the first article of the Apostles' Creed ("I believe in God, the Father almighty, Creator of heaven and earth"). The Reformed confessions and catechisms also teach some other parts of the doctrine of providence in various places which appertain to the divine work of redemption, such as, for examples, the doctrines of sanctification, perseverance, spiritual warfare, and the church.

In these preeminent and pivotal teachings of creation and providence, the Reformed confessions affirm the indivisibility of the divine works *ad extra*, despite the distinguishable economy of tasks in the Godhead. The Holy Spirit is depicted as one of the divine persons of the Trinity who assumes a different—but not less significant—role than those of the Father and the Son in creation and providence. The creation and providence of the whole universe, as the execution of God's eternal decrees, are no less the work of the Holy Spirit than of the Son and the Father.

The Holy Spirit and the Doctrine of Creation

The book of Genesis opens with a clear testimony about the creation of the world and the activities of God in it: "In the beginning God created the heavens and the earth. Now the earth was formless and empty, darkness was over the surface of the deep, and the Spirit of God was hovering over the waters" (Gen. 1:1-2). Reflecting upon the creation account in Genesis and some other passages, such as Jer. 10:12; Ps. 104: 24; Jn. 1:2-3; Rm. 1:20; Col. 1:16; Heb. 1:2; 11:3, the Reformed confessions testify to this scriptural teaching, that the whole world was created by God and thus has a beginning. They also affirm that the God who created the world out of nothing (*ex nihilo*) is the Triune God—the Father, Son, and Holy Spirit.

Creation as the Work of the Whole Trinity

Concerning God, the FHC asserts that "there is one only, true, living and almighty God, one in essence, threefold according to the persons, Who has created all things out of nothing by His Word, that is, by His Son, and by His providence justly, truly and wisely rules, governs and preserves all things."[2] The CECG echoes the same conviction that the Lord God, "one in substance and three in persons, Father, Son and Holy Ghost," has created out of nothing "heaven, earth, and all things therein contained."[3]

The creation of the world is not the work of one or two, but of all three persons of the Trinity who work indivisibly. The FC emphasizes this and states, "We believe that God, in three co-working persons, by his power, wisdom, and incomprehensible goodness, created all things."[4] Calvin and

---

2. FHC VI.
3. CECG I.
4. FC VI. See also SC I; BC XII; TNA I.

Beza, two of the framers of the FC, also affirm this in their other works. Calvin states in his *Institutes* that God in the creation account "sets forth for us His eternal Wisdom and Spirit."[5] For Calvin, Ps. 33:6 is an express testimony for the involvement of the Holy Spirit in the creation of the world; the universe was "no less the work of the Holy Spirit than of the Son."[6] Beza maintains in his *Sum of the Christian Faith* that the Father created all things by his eternal Word, that is his Son, and his infinite and substantial power and virtue, that is the Holy Spirit, who proceeds from the Father and the Son.[7]

Bullinger in the SHC also affirms the participation of the whole Trinity. Citing Ps. 33:6, "By the word of the Lord the heavens were made, and all their host by the breath of his mouth," he states that "This good and almighty God created all things, both visible and invisible, by his co-eternal Word, and preserves them by his co-eternal Spirit."[8] Bullinger expands this discussion in his sermon in his *Decades*. He argues that one is not to think of three Gods, but one God in three persons who works indivisibly in their actions.

> . . . we must think the Creator of all things to be such an one, as by his Son, that is, by his eternal Wisdom, hath created all things both visible and invisible; yea, and that of nothing too: and doth moreover at this very present sustain, nourish, rule, and preserve all things by his everlasting Spirit, without which every thing would presently fall to ruin, and come to nought. We do herein therefore confess also the providence of our eternal God, and his exceeding wise government.[9]

---

5. Calvin, *Institutes*, I.xiv.2.
6. Calvin, *Institutes*, I.xiii.15; I.xiv.20.
7. Beza, *A Briefe and Piththie [sic] Sum of the Christian Faith*, II.2; *A Confession of Faith*, VII.
8. SHC VII.1.
9. Bullinger, *Decades*, I.vii (126).

The use of the inclusive term of "God" in the Reformed Confessions also confirms the assertion that the creation of the world is the work of all persons of the Trinity, the Triune God. The notion of the Father as "the Creator or Maker of heaven and earth," as found in the Apostles' Creed, is never meant by the Reformed confessions to attribute the work of creation exclusively to the Father to the exclusion of the roles of the other persons of the Trinity—namely, the Son and the Holy Spirit—in creation. Rather, the Father is commonly thought of as the origin of all things. In his CC45 Calvin explicates this:

> Since there is but one God, why do you mention the Father, Son, and Holy Spirit, who are three? Because in the one essence of God, we have to look on the Father as the beginning and origin, and the first cause of all things; then the Son, who is Eternal Wisdom; and the Holy Spirit who is His virtue and power shed abroad over all creatures, but still perpetually resident in Himself.[10]

The Westminster Standards maintain the same language. The WCF explicitly states that "God the Father, Son and Holy Ghost, for the manifestation of the glory of his eternal Power, Wisdom and Goodness," in the beginning "create, or make of nothing the World and all things therein, whether visible or invisible, in the space of six days and all very good."[11] In the same manner, the WLC simply defines the work of creation as "that wherein God did in the beginning, by the word of his power, make of nothing, the world and all things therein, for himself," after acknowledging beforehand that by the word "God" the Catechism means the "three persons in the Godhead, the Father, the Son, and the holy Ghost," that is, the "one, true,

---

10. CC45 Q/A 19. As Heppe also states, "The Triune God is the Creator, but in such a way that the Father as the 'source of the Trinity' is also the proper source of the works of creation, which he has executed through the Son and the H. Spirit." Heppe, *Reformed Dogmatics*, 191.
11. WCF IV.1; WSC Q/A 9.

eternal God, the same in substance, equal in power and glory; although distinguished by their personal properties."[12]

Even if a Reformed confession seems to attribute the work of creation only to the Father, it is never meant by its framers to exclude or mitigate the roles of the Son and the Holy Spirit in creation. The HC seems at first to attribute the work of creation to the Father alone when it divides the Apostles' Creed into three parts and attributes the work of creation to the Father, while attributing the work of redemption and sanctification to the Son and the Holy Spirit, respectively.[13] Moreover, on the question "What do you believe when you say, 'I believe in God, the Father almighty, creator of heaven and earth?,'" the catechism clearly states that it is "the eternal Father of our Lord Jesus Christ, who out of nothing created heaven and earth and everything in them."[14] The biblical references for the article, for examples, Gen. 1:1-2; Ps. 33:6; 104:30, which are the integrated part of the article, however, show that the Father is never meant to be the single agent in creation.

Commenting on the aforementioned articles of the catechism, Olevianus, in his commentary, maintains the inclusive use of the term "God." God is "the highest good, the source of everything good," and he is "the Father, His only Son, and the Holy Spirit" who has revealed himself as the one "who out of nothing created heaven and earth and everything in them and preserves them."[15] Ursinus, in his comment on the same articles of the catechism, even makes clear the involvement of all three persons of the Trinity in creation. In his repudiation of the objection that the attribution of creation to the Father in the Apostles' creed and thus in the catechism may lead to the exclusion of the Son and the Holy Spirit in creation, Ursinus argues for the indivisibility of God in all their works. He contends that "the creed attributes creation to the Father, redemption to the Son, and sanctification to the Holy Ghost, not exclusively, or in such a manner as that these works

---

12. WLC Q/A 8, 9, 15.
13. HC Q/A 24.
14. HC Q/A 26.
15. Olevianus, *A Firm Foundation*, Q/A 17.

do not belong to all the persons of the Godhead."[16] Ursinus states further that in different works to different persons in the Godhead, one must not overlook "the distinction and the order of working which is peculiar to the persons of the Godhead." He goes on to say, "The work of creation is attributed to the Father, not exclusively, nor to him alone, but because he is the fountain of Divinity, and of all divine works, and so of creation; for he created of himself all things by the Son and Holy Ghost."[17] To another objection, that since the works which the persons of the Godhead perform in reference to creatures are indivisible, then they cannot be attributed to any one person of the Trinity without respect to the other persons, Ursinus gives a succinct yet clarifying reply. He argues that the indivisibility of the works of God does not necessarily rule out the attribution of the works of God to the persons of the Godhead when the order and manner of working of each person is properly understood.

> The works of the Trinity are indivisible, but not in such a sense as to destroy the order and manner of working peculiar to each person of the Godhead. All the persons of the Godhead perform certain works in reference to creatures, but yet this order is preserved, that the Father does all things of himself through the Son and Holy Spirit; the Son does all things of the Father through the Holy Spirit; and the Holy Spirit does all things of the Father and the Son through himself. In this way, therefore, all the persons of the Godhead create, redeem, and sanctify; the Father mediately through the Son and the Holy Spirit; the Son mediately through through the Holy Spirit; and the Holy Spirit through immediately through himself, but mediately through the Son, as he is the Mediator.[18]

Regarding the attribution of creation to God the Father, Ames, in his commentary on the HC, *A Sketch of the Christian's Catechism,* maintains

---

16. Ursinus, *The Commentary*, 119.
17. Ursinus, *The Commentary*, 120.
18. Ursinus, *The Commentary*, 120.

that all divine external works are attributed equally to the three persons of the Trinity.[19] The attribution pertains only to the order, namely "the order of origination," not "a temporal or natural order." In Ames' own words,

> Therefore, works in which the origin of things is especially clear by appropriation, like creation, are attributed to the Father. Secondary works, in which stewardship or administration is especially clear, like redemption, are attributed to the Son. And final works, in which perfection and consummation are revealed, like sanctification and glorification, are attributed to the Holy Spirit.[20]

Through their affirmation of the *ex nihilo* biblical account of creation, the Reformed confessions maintain that the world was created by God alone. It means that God alone is capable of creating the world *ex nihilo*. God is known first by his handiwork. As the BC declares, the invisible things of God are manifest in his works of "creation, preservation, and government of the universe."[21] For the Reformed, the importance of the distinction between the Creator and the creatures cannot be overstressed. This implies that there is not any less-than-God intermediary being involved in creation, but rather, the divine persons of the Trinity. The Reformed confessions strongly argue that since Scripture ascribes creation to both the Son and the Holy Spirit as well as to the Father, they are equal in divinity, glory, and majesty and no less God than the Father. No creature is to be worshipped. To worship anything other than God, whether angels or any other creature, is an abomination and idolatry.[22] To attest to the scriptural teaching of the plurality of persons in the Godhead and the deity of the Holy Spirit, the Reformed confessions also attribute creation to the Holy Spirit.

On the question, "Since there is but one God, why do you speak of three: Father, Son, and Holy Spirit?," the HC answers and points out

---

19. Ames, *A Sketch of the Christian's Catechism*, 45-46.
20. Ames, *Sketch*, 47.
21. BC II; FC II.
22. For examples, see GC II; SHC V.1; WCF II.2.

that "God has revealed himself in his Word" in that way, that "these three distinct persons are one, true, eternal God."[23] As Ames acknowledges in his commentary on the HC, the Spirit, who was moving upon the waters in the day of creation, is the efficiency of God with which God created all things and sustains and preserves all things that he has once created.[24] The Spirit is therefore God, equal in honor, power, and glory to the Father and the Son, to whom worship is properly due.

The BC, when arguing for the divinity of every Person in the Godhead, also enumerates the scriptural passages that testify to the participation of all divine persons in creation, the baptism of Jesus, the formula of baptism for believers, and others.[25] The WCF similarly declares that the one God in three persons—Father, Son, and the Holy Spirit—but of one substance, power, and eternity, is "the alone fountain of all being, of whom, through whom, and to whom are all things, and hath most Sovereign dominion over them, to do by them, for them, or upon them, whatsoever himself pleaseth."[26] The WLC also contends, "The Scriptures manifest that the Son and the Holy Ghost are God equal with the Father, ascribing unto them such names, attributes, works, and worship, as are proper to God only," and that creation is the work of God alone.[27] Dickson, in his commentary of the WCF, confirms this. On the question, "Is the Holy Ghost God?," Dickson gives an affirmative answer. Among other Scriptural proofs that he presents, Dickson also points out that the Holy Spirit is God because he is "to be worshipped as God" and he is "omnipotent, the maker, and preserver of all things."[28]

The Holy Spirit's Creational Activities

The Reformed confessions have made sufficiently clear that the Holy Spirit is as equally divine as the Father and the Son. By virtue of the indivisibility

---

23. HC Q/A 25.
24. Ames, *Sketch*, 52.
25. BC IX. See also CECG I; FC VII; SC I; TNA I.
26. WCF II.2; IV.1.
27. WLC Q/A 11, 15.
28. Dickson, *Truths Victory over Error*, II.6 (29).

of the divine operations *ad intra* and *ad extra*, the Holy Spirit is also called the *Creator Spiritus*. It is so because the Holy Spirit has a unique role in the creation of the world. Following the treatment of Scripture which itself does not give a clear description of the unique role of the Holy Spirit in creation, some Reformed confessions only testify to the role of the Holy Spirit by pointing out his creational activities found in various places in Scripture.

In CC37, Calvin emphasizes the oneness of God, that is, the indivisibility of the Godhead, in the Christian profession of the Trinity, namely, that "when we name the Father, Son, and Holy Spirit, we do not imagine three Gods." He states further,

> But the Scripture and the very experience of piety shows us, in the very simple essence of God, God the Father, his Son, and his Spirit, in such a way that our intellect cannot conceive the Father without comprehending at the same time the Son (in whom brightly shines the vivid image of the Father) and the Spirit (in whom appear the power and virtue of the Father).[29]

For Calvin, that God the Father created the world through his Spirit means that the divine power which operates in the creation of the world is ascribed to God in general, but also duly ascribed to the Holy Spirit in particular. And the Holy Spirit does not work everything of himself, but of the Father and the Son. The Holy Spirit is "the power and virtue of the Father (and of Christ)" through whom the Father and Christ not only created the world, but also do all things.

> For Christ by virtue of his Spirit works all that which is good, in whatever place that be. By the power of the Spirit, Christ makes, upholds, maintains, and vivifies all things; by it he justifies, sanctifies and purifies, calls and attracts us to himself in order that we may obtain deliverance.[30]

---

29. CC37 XX.
30. CC37 XX.

The Holy Spirit and the Doctrine of Creation and Providence 115

In his *Institutes*, Calvin explicates this further. While arguing for the divinity of the Holy Spirit, Calvin shows how the divinity of the Holy Spirit is demonstrated in his works, namely, creation, providence, and redemption. For Calvin, the testimony of Moses in the creation account (Gen. 1:1-2) clearly demonstrates the involvement of the Holy Spirit and thus his divinity, that is, that "the Spirit of God was spread over the deeps." Calvin then contends that the passage shows "not only that the beauty of the universe (which we now perceive) owes its strength and preservation to the power of the Spirit but that before this adornment was added, even then the Spirit was occupied with tending that confused mass."[31] He goes on to assert,

> For it is the Spirit who, everywhere diffused, sustains all things, causes them to grow, and quickens them in heaven and in earth. Because he is circumscribed by no limits, he is excepted from the category of creatures; but in transfusing into all things his energy, and breathing into them essence, life, and movement, he is indeed plainly divine.[32]

It is the Spirit that transfuses his energy into all things and gives life to animate creatures and beauty to all which he has once created, without whom none was created and able to exist and live by itself. Calvin also avers,

> From this history [of creation] we shall learn that God by the power of his Word and Spirit created heaven and earth out of nothing; that thereupon he brought forth living beings and inanimate things of every kind, that in a wonderful series he distinguished as innumerable variety of things, that he endowed each kind with its own nature, assigned functions, appointed places and stations; and that, although all were subject to

---

31. Calvin, *Institutes*, I.xiii.14.
32. Calvin, *Institutes*, I.xiii.14.

corruption, he nevertheless provided for the preservation of each species until the Last Day.³³

Calvin insists on the active participation of the Holy Spirit since the beginning of creation and holds that "beauty and order" are the Holy Spirit's bestowal. Against the antitrinitarian heresies particularly propounded by Servetus, which see the Holy Spirit merely as "the shadow of deity," among other things, Calvin also contends for the creative role of the Holy Spirit in establishing beauty and order,

> Moreover, although no mention is made of the Spirit except in the history of the creation of the universe, nevertheless the Spirit is introduced here, not as a shadow, but as the essential power of God, when Moses tells that the as yet formless mass was itself sustained in him [Gen. 1:2]. Therefore it then has become clear that the eternal Spirit had always been in God, while with tender care he supported the confused matter of heaven and earth, until beauty and order were added.³⁴

Also, to the Holy Spirit is properly assigned "the power and efficacy" of divine operations, "the power whereby [God] executes the decrees of his plan."³⁵

---

33. Calvin, *Institutes*, I.xiv.20. In his comment on Acts 17:28, Calvin states, "For the power of the Spirit is spread abroad throughout all parts of the world, that it may preserve them in their state; that he may minister unto the heaven and earth that force and vigour which we see, and motion to all living creatures. . . . God doth, by the wonderful power and inspiration of his Spirit, preserve those things which he hath created of nothing." Calvin, *Commentary upon the Acts of the Apostles*, ed. Henry Beveridge, vol. 2 (Grand Rapids: Eerdmans, 1949), 168. See "The Lausanne Articles (1536)," in Cochrane, *Reformed Confessions of the Sixteenth Century* (hereinafter LA), III: ". . . by the virtue of [Christ's] Holy Spirit fills, sustains, governs and vivifies all things."

34. Calvin, *Institutes*, I.xiii.22. See also M. Eugene Osterhaven, *The Faith of the Church: A Reformed Perspective on Its Historical Development* (Grand Rapids: Eerdmans, 1982), 164-167.

35. Calvin, *Institutes*, I.xiii.18. See Ames, *Sketch*, 47, 52. Ames points out that the Spirit of God is the efficiency of God with which God created all things and sustains and preserves all things that he has once created.

Along the same train of thought, the FC, of which Calvin was one of the framers, later also asserts that the Holy Spirit assumes a role as divine "virtue, power, and efficacy," whereas the Father is "first cause, principle, and origin of all things" and the Son is "his Word and eternal wisdom."[36] Later, in the next article, the FC affirms that "God, in three co-working persons, by his power, wisdom, and incomprehensible goodness, created all things, not only the heavens and the earth and all that in them is, but also invisible spirits."[37] Beza, in his *Sum of the Christian Faith*, asserts that the Holy Ghost is "the coeternall and consubstantiall power of the Father and the Sonne, in whom he is resident and from whom he proceedeth."[38] The Holy Spirit is the creator of the world as well as of faith. He is the "infinite force" and his virtue is "declared in the creation and preservation of all creatures from the beginning of the world."[39]

The Holy Spirit and the Doctrine of Providence

Intimately connected with the doctrine of creation is the subject of providence. The doctrine of providence has the relationship between God the creator and his creatures as its *locus*. Insofar as the relationship between God and his creatures is concerned, the idea of God's providence permeates almost every topic in dogmatics. This supposedly includes every action of God toward every single creature in every single event.[40] Nevertheless, most of the Reformed confessions still either mention, define, or discuss explicitly God's providence as a separate doctrine, focusing primarily on the

---

36. FC VI.
37. FC VII. The ascription of the power of God by which God created the whole world to the Holy Spirit can also be found in the CECG I; BC VIII. Bullinger in the SHC III.4 calls the Holy Spirit as "the power of the Most High" with reference to Lk. 1:35; see also Bullinger, *Decades*, IV.iv (174).
38. Beza, *A Briefe and Piththie [sic] Sum of the Christian Faith*, IV.1.
39. Beza, *A Briefe and Piththie [sic] Sum of the Christian Faith*, IV.2.
40. As Bavinck rightly states, "Though the doctrine of providence logically covers the entire scope of all God's decrees, extending to all topics covered in dogmatics, it is preferable to restrict the discussion to God's relation to his creation and creatures." Bavinck, *Reformed Dogmatics*, II, 591.

ways God relates to his creatures. In the Reformed Confessions, one may find the statements regarding the doctrine either exclusively in a separate section or along with other doctrines, such as the doctrine of creation and the doctrine of the Trinity. The Reformed catechisms usually discuss the doctrine of providence under the first article of the Apostles' Creed, "I believe in God, the Father almighty, creator of heaven and earth," with its relation to the doctrine of creation.

Providence as the Work of the Whole Trinity

In their treatment of the doctrine of providence, the Reformed confessions declare that, along with creation, providence is the work of the Triune God. The authorship of God over creation and providence is defended by pointing to the intimate connection between both. As they do in the doctrine of creation, the Reformed confessions maintain the use of the inclusive term "God" to denote the participation of the whole Trinity, and thus also of the Holy Spirit, in the providence of the world. Insofar as God is the Triune God, providence is the work of all persons of the Trinity.

The Reformed confessions contend that God the Creator did not only create the universe, but also maintains, preserves, and governs it. The BC asserts,

> He has given all creatures their being, form, and appearance, and their various functions for serving their Creator. Even now he also sustains and governs them all, according to his eternal providence, and by his infinite power, that they may serve man, in order that man may serve God.[41]

The WCF states that "God the Father, Son, and Holy Ghost" is pleased, "for the manifestation of the glory of his eternal Power, Wisdom and Goodness, in the beginning to create, or make of nothing the World, and all things therein." Later, the WCF affirms that the same God, "the great Creator of all things, doth uphold, direct, dispose, and govern all creatures,

---

41. BC XII.

actions, and things, from the greatest even to the least, by his most wise and holy Providence."⁴² Similar assertion can easily be found in other Reformed confessions.⁴³

For the Reformed in general, providence does not only logically succeed creation, but it is also inseparable from creation. Intimately joined with creation, providence is also seen as a continued or continuous creation (*continuata creatio*).⁴⁴ In CC37 Calvin asserts that by calling God creator of heaven and earth, one must understand that "he perpetually upholds, maintains, and gives life to all that which he has once created."⁴⁵ Later, in CC45, Calvin explicates further that the term "Creator" does not only signify God's work in bringing all things into existence, but also his providence, namely, his preservation and government over all things. As Calvin states, "Therefore, in that He is Creator of heaven and earth, it is His to rule the whole order of nature by His goodness and power and wisdom."⁴⁶ In his *Institutes* Calvin avers, "For unless we pass on to his providence . . . we do not yet properly grasp what it means to say: 'God is Creator.'"⁴⁷ Behind this

---

42. WCF IV.1; V.1.
43. See CC37 XX ("I believe in God, the Father almighty, creator of heaven and earth"); CC45 Q/A 21-27; CECG I; FC VIII; SC I; TNA I; HC Q/A 26-27; SHC VI.1; VII.1; WLC Q/A 14, 15, 18; WSC Q/A 8, 9, 11.
44. See Ames, *The Marrow of Theology*, I.ix.18; Heppe, *Reformed Dogmatics*, 257-258. Muller notes that the notion of "continued creation" (*continuata creatio*) was inherited by the Reformed and the Lutheran orthodox from the medieval scholastics. According to this medieval scholastics definition, "creation and providence is a purely rational one arising from our finite, temporal way of understanding the eternal and simple acts of God: the human mind understands by means of rational distinctions and divisions that which is essentially simple and indivisible." Muller, *God, Creation, and Providence in the Thought of Jacob Arminius: Sources and Directions of Scholastic Protestantism in the Era of Early Orthodoxy* (Grand Rapids: Baker, 1991), 247; Benjamin Wirt Farley, *The Providence of God* (Grand Rapids: Baker, 1988), 27-30. Bavinck contends that when "the earlier theologians" used the language of "continued creation," they should not be understood as erasing the difference between creation and providence and thereby leaning toward a pantheistic definition of creation, as Hodge fears. Rather, they all regarded providence "as simultaneously also an act of causing creatures to persist in their existence, as a form of preservation that presupposes creation." Creation and providence are "one single act and differ only in structure." Bavinck, *Reformed Dogmatics*, II, 606-607; Charles Hodge, *Systematic Theology*, 3 vols. (New York: Charles Scribner's Sons, 1888), I, 577ff.
45. CC37 XX ("I believe in God, the Father almighty, creator of heaven and earth").
46. CC45 Q/A 27.
47. Calvin, *Institutes*, I.xvi.1.

emphasis on the inseparability between creation and providence lies a concern over a particular understanding of creation, which believes that, once created, all things continue to exist apart from God's power.[48] For Calvin, not only is this way of understanding creation and providence "carnal," it also falls short of what Scripture has testified to regarding God's providence, for examples, Ps. 33:13; 104:27-30; Matt. 10:29.[49] The heavens, the earth, and all creatures, Calvin insists, "do not continue in their being" apart from God's power, the same power by which God created the universe.[50]

On the question "What do you believe when you say, 'I believe in God, the Father almighty, creator of heaven and earth'?" the HC also asserts that the idea of providence is included in the confession of God as Creator. The eternal Father, who created out of nothing heaven and earth and everything in them, "still upholds and rules them by his eternal counsel and providence."[51] "Providence is the almighty and ever present power of God by which he upholds . . . and so rules [all creatures]" that all things do not come to pass by chance, but from "his fatherly hand."[52] Even further, the HC maintains that all "creatures are so completely in his hand that without his will they can neither move nor be moved."[53] As Ursinus explicates in his commentary of the HC, the providence of God is "nothing else than a continuation of the creation." Providence is different, yet inseparable, from creation. It is a sure conviction of the Reformed that "as nothing could ever have existed except by the creating power of God; so it is impossible that any thing should exist, even for a moment, without his government and preservation." Hence, Ursinus goes on to assert, "we cannot have a full and

---

48. Calvin, *Institutes*, I.xvi.1.

49. Calvin, *Institutes*, I.xvi.1. Bullinger warns against the Epicureans who "deny the providence of God," and all those who say that "God is busy with the heavens and neither sees nor cares about us and our affairs." SHC VI.3.

50. CC45 Q/A 27. Cf., Leo Scheffczyk, *Creation and Providence*, trans. Richard Strachan (New York: Herder and Herder, 1970), 176ff. For Scheffczyk, a separate doctrine of providence is warranted only if the world is seen as entirely independent of God. He contends, "A separate doctrine of Providence makes sense only where the world is seen as something ontic, possessing a relatively independent being *vis-à-vis* God, so that God must also set it a goal and assume its governance."

51. HC Q/A 26.

52. HC Q/A 27.

53. HC Q/A 28.

correct knowledge of the creation unless we, at the same time, embrace the doctrine of divine providence."⁵⁴

On the one hand, the intimate connection between creation and providence as understood by the Reformed and confessed in the Reformed Confessions attests to the continuity—or, simultaneity—between creation and providence. On the other hand, it also attests to the same Authorship of both creation and providence; both are the work of the Triune God—the Father, Son, and Holy Spirit. The participation of the Holy Spirit in the providence of the world is thus confirmed.⁵⁵ However, even though it is never the intent of the framers of the Reformed confessions to give a full and detailed treatment of the doctrine with regard to the participation of each Person of the Trinity in divine providence, the Reformed confessions do give some explicit statements regarding the specific role of the Holy Spirit as they outline the doctrine of divine providence.

The Unique Role of the Holy Spirit in Providence

The Reformed confessions, as well as the Reformed orthodox theologians, unambiguously affirm the doctrine of providence and are seemingly in substantial agreement, despite some existing differences in definitions.⁵⁶

---

54. Ursinus, *The Commentary*, 147.
55. See Rohls, *Reformed Confessions*, 55.
56. Some confessions understand God's providence as the acts of God preserving, ruling, and governing all his creatures or the effectual execution of God's decrees; see for examples: CECG I; FC VIII; SC I; BC XIII; WCF VI.1; WLC Q/A 18; WSC Q/A 11. Some others, such as the HC and SHC define God's providence as God's power; see HC Q/A 27; SHC VI.1-2. Yet some other Reformed, such as Ursinus and Ames, define God's providence as God's counsel, his dispensation and appointment; see Ursinus, *The Commentary*, 151; Ames, *The Marrow of Theology*, I.ix.1. The difference in definitions, however, is not a matter of substantial disagreement or contradiction, but merely of emphasis. The issue concerning definition is resolved quickly once Turretin's explication comes into view. Turretin states that the Greek term for providence (*pronoia*) embraces three things: *prognōsin* (the knowledge of the mind), *prothesin* (the decree of the will), and *dioikēsin* (the efficacious administration of the things decreed). Hence divine providence "can be viewed either in the antecedent decree or in the subsequent administration or execution." Turretin continues to say, "The former is the eternal destination of all things to their ends; the latter is the temporal government of all things according to the decree. The former is an immanent act in God; the latter is a transitive action out of God." Both are inseparably joined. Creation and providence are none other than the execution of God's eternal decrees. Even though Turretin later preferred the latter in his discussion of the doctrine, the former is by no means denied or neglected. Turretin, *Institutes of Elenctic*

In brief, the Reformed understand the divine act of the Triune God in providence—that is, the way God the Creator relates to his creatures—as comprising a threefold activity: preservation (*conservatio*), concurrence (*concursus*), and government (*gubernatio*).[57] Preservation is the act of God that sustains or maintains the existence, essence, and natural faculties of all created things. Whereas by his act of preservation God sustains the being of things, by his act of concurrence God sustains the actions of things, particularly contingent beings. In Muller's words, "the *concursus divinus*" is "the divine willing of all things that operates concurrently with and that therefore concurs in and, in effect, sustains the willing of all rational creatures," or,

> ... the movement of the divine first cause in all finite operations in such a way as to sustain the created thing in its operation and to provide it with the capability of doing its own work and gaining its own ends, even as the ultimate purpose of all things is being worked out in particular finite acts.[58]

Government refers to the act of God that guides and orders all things so that they reach their appointed end, for which they were ordained by God, that is, to glorify God.

Although the Reformed confessions generally attribute all the acts of providence to the Triune God, one might also find in some Reformed confessions that the work of providence is attributed particularly to the Son and the Holy Spirit. The Father creates and preserves through the agency of the Son and the Holy Spirit.[59] Besides attesting to the different roles that each Person of the Trinity plays, which has been discussed in chapter 2, the following Reformed confessions attribute specifically the work of providence

---

Theology, VI.i.2. For a helpful discussion on the definition of providence, see Bavinck, *Reformed Dogmatics*, II, 591-598, 604-608.

57. See Heppe, *Reformed Dogmatics*, 256-264; Muller, *God, Creation, and Providence*, 247.

58. Muller, *God, Creation, and Providence*, 178, 253.

59. Rohls, *Reformed Confessions*, 55. Rohls notes this notion, but does not elaborate or discuss it further.

to the Holy Spirit as well as to the Son. The FCB confesses that "God has created all things by His eternal Word, that is, by His only-begotten Son, and preserves and strengthens all things by His Spirit, that is, by His power; and therefore, God sustains and governs all things as He created them."[60] Explicating the article of faith "I believe in the Holy Spirit" in the Apostles' Creed, Calvin states in CC37, "By the power of the Spirit, Christ makes, upholds, maintains, and vivifies all things;" by the same power of the Spirit, Christ also works salvation in the lives of the elect.[61] Calvin makes a similar assertion in CC45. Calling the Holy Spirit God's "virtue and power shed abroad over all creatures," Calvin also identifies the almighty power of God as God's providence, by which "He disposes all things" "governs the world by His will, ruling all as it seems good to Him."[62] He goes on to assert that "as the world was made by God in the beginning, so now is preserved by him in its estate, so that the heavens, the earth and all creatures do not continue in their being apart from this power." God rules "the whole order of nature by His goodness and power and wisdom."[63]

The BC appears to follow Calvin in attributing the infinite power of God to the Holy Spirit. In its article concerning the Trinity, the BC confesses that the Father is the cause and origin of all things, the Son is the Word and Wisdom, while the Holy Spirit is the eternal power and might that proceeds from the Father and the Son.[64] Having made this distinction and having affirmed the indivisibility of the Triune God in all his works, the BC confesses that the same God, who "has given all creatures their being, form, and appearance, and their various functions for serving their Creator," also "sustains and governs them all, according to his eternal providence, and by his infinite power."[65]

---

60. FCB I.

61. Calvin also maintains that "all that which is good, in whatever place that be," is the work of Christ by virtue of the Holy Spirit. CC37 XX ("I believe in the Holy Spirit").

62. CC45 Q/A 19, 23.

63. CC45 Q/A 27.

64. BC VIII.

65. BC XII. HC Q/A 27 states that providence is "the almighty and ever present power of God by which he upholds, as with his hand, heaven and earth and all creatures, and so rules them."

In the SHC, Bullinger affirms the participation of all divine persons in both creation and providence and declares, "This good and almighty God created all things, both visible and invisible, by his co-eternal Word, and preserves them by his co-eternal Spirit."[66] Bullinger explicates this point further in a sermon documented in his *Decades*, when he comments on the the first article of the Apostles' Creed. He states,

> . . . we must think the Creator of all things to be such an one, as by his Son, that is, by his eternal Wisdom, hath created all things both visible and invisible; yea, and that of nothing too: and doth moreover at this very present sustain, nourish, rule, and preserve all things by his everlasting Spirit, without which every thing would presently fall to ruin, and come to nought. We do herein therefore confess also the providence of our eternal God, and his exceeding wise government.[67]

The world does not stand and endure by any power of its own, since it has no self-subsisting power.[68] Unless sustained by the power of the Holy Spirit, all creatures simply cease to exist.

The Holy Spirit in the Special Providence over the Church

As discussed above, the Reformed confessions teach that the work of providence in general is duly attributed to the Holy Spirit as well as to the Father and the Son. In addition to that, the role of the Spirit in divine providence becomes more apparent when some of the Reformed confessions address special providence, namely, divine preservation and government over

---

66. SHC VII.1; Rohls, *Reformed Confessions*, 55.
67. Bullinger, *Decades*, I.vii (126).
68. Bullinger, *Decades*, IV.iv (174). Commenting on Genesis 1:2 regarding the first day of creation, Calvin asserts that "before God had perfected the world it was an indigested mass" and that "the power of the Spirit was necessary in order to sustain it." Citing Ps. 104:29-30 as a support, Calvin contends that "as soon as the Lord takes away his Spirit, all things return to their dust and vanish away." Calvin, *Commentaries on the Book of Genesis*, trans. John King, vol. 1 (Grand Rapids: Eerdmans, 1948), 73-74.

the church, particularly the issues of spiritual warfare and the ministries of ministers.

The Holy Spirit works in the church as well as in the life of individuals. The Reformed confessions declare that God preserves and governs his church—the communion of the elect—with his Word and Spirit. In CC45 Calvin states that God's Kingdom is "spiritual, and consists in the Word and Spirit of God, and includes righteousness and life."[69] The SC confesses, "God preserved, instructed, multiplied, honored, adorned, and called from death to life" his church in all ages "since Adam until the coming of Christ in Jesus in the flesh."[70] Likewise, the HC explicitly remarks that it is through his Word and Spirit that Christ "gathers, protects, and preserves for himself" his church.[71] God's reign over his church is spiritual and ethical in nature as it pertains not to the worldly authorities or powers, but to the work of the Holy Spirit in the lives of believers.

Bullinger illustratively asserts that the whole body receives life from the head, and from its spirit the body is governed in all things and receives increase that it may grow up. Therefore, the church cannot have any head other than Christ. And the church as the spiritual body of Christ, therefore, cannot be governed "by any other spirit than by the Spirit of Christ."[72] However, the Holy Spirit never works apart from the Word of God in governing the church. While Scripture reveals the will of God for his church and as such it serves as the objective rules by which God governs his church, the Holy Spirit works subjectively in the hearts of believers to quicken their faith, illumine, and move them to walk according to the Word of God.[73]

---

69. CC45 Q/A 37. In his exposition of the Lord's Prayer in CC37 Calvin teaches that God reigns over his own, i.e., his church, by his Holy Spirit as such that believers are to pray that the Holy Spirit "may will in us, through whose inspiration we may learn to love all things pleasing him and to hate and to detest all that which displeases him." CC37 XXIV (The Third Petition); CC45 Q/A 271-273. Or, in the words of the HC, Christians ought to pray: "Rule us by your Word and Spirit in such a way that more and more we submit to you." HC Q/A 123.

70. SC V; see BC XXVII.

71. HC Q/A 54; see also Ursinus, *The Commentary*, 286; Dickson, *Truths Victory over Error*, XXV.5 (248).

72. SHC XVII.6.

73. Ursinus, *The Commentary*, 277-278.

Therefore, as the GC teaches, Scripture alone as a whole is to be followed as the "rule of faith and religion" for "our spiritual government."[74]

Spiritual Warfare

The notion of the Kingdom of God in the Reformed confessions also confirms God's preservation and government by his Spirit over the church as well as other creatures, including the devils. God's Kingdom is a realm in which God alone rules and exercises dominion over all creatures, especially his church. God reigns over all things and all creatures, good and evil. However, the spiritual government of God over the church is distinguished from the divine government over the wicked and devils. Regarding the wicked and the devils, Calvin asserts in CC45 that although God "does not guide them by His Holy Spirit, nevertheless He curbs them by His power, so they cannot budge unless He permits them. He even constrains them to execute His will, although it is against their own intention and purpose."[75] The Kingdom of God in the second petition of the Lord's prayer, for Calvin, consists principally of two things: "that He leads His own, and governs them by His Spirit, and on the other hand casts down and confounds the reprobate who refuse to subject themselves to His rule, and so makes it clear that there is no power which can resist His power."[76] It appears that, when making a contrast between divine government over the church and over the wicked, Calvin uses an explicit reference to the Holy Spirit to denote God's positive and special providence towards his church, whereas a reference to God's power is to denote God's general providence towards his creatures, which includes the wicked and the devils.[77]

Nowhere does Calvin indicate that there are two different divine powers when it comes to governing power. The difference is only in manner. There

---

74. GC I; see also BC XXX; TNA XX.
75. CC45 Q/A 28.
76. CC45 Q/A 268; CC37 XXIV (The Second Petition and The Third Petition).
77. When Calvin discusses "divine permission" in his *Institutes*, he clearly maintains that "Satan and all the impious are so under God's hand and power that he directs their malice to whatever ends seems good to him, and uses their wicked deeds to carry out his judgments." Calvin also holds that although "often by means of Satan's intervention that God acts in the wicked," "Satan performs his part by God's impulsion and advances as far as he is allowed." Calvin, *Institutes*, I.xviii.1-2.

are not two different kinds of God's governing power, that of the Spirit and that of another. Calvin clearly acknowledges that the Holy Spirit is God's virtue and power; the Holy Spirit is God's almighty power working in his providence.[78] In CC37, when explicating the sixth petition of the Lord's prayer, "Lead us not into temptation, but deliver us from evil," Calvin makes a distinction between God's power and other opposing powers, but not between two different governing powers. He asserts that believers ought to pray so that they, "being firm and robust by the strength of the Lord," may constantly "stand against all powers combating us."[79] In CC45, Calvin also uses both references—to the Holy Spirit and his power—to denote God's preservation and positive government over believers. God leads believers away from temptation and delivers them from evil by giving them "strength to resist," sustaining them by his hand, and taking them into his safe keeping, in order to defend and lead them. How is this done? Calvin answers, "When He governs us by His Spirit, to make us love the good, and hate the evil, follow justice, and flee from sin. By the power of His Spirit, we may overcome the devil, sin and the flesh."[80]

A similar distinction can be found in the HC. The HC asserts that the second petition of the Lord's prayer, "Your kingdom come," is a request that God may rule believers with his Word and Spirit, preserve and increase his church, and destroy the devil's work.[81] Ursinus in his commentary of the HC points to the different manners in which God governs over his church and over the wicked and the devils. He uses different tones when addressing these two kinds of God's government. He enumerates the way God carries out his government over his church in a positive manner: the sending of the Son into the world, the institution and preservation of his ministry, the gathering of the church from the whole human race by the preaching of the Word and by the power of the Spirit, the preservation of the church notwithstanding the fierce assaults of enemies, the raising of the church to everlasting life, and the glorification of the church in eternal

---

78. CC45 Q/A 19.
79. CC37 XXIV (The Sixth Petition).
80. CC45 Q/A 289-290.
81. HC Q/A 123; Ursinus, *The Commentary*, 632-633.

life. Towards the wicked and the devils, God's government is exercised in a negative manner, such as casting all enemies of the Kingdom into everlasting condemnation, rejecting them, and bringing to an end all wickedness and ungodliness of every description; the wicked and the devils are regarded as those from whom the church is to be delivered.[82]

The power of the Holy Spirit curbs and restrains the wicked and the devils from harming the elect unless God permits them. Also, the Holy Spirit works in believers, helping them as they engage in spiritual warfare against spiritual enemies by governing and empowering them. The Holy Spirit makes believers hate evil and flee from sin; he dwells in them and continues to assist them in their continual spiritual battle so that they may triumph over the devil, sin, and the flesh, and attain victory.[83] The holy church, the BC confesses, is washed by Christ's blood and "sanctified and sealed by the Holy Spirit" that they may be "preserved by God against the rage of the whole world."[84] Among other marks, the BC teaches that true Christians are marked by their fleeing from sin, crucifying the flesh and its works: "Though great weakness remains in them, they fight against it by the Spirit all the days of their lives, appealing constantly to the blood, suffering, death, and obedience of the Lord Jesus, in whom they have forgiveness of their sins, through faith in him."[85]

Similarly, the HC asserts that Christ, by his power, that is, the Holy Spirit, "defends us and keeps us safe from all enemies."[86] As the HC also teaches, the sixth petition of the Lord's prayer means that believers, acknowledging their weaknesses and the enemies' tenacity to attack them,

---

82. Ursinus, *The Commentary*, 633-637. See also Olevianus, *A Firm Foundation*, Q/A 36. Olevianus also maintains that God governs the demons in a different manner than he does the angels. Commenting on the HC Q/A 27, Olevianus holds that God's providence also rules over the invisible creatures, namely, the angels and the demons. He then goes on to note the difference between God's ruling over both of them. God uses the angels to "serve and protect His believers." But, regarding the demons, Olevianus points out that, "although [God] does not rule the demons (which seek to undo the salvation of the elect) with His Spirit as He does the angels, by His power and wisdom He still employs them in such a way that they cannot even move except as it pleases Him."

83. CC45 Q/A 42, 290; SC XIII; WCF XIII.3

84. BC XXVII.

85. BC XXIX.

86. HC Q/A 51.

ought to constantly plead for the Holy Spirit's strength to uphold and make them strong so that they may firmly resist their enemies and gain complete victory in their spiritual struggle.[87]

Bullinger in SHC also emphatically remarks that the Gospel teaches how "vigilant and diligent" believers ought to be in this spiritual warfare against sin, and to strive for newness of life. Spiritual idleness opposes the teaching of the Gospel as much as it opposes the inner urge of the Holy Spirit in the renewal process of believers. Believers are called by God through the Holy Spirit to hate their sins and sinful lives as much as to live zealously a new virtuous life all the rest of their lives.[88]

Thus, as the CoD states, believers are to continually humble themselves before God, "to put the flesh to death more and more"—things that they, by nature, are unable to do—and they can only succeed with the help of "the Spirit of supplication and by holy exercises of godliness."[89] In their continual fight against sin, due to their weaknesses remaining in them, as the CoD states, "God preserves in those saints . . . his imperishable seed from which they have been born again," so that even when they fall, they will not fall away from grace. By his Word and Spirit God "certainly and effectively renews them to repentance so that they have a heartfelt and godly sorrow for the sins they have committed; seek and obtain, through faith and with a contrite heart, forgiveness in the blood of the Mediator."[90] It is not in human merit, nor in human power, that the preservation of believers is securely anchored. Rather, it is by virtue of God's undeserved

---

87. HC Q/A 127.

88. SHC XIV.1; see also V.12, 13. In the Tarczal-Torda Confession, as Barth notes, Beza also teaches that it is the Spirit, the Paraclete, who "guides us to hate sin, to hold the world in contempt, to call the Father with inexpressible sighs, to forget ourselves and to become even firmer." In the chapter "On the Church," Beza defines the church as the "assembly and multitude of elect persons" who fight "the battle of the Spirit against the flesh." Barth, *The Theology of the Reformed Confessions*, 120.

89. CoD V.2; see also WCF XIII.1-3; WLC Q/A 195. The Holy Spirit helps take away from believers weaknesses, blindness, and so on that prevent them from praying and approaching God.

90. CoD V.7.

mercy manifested in his immutable plan and unfailing promise that "the sealing of the Holy Spirit can neither be invalidated nor wiped out."[91]

The WCF confesses that believers, in whom God's Word and Spirit dwell, engage in "a continual and irreconcilable war" against the flesh, in every part of which "some remnants of corruption" still abides. However, having a new heart and a new spirit created in them, "the dominion of the whole body of sin is destroyed, and the several lusts thereof are more and more weakened and mortified," and believers are "more and more quickened and strengthened in all saving graces, to the practice of true holiness."[92] Although the remaining corruption may prevail for a time, true believers are enabled to overcome the spiritual war and grow in grace and holiness through "the continual supply of strength from the sanctifying Spirit of Christ."[93] As the WLC also states, true believers may fall into sin and grieve the Holy Spirit, but they are "never left without such a presence and support of the Spirit, as keeps them from sinking into utter despair."[94] Believers find necessary support in the Word of God to endure temptations and war against sin, but it is the Holy Spirit who makes the reading and the preaching of the Word an effectual means of "strengthening them against temptations and corruptions; of building them up in grace, and establishing their hearts in holiness and comfort through faith unto salvation."[95]

Human Ministers and Ministries as Outward Means

Regarding the way God executes his providence over his church, it should also be noted that in preserving and governing his church, God uses his ministers and their ministries as outward means.[96] "Not that God is bound

---

91. CoD V.8.
92. WCF XIII.1-2.
93. WCF XIII.3; VIII.8.
94. WLC Q/A 81; see also TNA XVI; WCF XVII.3; XVIII.4; WLC Q/A 105.
95. WLC Q/A 155.
96. With respect to the use of creatures or second causes, divine acts of providence can be distinguished into acts that are immediate and mediate. Immediate providence consists in God's provision for things, i.e., accomplishing all things that come to pass through his power over all being, directly without the use of means or second causes. And mediate providence is when God provides for things indirectly, that is by the use of means or second causes as the mediating subjects. Another distinction of providence is also made

to such aid and subordinate means, but because it pleaseth him to govern us by such restraints," the FC states.[97] In the Old Testament God sent certain people to undertake various offices in the name of God; they were prophets, judges, priests, and kings to preserve and govern his church.[98] In the New Testament he called unto his service certain people to be apostles, pastors, elders, and deacons for the same purpose.[99] The Reformed confessions regard pastors as preeminent among the ministers because of the ministries attached to their office as the ministers of the Word of God, such as preaching the Gospel, feeding the sheep of Jesus Christ, protecting them from false doctrines, administering sacraments, and the building up of the church.[100] Some Reformed confessions even consider the government of the church to be a task shared by some ecclesiastical offices, for examples, pastors, overseers, elders (presbyters), evangelists, teachers, and deacons.[101]

In complete agreement, the Reformed confessions teach that the power, authority, credibility, and efficacy of the outward means do not reside in the offices, ministers, or outward administrations in themselves, but in the Word of God and the Holy Spirit. As the GC confesses, the Word of God endows these ministers with power or authority "to conduct, rule, and govern the people of God." Only if the ministers are faithful in the Word of God, "they have power to command, defend, promise, and warn" them.[102] As Calvin states, the power given to ministers is "wholly contained in and

---

by the Reformed with respect to the law of nature embedded in the created order, that is between ordinary and extraordinary providence. While in the former, God's providence is carried out in accord with the law of nature common to all things, or the very nature of things, in the latter, God's providence is done beyond the usual and appointed order, e.g., miracles. For the definitions and other various distinctions of providence, see, for examples, WCF V.2-3; Ursinus, *The Commentary*, 152; Ames, *The Marrow of Theology*, I.ix.3-12.

97. FC XXV; see also CC37 XXX; CC45 Q/A 306-307; SHC XVIII.1; WCF XXV.3; XXX.1-2.

98. SC V; SHC XVIII.3.

99. WLC Q/A 63; SHC XVIII.5.

100. In Calvin's words, "it is necessary that there be pastors ordained to the churches, pastors who teach the people both in public and in private the pure doctrine, administer sacraments, and by their good example instruct and form all to holiness and purity of life." CC37 XXX. See also TC XIII; FHC XVI.

101. FC XXIX; BC XXXI; SHC XVIII.5.

102. GC XX; see also FC XXV; SC XXII; SHC XVIII.1.

limited to the ministry of the word," and that Christ gives the power not to the ministers but to his word.[103] Insofar as these ministers are faithful to the Word of God, their source of authority, they begin to be instruments of the Holy Spirit, and thus ought to be received as messengers and ambassadors of God.[104] Not only does the Spirit never operate in the church contrary to the Word, the church is also never ruled by the Spirit apart from the Word, and vice versa, nor any church ministry conducted faithfully according to the Word ever without the presence and power of the Holy Spirit.[105]

This chapter has shown that the doctrines of creation and providence in the Reformed confessions bear witness to the distinct role that the Holy Spirit plays in relation to all that is created. The Holy Spirit is involved in both the creation and providence of the world and all things therein, actively preserving, governing, and directing them all to their appointed ends according to the will of God. The creation of the world is not the work of one or two, but of all three persons of the Trinity who work indivisibly. Thus the creation and providence of the whole universe are no less the work of the Holy Spirit than of the Son and the Father.

The Reformed confessions also testify to the unique role of the Holy Spirit in both creation and providence by pointing to his creational and providential activities. In creation, the Holy Spirit is portrayed as the power or virtue of the Father, through whom the Father and Christ not only created, but also do all things. It is the Spirit that transfuses his energy into all things, and gives life to animate creatures, and beauty to all which he has once created, without whom none was created and able to exist and live by itself. All that is good proceeds from the Father and Christ through the Holy Spirit. In providence, the Holy Spirit is seen as the infinite power of God that fills, strengthens, vivifies, preserves, and governs all things,

---

103. CC37 XXX; see also FHC XV; TC XIII. The TC XIII states that "there is no power in the Church except for edification" and that "no one is sufficient of himself to think anything as of himself, but his sufficiency is of God" who appointed them to be his ministers.

104. Calvin states, "But if pastors turn away from the word to their dreams and to the inventions of their own minds, already they are no longer to be received as pastors." CC37 XXX. See also Calvin, *Institutes*, IV.viii.3.

105. Calvin, *Institutes*, IV.viii.13.

without whom all things could never have existed. With regard to divine providence over the church, namely, the special providence, the role of the Holy Spirit is highlighted even more as the Holy Spirit brings salvation to the elect, preserves their faith amidst spiritual warfare against the wicked and the devils, and with the Word rules the elect. In preserving and governing his church, God uses his ministers and their ministries as outward means. Through the work of the Holy Spirit God calls his ministers, bestows upon them necessary gifts for their offices, and gives power, authority, and efficacy to their ministries. The power and presence of the Holy Spirit are always with the ministers who carry out their ministries faithfully according to the Word of God.

PART THREE

CHAPTER 5

The Holy Spirit and the Doctrine of the Church

The Church's Unity and the Diversity of Spiritual Gifts

The next part of this dissertation, that is, this and the following chapter, will focus on the role of the Holy Spirit in some aspects of the doctrine of the church that have not been dealt with in chapter 3. The teaching of the Reformed confessions regarding the church has several aspects. As chapter 3 has shown, the Holy Spirit is involved in the church from its very inception. He also gives identity and marks to the true church, and invigorates the church through sacraments. However, the roles of the Holy Spirit in some other aspects of the doctrine of the church in the Reformed confessions have not been adequately treated or acknowledged by scholars in the past. These aspects are the unity of the church, the diversity of spiritual gifts for the church, and the mission of the church. This and the next chapter will focus the discussion on the role of the Holy Spirit in those aspects of the doctrine of the church as treated in the Reformed confessions. This chapter will discuss the first two, and chapter 6 will deal with the third.

The Holy Spirit and the Church's Unity

The Reformed confessions are unanimous in teaching the unity of the church. Even though they do not give a developed presentation of the doctrine, they nonetheless present the essential principles according to which the church ought to implement, cultivate, and foster its unity. The confessions teach the unity of the church as twofold: the unity of believers both with God and with each other, vertical and horizontal unity. The former underlies and gives the proper foundation for the latter. Both are inseparable from each other as they are two aspects of one and the same reality. As the Holy Spirit regenerates, justifies, sanctifies, and thus makes individual believers partakers of Christ's redemption, he unites them with Christ and reconciles them with the Father. In the words of the SC, the church contains all the elect out of the entire human race, "who have communion and society with God the Father, and with His Son, Christ Jesus, through sanctification of His Holy Spirit."[1] However, the work of the Holy Spirit in this personal or individual salvation is only a part of the whole operation of the Holy Spirit. The work of the Holy Spirit in the life of believers as a church is an integral part of the same operation. Having been united with God in Christ, believers consequently become members of a distinct society, a communion of people that God himself has chosen and gathered by his Spirit from all over the world, in all ages. This communion is exclusively the people of God, the one holy catholic church.

In arguing for their doctrine of the holy catholic church, the Reformed confessions state this twofold sense of the church's unity, while noticeably acknowledging the role of the Holy Spirit in establishing this unity. The Reformed confessions teach some fundamentals on which the church's unity ought to be built, nurtured, and developed, and at the same time note how the Holy Spirit is deeply involved in this endeavor. The Holy Spirit gathers and unites believers with each other. Believers also find the reason for their unity in the fact that they are led by the same Spirit who lives in them and rules them to worship and serve the one same God. God uses the sacraments and works by his Spirit through the administration of sacraments to preserve and foster the church's unity.

---

1. SC XVI. See also WLC Q/A 65-66, 68. The unity of believers with Christ by virtue of the application of redemption wrought in the lives of individual believers by the Holy Spirit has been discussed in Chapter 3 and will not be discussed here.

Unity in Communion

The Reformed Confessions do discuss, albeit briefly, the nature of unity that believers have with each other in Christ through the work of the Holy Spirit in them. With the Apostles' Creed, the Reformed confessions declare that the holy catholic church is the communion of the saints, a fellowship of believers. This fellowship that believers have, namely, the unity of believers, goes beyond mere shared outward profession of faith or ideological level. It originates in the shared experience of the Holy Spirit, applying Christ's redemption in the lives of believers along with its implications. It should be remembered that believers are enabled to come to Christ and make genuine profession of faith only through the help of the Holy Spirit.

The TC confesses that the church of Christ, which is also frequently called "the kingdom of heaven," is "the fellowship of those who have enlisted under Christ and committed themselves entirely to his faith." Later the TC asserts further that the church is properly called the communion of saints because in this communion Christ reigns by his Spirit. "This [that is, the church] the Holy Ghost rules, from this Christ is never absent, but he sanctifies it to present it at length to himself blameless, not having spot or wrinkle."[2] The FCB similarly identifies this fellowship of the saints as "the spiritual assembly of believers," or "the gathering of believers in the Spirit," in which all are "citizens who truly confess that Jesus is the Christ, the Lamb of God who takes away the sin of the world, and who also confirm such faith by works of love."[3]

The GC also firmly holds that the communion of believers lies deeper than mere outward profession of faith by pointing to the work of the Holy Spirit that underlies the communion. There is only "one Church of Jesus Christ," the company of the faithful.[4] This church consists of believers, whom God gathers and receives into a communion with Christ through the agency of the Holy Spirit. As the GC asserts, God does not

---

2. TC II; XV. See also FHC XIV.
3. FCB V. Cf. The First Confession of Basel (1534) (in Dennison, *Reformed Confessions of the 16th and 17th Centuries*), V. Dennison provides a better translation of the Latin text for "the spiritual assembly of believers," i.e., "the gathering of believers in the Spirit."
4. GC XVIII; FC XXVII.

receive believers into "the communion of his son Jesus" because of any consideration of believers' "worthiness" or the merit of their works," but merely because of his "clemency and pity" that works in believers through his Spirit: regenerating them into "a new spiritual nature," mortifying "the evil desires" of the flesh," rendering their will "conformable to God's will," and delivering them from "the servitude of sin," under whose power they were held captive.[5]

The universality of the church goes beyond the boundaries of geography, ethnicity, language, and time, as the work of the Holy Spirit is not subject to those boundaries. As the SC confesses, "from the beginning there has been, now is, and to the end of the world shall be, one Kirk, that is to say, one company and multitude of men chosen by God."[6] This church is catholic, universal, because "it contains the chosen of all ages, of all realms, nations, and tongues." The SC describes further what it means by "the chosen," the elect, as those "who have communion and society with God the Father, and with His Son, Christ Jesus, through the sanctification of the Holy Spirit."[7] In other words, none shall have part of the communion of believers, but "those whom the Father has given unto His Son Christ Jesus, and those who in time to come to Him, avow His doctrine, and believe in Him."[8] And it is only by virtue of the Holy Spirit that believers may be brought into all truth and to believe in Christ. Without the Holy Spirit regenerating, inspiring, and sanctifying, all human beings because of their sinfulness "should remain forever enemies to God and ignorant of His Son, Christ Jesus."[9]

The BC defines the holy catholic church as "a holy congregation and gathering of true Christian believers, awaiting their entire salvation in Jesus Christ being washed by his blood, and sanctified and sealed by the Holy Spirit." To highlight the nature of the church's unity as a communion or fellowship of believers, it then continues to assert that, although the church

---

5. GC VIII; X.
6. SC XVI.
7. SC XVI.
8. SC XVI.
9. SC XII.

is "spread and dispersed throughout the entire world," all true believers are "still joined and united in heart and will, in one and the same Spirit, by the power of faith."[10]

When elaborating the meaning of the holy catholic church, the HC asserts that it is "a community chosen for eternal life and united in true faith," which Christ himself, "through his Spirit and Word, out of the entire human race, from the beginning of the world to its end, gathers, protects, and preserves for himself," and of this community, a true Christian is and always will be "a living member."[11] The holy catholic church, that is the invisible church, is the communion of those who are called, gathered, and sanctified by the Holy Spirit. In his commentary on the HC, Ursinus states that the church is called holy because the church is "sanctified by the blood and and Spirit of Christ" as the Holy Spirit "renews and delivers the church from the dregs of sins by degrees."[12] When drawing distinction between the church and the State, Ursinus points out the role of the Holy Spirit in the lives of those who are members of the church as the main distinguishing identifier of the church.[13] Later, regarding the cause of the difference between the church and the rest of mankind, Ursinus also states that the efficient cause of the difference is "the election of God," the Son is "the mediate executor of the will of the Father," the Holy Spirit is "the immediate executor."[14] The church consists of "those who embrace the gospel, and observe the sacraments according to divine appointment, and is governed by the Spirit and word of God."[15] Olevianus, in his commentary on the HC, similarly asserts that all members of the true church are members of Christ, united into one body through the Holy Spirit.[16] In his *Exposition*, Olevianus states that the church is "a new people" that the Father builds for himself in Christ by the power of the Holy Spirit, with whom he establishes

---

10. BC XXVII.
11. HC Q/A 54.
12. Ursinus, *The Commentary*, 289; Olevianus, *A Firm Foundation*, Q/A 134.
13. Ursinus, *The Commentary*, 291.
14. Ursinus, *The Commentary*, 292.
15. Ursinus, *The Commentary*, 291.
16. Olevianus, *A Firm Foundation*, Q/A 135.

a gracious covenant and to whom he communicates himself and all his benefits.[17] The Son of God "unites them to Himself like a bride, so that every true member of this people might have κοινωνίαν [fellowship] with Christ and mutual fellowship among themselves, both in this life and the one to come (1 John 1[:3])."[18] All believers share the same experience of being gathered out of the world, drawn into a communion with Christ as the Head, sanctified, and united to each other by the same Spirit.

Bullinger in the SHC teaches that the church is "an assembly of the faithful called or gathered out of the world; a communion . . . of all saints." By "saints" Bullinger means "those who truly know and rightly worship and serve the true God in Christ the Savior, by the Word and Holy Spirit, and who by faith are partakers of all benefits which are freely offered through Christ."[19] The conviction that there is only one church is derived from the fact that there is always one God, one Mediator between God and human beings, who is also the only Shepherd of the flock and Head of the whole body, and one Spirit, who works salvation and faith and unites all believers in one fellowship.[20]

In addition to the description of the communion of the saints, as the nature of the unity that believers have with each other in Christ through the Holy Spirit, the Reformed confessions also use biblical images or metaphors for the church to affirm the same unity. Two most common biblical images for the church that one could find in the Reformed confessions are "the body of Christ" and "the bride of Christ."[21] In using these biblical images, the Reformed confessions again acknowledge and point to the role of the Holy Spirit in uniting believers with God in Christ and with each other.

---

17. Olevianus, *An Exposition*, 129-130.
18. Olevianus, *An Exposition*, 130.
19. SHC XVII.1.
20. SHC XVII.2, 4.
21. The FHC uses another biblical image found in I Ptr. 2:4 ff. to illustrate the church: "living stones built upon the living rock;" FHC XIV. Besides "the body of Christ" and "the bride of Christ," the HSC also uses the same image as the FHC, but then also adds few other biblical images for the church: "the pillar and bulwark of the truth" (I Tim. 3:15), and "a flock of sheep" (Ezek. 34; Jn. 10); SHC XVII.5.

Believers are united to Christ, as members of one body are united to its head. Christ is the head from which the body and all its members receive their identity as members of Christ.[22] The TC portrays the church, the communion of saints which the Holy Spirit rules, as "a body compacted of various members, whereof each has his own work."[23] The GC states that God does not only receive believers as his children, but also as "members of his Son," who live in Christ by his Spirit.[24] In CC37 Calvin highlights this truth even more when he describes the universality of the church. He asserts that "all the elect are conjoined through the bond of faith in one church and society, in one people of God, of which Christ our Lord is the leader and prince and head, as of one body."[25] Calvin goes on to state that the church is one and catholic, that is, universal, because "there are not two or three churches, but all God's elect are united and conjoined in Christ in such a way that just as they depend on one head so they grow as in one body." As such, all the elect are "being composed as the members of one same body, being truly made one in as much as they live by the same spirit of God in one same faith, hope, and charity, being called to participate in one same inheritance of eternal life."[26]

The CECG affirms that the operation of the same Holy Spirit, who works in the lives of believers as members of the body of Christ, is the undergirding basis of the church's unity. Right after confessing belief in the Holy Spirit, who regenerates, sanctifies, rules, guides into all truth, and persuades all believers that they are "children of God, brethren to Jesus Christ, and fellow heirs with Him of life everlasting," the CECG declares, "I believe therefore and confess one holy Church which (as members of Jesus Christ the only Head thereof) agree in faith, hope, and love."[27]

The BC affirms the uniting role of the Holy Spirit in the church as the body of Christ. It holds that the holy catholic church is "still joined and

---

22. Eph. 4:16; I Cor. 12:13. See FHC XVIII; XIX.
23. TC XV.
24. GC XV.
25. CC37 XX; see also SC VIII.
26. CC37 XX ("I believe the holy Church universal, the communion of saints"); see also CC45 Q/A 97, 344; Calvin, *Institutes*, IV.i.2.
27. CECG III; IV.

united . . . in one and the same Spirit."[28] Being united in one and the same Spirit, believers ought to manifest this unity by regarding themselves as "members of each other in the same body," that is, the body of Christ.[29] The HC maintains the use of the body of Christ image when it teaches that a believer is called a Christian because by faith she is "a member of Christ."[30] Similarly, the CoD calls Christ "the head of all those chosen," into whose fellowship the elect are called and drawn effectively by God through his Word and Spirit.[31]

The WCF even explicitly asserts the role of the Holy Spirit in bringing about the twofold unity of the church as the body of Christ. "The Catholick or Universal Church which is invisible, consists of the whole number of the Elect, that have been, are, or shall be gathered into one, under Christ the Head thereof."[32] As Dickson explains the article, "the members of the Church Universal, considered as to their internal state, and condition, are united, and conjoyned together in one body, by one Spirit, and by one Faith; I Cor. 12. 13. Eph. 4. 4, 5."[33] The WCF also states that the elect are united to Christ their head "by his Spirit, and by Faith," so that they have "fellowship with him in his graces, sufferings, death, resurrection, and glory." It then confesses that, as members of one body, the elect are "united to one another in love" and "have communion in each others gifts and graces."[34]

Thus believers are united to each other by God in Christ through the Holy Spirit who lives in them, who applies God's grace of adoption in the lives of believers. Together, being quickened and renewed, believers are engrafted by the Holy Spirit into one single body, the body of Christ. By the same virtue of the Holy Spirit, not by mere solidarity of having a same

---

28. BC XXVII.
29. BC XXVIII.
30. HC Q/A 32.
31. CoD I.7.
32. WCF XXV.1.
33. Dickson, *Truths Victory over Error*, XXV.1 (236).
34. WCF XXVI.1.

religion, believers then become fellow children of God to each other and fellow members of the same body, of which Christ is the only Head.

Another biblical image that is commonly used by some confessions to illustrate the unity of the church is the image of the church as the holy bride of Christ.[35] The FCB confesses that there is only "one holy, Christian Church," which is also known as "the fellowship of the saints, the spiritual assembly of believers which is holy and the one bride of Christ."[36] For the FCB, the unity of the church ought also to be based on the fact that Scripture testifies to the one, holy bride of Christ. Christ is the groom and the church is his bride, restored from her fallenness and sanctified by the Holy Spirit.[37] In the same line of thought, the FHC uses the same imagery to stress both the unity of the church and the ongoing reality of the work of the Holy Spirit in sanctifying the church. The church, that is "the fellowship and congregation of all saints," is "Christ's bride and spouse which He washes with His blood and finally presents to the Father without blemish or any spot."[38]

As the body of Christ is one, the bride of Christ is one. The SC firmly holds that "from the beginning there has been, now is, and to the end of the world shall be, one Kirk," which is also called "the body and spouse of Christ Jesus." It should be noted that this spouse of Christ, although she contains the chosen of all ages, realms, nations, and tongues, is one. It consists of those, and only those, who have communion with God the Father and with his Son through the sanctification of the Holy Spirit.[39] The CoD and WCF also maintains a monogamous love of Christ toward his church as his only bride. The CoD remarks that from the beginning of the world to the present time, "the chosen are gathered into one, all in their own time, and there is always a church of believers founded on Christ's blood," a church that "steadfastly loves and persistently worships, and . . . praises [Christ] as her Savior who laid down his life for her on the cross,

---

35. Eph. 5:25 ff.; Rev. 21:9.
36. FCB V; see also TC II; XV.
37. FCB II.
38. FHC XIV; see also XIII.
39. SC XVI.

"as a bridegroom for his bride."[40] Without elaborating it, the WCF calls the catholic or universal church as "the Spouse, the Body, the fullness of Him that filleth all in all."[41]

Thus, believers of all ages in all places are united to Christ and to each other by the Holy Spirit as a communion of all saints. As the one body and bride of Christ, they are gathered and made one by the active work of the Holy Spirit. This sure belief of the work of the Holy Spirit in uniting believers leads the Reformed confessions to the conviction of the unifying visible marks of the true church, which are nothing but the outward manifestation of the works of the Holy Spirit through the church: the pure preaching of the gospel and the faithful administration of sacraments. These marks of the true church have been discussed in chapter 3.

Unity in Worship and Service

Another basis for the church's unity is the ongoing work of the Holy Spirit uniting believers in their worship and service as he rules them and inspires them to live as a community of saints. Whereas the church's unity does not stop in the inward renewal of each believer but finds expression in actuality, the Holy Spirit not only works in believers to gather them into the communion of the saints but also leads them to live up to their calling as God's community that worships God. Believers, as members of the same communion of saints, are ruled by the same Holy Spirit. They are regenerated and transformed by the Holy Spirit to worship and serve one God. The Holy Spirit dwells and lives in believers, ruling and guiding, sanctifying and assuring them that they are children of God, brethren of Jesus Christ, and fellow heirs with him, and leading them to live according to their identity.

The Holy Spirit brings unity among believers as he works in them, inspiring them to worship but one God in spirit and in truth. In the Reformed confessions, to worship God and serve him in spirit and truth are not to be understood merely as common purposes that unite churches of different traditions, to be exercised at the church's discretion. To worship and to serve God are God's sole calling for the church that is deeply

---

40. CoD II.9.
41. WCF XXV.1.

embedded in its nature and identity. They are the church's *raison d'être* that gives every reason for the church to pursue its unity. The GC declares that any assembly of people can only be called church as long as it assembles in the name of the Lord. As the GC later describes, this means that a church can only find its allegiance with the holy catholic church when they gather together in the name of the Lord and worship the same God, of which the pure and faithful preaching of the gospel and the proper administration of sacraments are the principal marks.[42] It should be noted that the GC has previously remarked that the church has only one God "to worship and serve, and in whom we are to put all our confidence and hope."[43] To worship God who is spirit, one is to serve him in spirit and truth (Jn. 4:23-24), as the GC also notes. Such worship is not within human natural capability. It is by the power of the Holy Spirit that human beings are enabled to overcome their corrupt nature and perversity of heart, to come to the right knowledge of God and be redirected in affections and reformed to the obedience of the righteousness of God.[44] The Holy Spirit actually helps believers worship God, and thus unites them in their worship, by rendering their will "conformable to God's will, to follow in his way and to seek what is pleasing to him."[45]

The SC explicitly remarks, "As we believe in one God, Father, Son, and Holy Ghost, so we firmly believe that from the beginning there has been, now is, and to the end of the world shall be, one Kirk." This means that there is only "one company and multitude of men chosen by God, who rightly worship and embrace Him by true faith in Christ Jesus." As the SC also points out later, the church is united as a community of saints by the fact that she worships one God and serves one Lord, that is Jesus Christ.[46] This assertion, however, is made after acknowledging previously that to have one God, to worship and honor him, to call upon him and reverence his holy Name, are things that can only be done by the help of the Holy

---

42. GC XVIII.
43. GC II.
44. GC IV; VIII.
45. GC VIII.
46. SC XVI.

Spirit, who dwells in believers' hearts.[47] The Holy Spirit works in believers, enabling and inspiring them to worship and serve God in unity.

Bullinger in the SHC makes a similar remark. He defines the church as "an assembly of the faithful called or gathered out of the world; a communion . . . of those who truly know and rightly worship and serve the true God in Christ the Savior, by the Word and Holy Spirit."[48] Believers, having the same faith and Spirit, are united as they share common disposition toward God. Bullinger holds that true believers, joined together with all the members of Christ, have the same desire to "worship but one God, and him alone they worship in spirit and in truth, loving him alone with their hearts and with all their strength, praying unto him alone through Jesus Christ."[49] Even though Bullinger does not explicitly refer to the Holy Spirit when he discusses the church's unity in relation to her worship, the work of the Holy Spirit is everywhere presupposed. Bullinger contends previously that it is the Holy Spirit who invigorates the body of Christ, as "the body receives increase" from its spirit.[50]

Unity under God's Rule and Government

The Reformed confessions also teach that, despite the diversity of its members, the church—as a company of believers, the body and bride of Christ—is united by the Holy Spirit who works in and rules the church. The previous chapter has discussed the role of the Holy Spirit in relation with God's government over the church from the perspective of the doctrine of providence, as treated in the Reformed confessions. Here the role of the Spirit can also be seen in God's government over the church from the perspective of the church's unity. As God rules and governs his church with his Spirit and Word, the church—that is, all believers in all quarters of the world and of all realms—has in principle the same rule and government of God. Consequently, believers are in an alliance with the same Lord and

---

47. SC XIII; XIV.
48. SHC XVII.1.
49. SHC XVII.12.
50. SHC XVII.6.

each other as they obediently follow God, who lives and rules in them through his Spirit and Word.

The LA expresses this belief when it aptly states that believers are named "the church of God" because they believe that they are "received by the blood of Jesus Christ alone," and that they "without vacillation believe and wholly establish and support themselves on the Word, which, having withdrawn from us in corporeal presence, nevertheless by virtue of his Holy Spirit fills, sustains, governs and vivifies all things."[51] Calvin teaches in CC37 that the church is made one inasmuch as she lives in obedience to the Holy Spirit. Calvin admits that the church's unity involves a process, a process of growth. All God's elect are "united and conjoined in Christ in such a way that just as they depend on one head so they grow as in one body, adhering one to the other, being composed as the members of one same body." Therefore, as Calvin states later, the catholic, universal church is "being truly made one in as much as they live by the same [S]pirit of God in one same faith, hope, and charity."[52]

The CECG also affirms that the Holy Spirit unites believers as he continually works in them. The Holy Spirit convinces believers of their new identity in Christ and inspires them to see fellow believers accordingly, as the Holy Spirit guides them into all truth. In the section on the Holy Spirit, the CECG asserts that the Holy Spirit does not only regenerate and sanctify, but also "rules and guides us into all truth, persuading us most assuredly in our consciences that we are children of God, brethren to Jesus Christ, and fellow-heirs with Him of life everlasting."[53]

The same teaching can also be found in the HC, although it is stated from a different point of view. On the question of why the Son of God is called Christ, the HC answers that he is called Christ because "he has been ordained by God the Father and has been anointed with the Holy Spirit" to be "our chief prophet and teacher," "our only high priest," and "our eternal king." As for the third, the HC adds that, as our eternal king,

---

51. LA III. See also FCB VI; GC XV.
52. CC37 XX ("I believe the holy Church universal, the communion of saints"); Calvin, *Institutes*, IV.i.2.
53. CECG III.

Christ "governs us by his Word and Spirit" and "guards us and keeps us in the freedom he has won for us."[54] This means that Christ, as the King and the sole Head of the church, manifests his Kingship, or Headship, by governing, guarding, and keeping his people, which is his church. Therefore, as the HC explicates further, by being called "a Christian" one professes publicly that she is a member of Christ and posits herself to be a subject to be governed by Christ, the Head.[55] As the HC continues to assert, in this sense a Christian shares in Christ's anointing. While Christ has been anointed by the Holy Spirit to be the King or Head of the church, believers are anointed to confess Christ's name, to present themselves to him as "a living sacrifice of thanks, to strive with a good conscience against sin and the devil in this life, and afterward to reign with Christ over all creation for all eternity."[56] In other words, a Christian is a member of Christ as much as she subjects herself to Christ and thus wills to be governed by Christ through his Holy Spirit.

Bullinger in the SHC states that, as the church cannot have any other head besides Christ, neither can it "be governed by any other spirit than by the Spirit of Christ."[57] Having affirmed Christ is the Head who governs his church by his Spirit, Bullinger then maintains the unity of the church under the government of its Head as he deals with the problem of dissensions and strife in the church. Despite manifold discords and contentions that divide churches, the true church never ceases to be the true church. Bullinger even holds that "it pleases God to use the dissensions that arise in the church to the glory of his name, to illustrate the truth, and in order that those who are in the right might be manifest (I Cor. 11:19)."[58] Bullinger then contends that not every church is part of the true church just because she claims herself to be such. The true church, therefore, has to bear the marks of the true church, that is, the pure preaching of the gospel and the proper administration of sacraments, which "all lead us unto Christ,"

---

54. HC Q/A 31.
55. HC Q/A 32, 54.
56. HC Q/A 32.
57. SHC XVII.6.
58. SHC XVII.10.

the sole Head of the true church.[59] Bullinger states further that those who are in the true church ought to also display in life that they belong to the true church. Besides worshiping one God in spirit and truth and showing genuine affection in loving God alone, true believers are so "joined together with all members of Christ by an unfeigned love" that their life brings a living testimony that they are "Christ's disciples by persevering in the bond of peace and holy unity."[60] Being governed by the Spirit of Christ under one rule, true believers are united to each other to live up to their calling as members of the same body, the body of Christ.

Sacraments as Outward Means for Preserving Unity

The Reformed confessions also teach that besides working in the lives of believers, guiding and ruling them, the Holy Spirit also works in the administration of sacraments to preserve the church's unity. Chapter 3 has discussed the strong emphasis that the Reformed confessions put on the role of the Holy Spirit in the ingrafting of the believers into Christ and the offering of all benefits of Christ in the sacraments. As chapter 3 has also already noted, scholars in the past who studied the theology of the Reformed confessions have identified this theme. However, what has not been given notice by these scholars is that the Reformed confessions also teach that sacraments are ordained by God to be effectual means for preserving the unity of the church through the same agency of the Holy Spirit. To describe the teaching of the Reformed confessions regarding the use of sacraments only in relation to the union of believers with Christ is a one-sided presentation and does not do justice to the teaching of the confessions regarding the theme as a whole. Just as the confessions understand the church's unity as twofold, that believers are in unity with both Christ and each other, so the use of sacraments to preserve the church's unity is also twofold. Albeit briefly, some confessions do explicitly teach that sacraments, properly and lawfully administered, are ordained by God, who works through his Holy Spirit, to preserve and foster the unity that believers have with each other as well as with Christ.

---

59. SHC XVII.11.
60. SHC XVII.12; see also FCB V; FC XXVI; XXVII.

As the SC teaches, sacraments were from the beginning ordained by God for and to be used by his church as a community as well as for individuals that constitute the church. The SC states that sacraments "were instituted by the Lord Jesus and commanded to be used by all who will be counted members of His Body." They were instituted by God to make "a visible distinction between his people and those who were without the Covenant," as well as "to exercise the faith of His children" and "to seal in their hearts the assurance of His promise, and of that most blessed conjunction, union, and society, which the chosen have with their Head, Christ Jesus."[61]

When Bullinger's SHC describes the holy catholic church and Christ as the sole Head of the church, it remarks that the observance of sacraments is an expression of the church's unity. Even though the role of the Holy Spirit is not explicitly mentioned in this particular theme or context, there is an implicit reference to the Holy Spirit. As was discussed in chapter 3 in the description of the role of the Holy Spirit in sacraments, it is Bullinger's conviction that the efficacy and power of sacraments lie in God himself, who works through his Holy Spirit. For Bullinger, true believers, "joined together with all the members of Christ by an unfeigned love," "participate in the sacraments instituted by Christ, and delivered unto us by his apostles, using them in no other way than as they received them from the Lord."[62] In another part of the same section, Bullinger points out that unity "consists not in outward rites and ceremonies, but rather in the truth and unity of the catholic faith." Insofar as ecclesiastical rites, including sacraments, are founded on the true and pure preaching of the catholic faith, they remain expedient to the unity of the church. Regarding this, he later concludes that "the true harmony of the Church consists in doctrines and in the true and harmonious preaching of the Gospel of Christ, and in rites that have been expressly delivered by the Lord."[63] In his treatment of the doctrine of sacraments, Bullinger also asserts that one of the purposes of God's giving sacraments to peoples of both Old and New Testaments is to unite his people. Sacraments are to be understood as "signs and seals of the grace

---

61. SC XXI.
62. SHC XVII.12.
63. SHC XVII.17; see also FHC XIV.

and promises of God." As such, the observance of sacraments, in both the Old and New Testaments, is meant to remind them of God's grace as well as their identity. Sacraments are to "call to mind and renew the memory of God's great benefits," to "distinguish the faithful from all the religions in the world," to be "received spiritually by faith" through the work of the Holy Spirit, and to "bind the receivers to the Church, and admonish them of their duty."[64] Sacraments bind their receivers to the church.

The Reformed confessions state further the role of the Holy Spirit in the preservation of horizontal unity through sacraments in their explications of the doctrines of holy baptism and the Lord's Supper. Calvin in CC37 brings to the fore the horizontal dimension resulting from the union between Christ and the people of God exhibited in the sacraments.[65] For Calvin, the sacrament of baptism has been given by God to help, first, the faith of believers in him, and, secondly, their profession of faith before others. As for the latter, being baptized means publicly declaring "to be numbered among the people of God, to the end that we, together with all believers, may serve and honor, with one some religion, one God."[66] Not only with Christ, to be baptized also means to be united with all believers, to be a member of the same communion of saints.

One can find the same train of thought expressed in the TNA and HC. The TNA states that they who receive the sacraments are united with Christ as well as with each other. When believers rightly receive baptism, they are "grafted into the Church." By receiving baptism, "the promises of the forgiveness of sin, and of our adoption to be the sons of God by the Holy Ghost, are visibly signed and sealed."[67] Believers are visibly received into the body of Christ through baptism. The HC similarly teaches that the sacrament of baptism is "the mark of covenant," that outwardly signifies the forgiveness of sins by the blood of Christ that they receive through the Holy Spirit.[68] The meaning of baptism, for the HC, lies in the notion of "to

---

64. SHC XIX.5; XX.2.
65. Hesselink rightly points this out, *Calvin's First Catechism*, 144; see also 151-152.
66. CC37 XXVIII.
67. TNA XXVII.
68. HC Q/A 70, 75.

be washed with Christ's blood and Spirit."[69] Believers are set apart by the Holy Spirit to be members of Christ. In other words, they are joined with other members of Christ by the Holy Spirit.

For Bullinger, baptism is a God-ordained sign of initiation, or consecration, and by it the elect are consecrated to God.[70] This consecration joins the elect to other members of the covenant people, the family of God. Thus, for Bullinger, to be baptized in the name of Christ means "to be enrolled, entered, and received into the covenant and family."[71] Through baptism, God adopts us to be his children and by a holy covenant joins them with himself in Christ.[72] Bullinger emphasizes again the aspect of the church's unity among believers in the sacrament of baptism when he states that "we are baptized into one body of the Church, that with all members of the Church we might beautifully concur in the one religion and in mutual services."[73] What is signified outwardly by the sacrament of baptism is what God through the Holy Spirit works inwardly in the believers who observe the sacrament. Joining believers to the family of God and to God in Christ is indeed the work of the Holy Spirit who operates through the administration of the sacrament of baptism.

The WCF holds that sacraments, as "holy Signs and Seals of the Covenant of grace, immediately instituted by God," put visible marks to those who belong to the church, to distinguish the church from the rest of the world and to engage them to the service of God in Christ.[74] Having declared that the efficacy of sacraments depends solely upon "the work of the Spirit" and "the word of institution," the WCF asserts that baptism plays its role in the church as a sign of "the solemn admission of the party baptized, into the visible Church," as well as "a sign and seal of the Covenant of Grace, of his ingrafting into Christ, of Regeneration, of Remission of sins, and of his giving up unto God, through Jesus Christ, to walk in newness of

---

69. HC Q/A 69-70.
70. SHC XX.1.
71. SHC XX.2; see also CECG IV.
72. SHC XX.3.
73. SHC XX.4. Those who separate themselves from the holy fellowship of the church thereby introduce alien and ungodly doctrines to the church. See FHC XXV; BC XXVIII.
74. WCF XXVII.1.

life."⁷⁵ All these things that baptism signifies are nothing but the work of the Holy Spirit. Thus, through the work of the Holy Spirit, baptism can be an effectual means to unite the church, as by baptism, members of Christ are visibly admitted to the church. The WLC remarks that, among other things, "being baptized by the same Spirit into one body," believers ought to "walk in brotherly love."⁷⁶

In the same way, the Reformed confessions also teach that God ordains the sacrament of the Lord's Supper to preserve the church's unity through the agency of the Holy Spirit. In CC37 Calvin maintains that the Lord's Supper "exhorts us to embrace each other mutually by such a unity as that which binds among themselves and conjoins together the members of one same body." Calvin then argues that there is no stronger reason to incite among believers a mutual love than when Christ "invites us not only by his example to give ourselves and to expose ourselves mutually one for the other, but inasmuch as he makes himself common to all, he makes us also all one in himself."⁷⁷ Even though no reference to the Holy Spirit can be found in the aforementioned articles of Calvin's catechism, it should be noted that underlying this teaching on the sacraments is Calvin's firm conviction that "the sacraments profit not a whit without the power of the Holy Spirit." Calvin states clearly in his *Institutes* that sacraments are "empty and trifling, apart from the action of the Spirit, but charged with great effect when the Spirit works within and manifests his power."⁷⁸

The TNA asserts that the sacrament of the Lord's Supper is "a sign of the love that Christians ought to have among themselves one to another," as well as a sign for their partaking of the body and blood of Christ.⁷⁹ The HC similarly teaches that "to eat the crucified body of Christ and to drink his

---

75. WCF XXVII.3; XXVIII.1; WLC Q/A 165.
76. WLC Q/A 167. When discussing the doctrine of adoption, Watson asserts that, among signs of true adoption, the children of God have "the Conduct of God's Spirit" and "an intire love to all God's Children." "We bear Affection to God's Children, though they have some Infirmities. . . . If we are adopted, we love the Good we see in God's Children, we admire their Graces, we pass by their Imprudencies." Watson, *A Body of Practical Divinity*, 138.
77. CC37 XXIX.
78. Calvin, *Institutes*, IV.xiv.9.
79. TNA XXVIII.

poured-out blood" means that through "the Holy Spirit, who lives both in Christ and in us, we are united more and more to Christ's blessed body."[80] As a result, "we forever live on and are governed by one Spirit, as members of our body are by one soul." The HC then quotes Paul's words in I Cor. 10:16-17 to emphasize the aspect of unity in the Lord's Supper:

> Is not the cup of thanksgiving for which we give thanks a participation in the blood of Christ? And is not the bread that we break a participation in the body of Christ? Because there is one loaf, we, who are many, are one body, for we all partake of the one loaf.[81]

In his commentary on the HC, Ursinus states even more clearly that for all members of the church, who are united in Christ by the Spirit, the sacraments—baptism and the Lord's Supper—serve as "bonds of mutual love," "cords that bind together the public assemblies which come together in the church," and "pledges of that communion which [C]hristians have with Christ in the first place, and then with each other."[82]

In the SHC, Bullinger maintains that when believers receive the elements of the Lord's Supper they exercise the sacramental eating of the body of the Lord, by which believers not only spiritually and internally participate in the true body and blood of the Lord by virtue of the Holy Spirit, but also outwardly receive the visible sacrament of the body and blood of the Lord. By participating in the sacrament, a believer "gives a witness before the Church, of whose body he is a member."[83] In the celebration of the Lord's Supper, the church is admonished to remember what the Holy Spirit has inwardly done to them, ingrafting them into the body of Christ and the communion they have through the sacrifice of Christ. Believers are "to be mindful of whose body we may have become members, and that, therefore,

---

80. HC Q/A 76.
81. HC Q/A 77.
82. Ursinus, *The Commentary*, 345.
83. SHC XXI.8.

we may be one of mind with all the brethren," as they persevere "in the true faith to the end of life and striving to excel in holiness of life."[84]

The WCF maintains the language of unity when it describes the sacrament of the Lord's Supper. It strongly asserts that the sacrament is to be observed in the church unto the end of the world. Besides the purposes of the sacrament to signify and seal all benefits of Christ offered and conveyed by it for the church's spiritual nourishment and growth, the sacrament also functions as a visible "Bond and Pledge of their Communion with [Christ], and with each other, as Members of his Mystical Body."[85] The participation of believers in the sacrament, as the WLC teaches, gives testimony to "their mutual love, and fellowship with each other, as members of the same mystical body."[86]

As discussed above, the role of the Holy Spirit in preserving and fostering the unity of believers with Christ and with each other is pivotal in the Reformed confessions. God through his Holy Spirit unites believers with each other to make a communion of saints, the body and holy bride of Christ. The Holy Spirit is the person of the Trinity who works in believers to rule and guide them according to the Word, and who operates in the faithful administration of sacraments as to make sacraments effectual means for bringing unity to believers as they are more and more united to Christ. The conviction of the church's unity founded on the work of God through his Holy Spirit is clearly evident in the confessions. Thus any company of people which claims to be a part of the holy catholic church, that is, the communion of saints, and thus professes itself to be in line with and governed by the Spirit, should be discerned by its fruit. If it is the true church, then it should maintain and be characterized by unity in the truth of the catholic faith and the proper administration of sacraments, plainly manifested in worship and service, in profession and action.

---

84. SHC XXI.11.
85. WCF XXIX.1.
86. WLC Q/A 168.

The Holy Spirit and the Diversity of Spiritual Gifts

As discussed earlier, the Reformed confessions are in a full agreement with each other in teaching that the catholicity of the church embraces the chosen from different places and times, realms and cultures, ages and traditions. God actively unites his people from all places and ages by ruling them with his Word and Spirit. The active role of God in bringing unity to his church, however, does not diminish the role of the elect in the same enterprise. God endows the church not only with the saving grace of redemption, but also with various spiritual gifts of ministry so that the church may unite under Christ as her head, experience her growth, and worship and serve God in the world (Eph. 4:7-13). He unites his church through his Spirit working inwardly in the lives of the elect. But God also works by the use of outward means, the ministry of all members of the body, on whom he bestows various spiritual gifts of ministry, each according to his own will. The confessions acknowledge and confess this biblical truth, and at the same time point to the role of the Holy Spirit in imparting the gifts and making them effectual to their appointed ends.

The Reformed confessions do not enumerate spiritual gifts or provide a complete list of them, as one may find in various places in Scripture, for instances, Rm. 12:4-8 and I Cor. 12:7-11. Nor did the framers of the Reformed confessions of the sixteenth and seventeenth centuries give a full treatment of spiritual gifts and make it a confessional norm. However, some confessions discuss spiritual gifts in relation to other doctrines such as the church, the church's offices or ministers, the sacraments, and the ascension of Christ. Chapter 3 has discussed that it is the power and authority of the Holy Spirit that accompanies the faithful ministry of the Word and the proper administration of sacraments and makes them vital and effectual for the church. The authority and efficacy of spiritual gifts do not rely on the persons to whom God imparts spiritual gifts but on God who works by his Spirit through them. Chapter 4 has pointed out that God uses his ministers and their ministries as an outward means in preserving and governing his church. This chapter will focus on the importance of spiritual gifts for the unity and growth of the church.

In the chapter concerning the office, dignity, and power of ministers in the church, the TC strongly maintains that "there is no power in the Church except for edification." The power and dignity of the church's ministers originate from God alone and are lavished upon them for the building up of the body of Christ. The TC also clearly states that "what constitutes fit and properly consecrated ministers of the Church, bishops, teachers and pastors, is that they have . . . received the power and mind to preach the Gospel and to feed the flock of Christ, and also the Holy Ghost who cooperates" in persuading hearts.[87]

The FHC also points out the edification motive in the bestowal of God's spiritual gifts and offices on his church. The ministers of God's Word are "God's co-workers," through whom God "strengthens and comforts men, but also threatens and judges them." The highest and chief thing in the office of ministers is the building up of the church that includes preaching repentance and sorrow for sins, improvement of life, and forgiveness of sins. In addition, ministers of the Word ought to pray for the people they serve, to apply themselves to and diligently study the Word of God, as well as to exercise the church discipline.[88] The FHC also notes that "all efficacy and power" of the ministries should be ascribed to God alone, "and only the imparting to the minister."[89] The FHC contends that this power and efficacy "never should or can be attributed to a creature," but to God who, through his Spirit, "dispenses it to those He chooses according to His free will."[90]

In CC37, Calvin clearly teaches that the diversity of spiritual gifts is meant to build a communion of believers, a body of believers. In this communion all members "participate all among themselves in all the things that they have, and yet each member has by itself particular properties and diverse functions." Calvin asserts that all the elect, as they live by the same Spirit of God, are "assembled and shaped in one body," and that any gift

---

87. TC XIII.
88. FHC XIX.
89. FHC XV.
90. The FHC uses 2 Cor. 6:4 ff. and Jn 20:21 ff. as references to point to the role of the Holy Spirit in empowering and bringing efficacy to the ministries of the Word. FHC XV; see also XIX.

that God bestows upon individuals in Christ through the Holy Spirit is to bring good for the whole body.[91] As Calvin also maintains, "if one believer has received any gift from God, all other believers are in some manner made participants in it, although God's dispensation of the gift may be given peculiarly to one person and not to others."[92] In his *Institutes*, Calvin explicates even further and states that "the saints are gathered into the society of Christ on the principle that whatever benefits God confers upon them, they should in turn share with one another." Deriving from the same principle, Calvin points out that "all those who, by the kindness of God the Father, through the working of the Holy Spirit, have entered into fellowship with Christ, are set apart as God's property and personal possession; and that when we are of their number we share that great grace."[93] Calvin is obviously thinking of the apostle Peter's words in 1 Pet. 4:10 when he notes that whatever benefits that God has entrusted to believers should be "applied to the common good of the church," and that "all the gifts we possess have been bestowed by God and entrusted to us on condition that they be distributed for our neighbors' benefit."[94] Commenting on 1 Cor. 12:1-12, Calvin develops this principle further. He clearly states that the purpose believers are adorned with spiritual gifts is for "the edification of their brethren."[95]

The CECG affirms that God through his Spirit gives the church spiritual gifts for her own edification. The gifts of God, whether they are temporal or spiritual, are to be used "to the profit and furtherance" of the church.[96] Similarly, the FC asserts that Christ has established an order by which God governs his church and ordains "pastors, overseers, and deacons," so that

---

91. CC37 XX ("I believe the holy catholic Church universal, the communion of saints"); see also CC45 Q/A 41, 42, 91, 98.
92. CC37 XX ("I believe the holy catholic Church universal, the communion of saints").
93. Calvin, *Institutes*, IV.i.3.
94. Calvin, *Institutes*, III.vii.5.
95. Calvin, *Commentary on the Epistles of Paul the Apostle to the Corinthians*, trans. John Pringle, vol. 1 (Grand Rapids: Baker Books, 2003), 395.
96. CECG IV.

by the exercise of their spiritual gifts all members of the church, "great and small may be edified."[97]

In the same line of thought, the BC even states that the responsibility to build up the church does not rest only on the shoulders of people entrusted with certain offices in the church. Rather, all people are obliged to serve and "build up one another according to the gifts God has given them as members of each other in the same body,"[98] so that the unity of the church may be preserved. Here the conjunction between the use of spiritual gifts for the edification and the unity of the church is affirmed. The same conjunction is also present in the HC. When discussing the article in the Apostles' Creed, that Christ is "seated at the right hand of God," the HC asserts that by his ascension Christ shows that "he is the head of his church, and that the Father rules all things through him."[99] And as the HC explains, his ascension benefits believers in two ways: "First, through his Holy Spirit he pours out his gifts from heaven upon us his members. Second, by his power he defends us and keeps us safe from all enemies."[100] The gifts that Christ pours out through his Holy Spirit upon his members are not gifts given for individual purposes. Instead, they are given for the building up of "the communion of saints." When explaining the sense in which "the communion of saints" should be understood, the HC also states that, as members of this community, believers "share in Christ and in all his treasures and gifts," and that "each member should consider it a duty to use these gifts readily and cheerfully for the service and enrichment of the other members."[101] Olevianus, in his commentary on the HC, adds that all members of this community are bound to each other and ought to have compassion on fellow members in their afflictions.[102]

The conjunction between the use of spiritual gifts for the edification and the unity of the church can be seen even more clearly in the WCF. The WCF

---

97. FC XXIX.
98. BC XXVIII.
99. HC Q/A 50.
100. HC Q/A 51; see also WLC Q/A 54.
101. HC Q/A 55.
102. Olevianus, *A Firm Foundation*, Q/A 136.

confesses that "Christ hath given the Ministry, Oracles, and Ordinances of God, for the gathering, and perfecting of the Saints, in this life to the end of the World: and doth by his own presence and Spirit, according to his promise, make them effectual thereunto."[103] In the chapter on the communion of saints, the WCF states further that all saints, being united to Christ as their Head and to one another in love, "have communion in each other's gifts and graces, and are obliged to the performances of such duties, public and private, as to conduce to their mutual good, both in the inward and outward man."[104]

As the Reformed confessions teach, then, God endows the church not only with the saving grace of redemption, but also with various spiritual gifts of ministry so that the church may unite under Christ by the exercise of those gifts. The diversity of spiritual gifts is meant to edify and bring unity to the church. And since it is God who bestows spiritual gifts upon his church through his Spirit, the eminence of spiritual gifts never rests in themselves or in the individuals who receive them, but in God who imparts and utilizes them to achieve their God-appointed ends, whereas their power and efficacy originate solely from God who works through his Spirit. Moreover, the importance of spiritual gifts, by consequence, never resides in individuals, but in their achieved ends, that is, for the edification and the unity of the church.

---

103. WCF XXV.3.
104. WCF XXVI.1.

CHAPTER 6

The Holy Spirit and the Doctrine of the Church

The Church's Evangelistic Mission

Another aspect of the work of the Holy Spirit that has not received due attention from scholars of the past who have studied the theology of the Reformed confessions is that which is related to the mission of the church. The lack of attention given to this particular aspect is perhaps due to the generally negative view of so many historians in the past concerning the Reformers—and thus their immediate successors—with respect to missions and evangelism. The claim of Gustav Warneck, a Protestant missiologist, suffices to exemplify this negative sentiment:

> We miss in the Reformers not only missionary action, but even the idea of missions, in the sense in which we understand them to-day. And this not only because the newly discovered heathen world across the sea lay almost wholly beyond the range of their vision, though that reason had some weight, but because fundamental theological views hindered them from giving their activity, and even their thoughts, a missionary direction.[1]

---

1. Gustav Warneck, *Outline of a History of Protestant Missions from the Reformation to the Present Time*, 3rd English edition, trans. from the 8th German edition by George Robson (Edinburgh: Oliphant Anderson & Ferrier, 1906), 9. See also for examples: Kenneth

In connection with the Reformed confessions, Donald MacGavran, a former professor at the Fuller School of World Missions, makes a similar remark. He complains about the "silence" of the Protestant creeds regarding "the missionary function of the Holy Spirit." To support his claim, he states two reasons why, for nearly three hundred years, "the Protestant churches had practically no missionary conscience at all." They are the isolation of Europe from the non-Christian world, by Islam on the south and east and the Spanish and Portuguese navies on the west, and the preoccupation of Protestantism in reforming the church in Europe. MacGavran states, "Protestantism was busy reforming the church rather than bringing the nations of Asia, Africa, and Latin America to faith in and obedience to the gospel."[2]

The aforementioned claims regarding the lack of missionary efforts and missionary conscience in both the theology and practice of the Reformed churches in the sixteenth and seventeenth centuries do not go uncontested. As the interest of research on the Reformation period grows, an increasing number of scholars find that the negative judgment of Reformers with respect to missions is more untenable.[3] With respect to the critique

---

Scott Latourette, *A History of Christianity,* First edition (New York: Harper & Brothers, 1937-1945), 926; *A History of the Expansion of Christianity,* Vol. 3 (New York: Harper & Brothers, 1939), 25-27; J. Herbert Kane, *Understanding Christian Missions,* 3rd ed. (Grand Rapids: Baker, 1982), 140. For a more extensive list of secondary literature in the past that discusses the pro and con debates made by many scholars concerning the Reformation's view of missions, see Hans Kasdorf, "The Reformation and Mission: A Bibliographical Survey of Secondary Literature," *Occasional Bulletin of Missionary Research* 4, no. 4 (October 1980): 169-175; Ho-Jin Jun, "Reformation and Mission: A Brief Survey of the Missiological Understanding of the Reformers," *ACTS Theological Journal* 5 (1994): 160-178.

2. Donald MacGavran, "A Missionary Confession of Faith," *Calvin Theological Journal* 7, no. 2 (November, 1972): 141. See also Richard R. De Ridder, *Discipling the Nations* (Grand Rapids: Baker, 1975), 212-214.

3. Warneck met his first opponent in Paul Drews as early as 1897. Drew holds that the Reformers' idea of mission can in no way be brought into harmony with the modern concept, and that the disjunction between them is not in motive but in method. Paul Drews, "Die Anschauungen reformatorischer Theologen über die Heidenmission," *Zeitschrift für praktische Theologie* 28 (1897): 1-26, 193-223, 289-316. R. Pierce Beaver gives a good yet brief account of the pioneer Protestant project of colonization and missionary activity off the coast of Brazil during the years 1555 to 1560. R. Pierce Beaver, "The Genevan Mission to Brazil," in *The Heritage of John Calvin,* ed. John H. Bratt (Grand Rapids: Eerdmans, 1973), 55-73. To name but a few, see also Karl Holl,

specifically aimed at the Reformed confessions, especially MacGavran's claim, Robert Recker, Klooster, and Hoekema each wrote an article to argue from the perspective of the BC, HC, and CoD respectively that the Reformed confessions, carefully observed, are not totally deficient in missionary conscience.[4] They all agree that the Protestant foreign missionary forces in the sixteenth and seventeenth centuries, due to their particular historico-political and geographical settings, were not as robust as their Roman Catholic counterpart with its constellation of missionary orders and agencies. However, that does not mean that the Protestant churches and leaders lacked a missionary conscience. Nor did they lack a theology and practice of missions. Insofar as the confessional documents are concerned, Recker, Klooster, and Hoekema maintain that what could be considered as lacking in the confessions with regard to missions is the modern idea or concept of mission with its emphasis on foreign mission, but not the fundamental and biblical theology of mission.

Moreover, the term "evangelism" is also a modern term. None of the confessions of the sixteenth and seventeenth centuries use the term to signify efforts to share the gospel with others. However, the absence of the term does not mean the absence of the concept of evangelism in the confessions. As this chapter will demonstrate, a careful reading of the confessions shows that the confessions do not lack in passion for evangelism when it is

---

"Luther und die Mission," *Neue Allgemeine Missionszeitschrift* 1 (1924): 36-49; Walter Holsten, "Reformation und Mission," *Archiv für Reformationsgeschichte* 44 (1953): 1-32; Hendrik Bergema, "De betekenis van Calvijn voor de Zending en de Missiologie," *Vox Theologica*, 20 (November 1958): 44-54; J. Vanden Berg, "Calvin and Missions," in *John Calvin: Contemporary Prophet,* ed. Jacob T. Hoogstra (Grand Rapids: Baker, 1959), 167-183; Charles Chaney, "Missionary Dynamics in the Theology of John Calvin," *Reformed Review* 17 (1964): 24-38; Sidney H. Rooy, *The Theology of Missions in the Puritan Tradition* (Delft: W. D. Meinema, 1965); Jan A. B. Jongeneel, "The Missiology of Gisbertus Voetius: The First Comprehensive Protestant Theology of Missions," *Calvin Theological Journal* 26, no. 1 (April 1991): 47-79; Muller, "'To Grant This Grace to All People and Nations': Calvin on Apostolicity and Mission," in *For God So Loved the World: Missiological Reflections in Honor of Roger S. Greenway*, ed. Arie C. Leder (Belleville: Essence Publishing, 2006), 211-232.

4. Robert Recker, "An Analysis of the Belgic Confession as to Its Mission Focus," *Calvin Theological Journal* 7, no. 2 (November, 1972): 158-180; Klooster, "Missions—The Heidelberg Catechism and Calvin," *Calvin Theological Journal* 7, no. 2 (November, 1972): 181-208; Anthony A. Hoekema, "The Missionary Focus of the Canons of Dort," *Calvin Theological Journal* 7, no. 2 (November, 1972): 209-220.

understood as the propagation of the gospel of salvation. In this regard, the church's evangelistic mission will be understood in this chapter to mean the mission of the church in propagating and proclaiming the gospel.

In agreement with the contention of Recker, Klooster, and Hoekema, this chapter will provide primary source documentation from a wider collection of the major Reformed confessions of the sixteenth and seventeenth centuries, especially with regard to the role of the Holy Spirit in the church's mission. However, some themes of the church's mission overlap with other doctrines and have been dealt with in previous chapters. In relation to the doctrine of salvation, chapter 3 has demonstrated that the Holy Spirit accompanies the pure and faithful preaching of the gospel and makes it an effectual means for the salvation of the elect. He restores, quickens, and renews the sinful human heart, convinces and humbles sinners by the preaching of the gospel so that they are thereby made willing and able freely to answer God's call, accept, and embrace the grace offered and conveyed in it. In relation to the doctrine of the church, the confessions also teach that the pure preaching of the gospel, along with the proper administration of sacraments, is one of the most prominent marks of the true church. Chapter 5 has shown that the Holy Spirit gathers all the elect and joins them into this church, works in and and governs this communion of believers, and hence distinguishes her from the rest of human societies. The whole enterprise of gathering and uniting all the elect in all ages and places dispersed throughout the world to the one holy catholic church is the work of God alone, who through his Spirit bestows various spiritual gifts of human ministry for the edification of the church. Moreover, it is the Holy Spirit who lavishes necessary gifts on the ministers of the Word and grants authority to preach the gospel of salvation.

This chapter will discuss the role of the Holy Spirit in the propagation of the gospel, the evangelistic mission of the church, as treated in the Reformed confessions. It will particularly deal with the role of the Holy Spirit in the calling out of sinners to life through the propagation and proclamation of the gospel. In full agreement with each other, the confessions assert that it is God who initiates the proclamation of the gospel, the church's evangelistic mission. Through his Spirit, God externally calls sinners to salvation by sending his church to carry out his mission. God carries out this mission primarily by appointing some to assume the office of minister of the Word. A few confessions, however, also teach that God calls his church, that is, all believers, to bring the gospel message to their neighbors through their good works, a call that today is often signified by the term "personal evangelism."

The Church's Mission as the Missio Dei

All Reformed confessions teach that salvation is initiated by and carried out by God through his Son and Spirit. Because of the fall and disobedience of their first parents, humans have a corrupt nature from conception. Without God himself working salvation in them, none will be able or willing to come to God. The confessions attribute the calling out of sinners, which is at the heart of the church's evangelistic mission, exclusively to God the Father, who works through his Son and Spirit. The mission of the church originates in God. Therefore, it is primarily not the activity of the church but the activity of God through the church; it is the mission of God, the *Missio Dei*.

In CC37 Calvin clearly states that humans in their sinful nature are completely unable by their own power to turn to and come to God.[5] Only Christ, through the power of the Holy Spirit, "calls and attracts us to himself in order that we may obtain deliverance."[6] In his *Institutes* Calvin describes it more clearly. Citing several biblical passages (I Cor. 2:14, 16; Rm. 11:34; Jn. 6:44-45; Jn. 1:18; 5:37), Calvin then concludes that "we cannot come to Christ unless we be drawn by the Spirit of God."[7] It is God who draws the elect to himself by the power of the Spirit. Calvin also discusses God's mission in terms of the expansion of the Kingdom of God when he describes the second petition of the Lord's Prayer. In CC37 Calvin clearly maintains that the church's mission comes to fruition solely because of God's reign, as God is actively "guiding and governing his own by his

---

5. CC37 IV.
6. CC37 XX ("I believe in the Holy Spirit").
7. Calvin, *Institutes*, III.ii.34; see also III.ii.35.

Holy Spirit." Praying that God's reign may come means praying that "the Lord may from day to day multiply the number of his faithful believers . . . and that he may continually spread on them more largely the affluence of his graces, whereby he may live and reign in them more and more."[8] Calvin expands the discussion further in his *Institutes*. He asserts that the second petition urges believers to "daily desire that God gather churches unto himself from all parts of the earth; that he spread and increase them in number; that he adorn them with gifts; . . . that he cast down all enemies of pure teaching and religion."[9] In his commentary on *A Harmony of the Evangelists*, Calvin states even more clearly that by the second petition believers also ask that God "may remove all hindrances, and may bring all men under his dominion, and may lead them to meditate on the heavenly life." He then adds, "This is done partly by the preaching of the word, and partly by the secret power of the Spirit." The Word—that is, the preaching of the gospel—and the Spirit "must be joined together, in order that the *kingdom* of God may be established."[10]

The SC agrees with Calvin in stressing that the calling of sinners to life—and thus the multiplication of the number of believers—is solely the active work of God himself. The confession states that God "preserved, instructed, multiplied, honoured, adorned, and called from death to life His Kirk in all ages since Adam until the coming of Christ Jesus in the flesh."[11] The confession adds later that it is the Holy Spirit who guides the elect into all truth and gives faith to them. Otherwise, they will never be able to respond to the gospel of Christ and thereby "should remain forever enemies to God and ignorant of His Son, Christ Jesus" without the Holy Spirit.[12]

Moreover, God is not only the initiator or the origin of the church's mission but also the first missionary, the first proclaimer of the gospel. As

---

8. CC37 XXIV ("The Second Petition").
9. Calvin, *Institutes*, III.xx.42.
10. Calvin, *Commentary on a Harmony of the Evangelists, Matthew, Mark, and Luke*, trans. William Pringle, vol. 1 (Grand Rapids: Baker, 2003), 320; emphasis his.
11. SC V.
12. SC XII.

cited above, the SC confesses that God "called" his church since Adam. The HC concurs and asserts even more descriptively,

> God himself began to reveal the gospel in Paradise; later, he proclaimed it by the holy patriarchs and prophets, and portrayed it by the sacrifices and other ceremonies of the law; finally, he fulfilled it through his own dear Son.[13]

In his commentary on the HC Ursinus explicates this further and argues, with the HC, that the gospel is not a new doctrine, but was already revealed in Paradise immediately after the fall. For Ursinus, the gospel can be distinguished into two senses with respect to the coming of the Messiah in the flesh, signifying either "the doctrine concerning the promise of grace, and the remission of sins to be granted freely, on account of the sacrifice of the Messiah, who had not as yet come in the flesh" or "the doctrine of the Messiah as already come."[14] However, Ursinus and the HC hold to a definition of the gospel that embraces both senses. Meanwhile, Ursinus emphasizes the active role of God in revealing the gospel, regardless of its varied dispensations throughout time. Both the promises and prophecies which relate to the Messiah and the testimony of the Apostles establish the same thing, that it is God who "will have us know that there was, and is from the beginning to the end of the world, only one doctrine, and way of salvation through Christ."[15] This is the gospel through which "the Holy Spirit works effectually in the hearts of the faithful, kindling and exciting in them, faith, repentance, and the beginning of eternal life."[16] Olevianus fully concurs with Ursinus and gives an explicit remark on the active engagement of God in conferring the gospel to human sinners. The gospel is "the good news that delights the heart of the poor condemned sinner;" it is "a revelation of the fatherly and immutable will of God, in which He promised us, who are unworthy, that all our sins have been washed

---

13. HC Q/A 19.
14. Ursinus, *The Commentary*, 101-102.
15. Ursinus, *The Commentary*, 102.
16. Ursinus, *The Commentary*, 101-102.

away and pardoned not just for the rest of our life but, indeed, forever."[17] God has not only given his promise of salvation, but also "carries out this promise by giving His Son to die for us and by raising Him." Olevianus then states, "Along with that [that is, the death and resurrection of Christ], God through Christ both promises us in the gospel and then actually gives us the Holy Spirit." He adds further, "All of this God freely offers and gives to us in the gospel, without any regard to our past, present, or future merit or piety."[18]

Similar teaching can also be found in the SHC. As reflected in the confession, Bullinger holds that, although the promises of the gospel, that is, the "evangelical promises," were given through different dispensations, God is the first and primary revealer of those promises. God revealed the promises of the gospel to the ancient fathers of Israel who were both before and under the law. He also revealed the same promises through his prophets in the holy Scriptures. Then, by "John the Baptist," "Christ the Lord himself, and afterwards by the apostles and their successors" the gospel is preached to people "in the world that God has now performed what he promised from the beginning of the world, and has sent, nay more, has given us his only Son and in him reconciliation with the Father, the remission of sins, all fulness and everlasting life."[19] In his *Decades* Bullinger further explicates the definition of the gospel and explicitly emphasizes that God is the author and the first preacher of the gospel. He defines the gospel as, first of all, "tidings come from heaven, and not begun on earth," because "God our heavenly Father did himself first preach that tidings to our miserable parents after their fall in paradise, promising his Son, who, being incarnate, should crush the serpent's head."[20] He then quotes several passages, such as Heb. 1:1-2; Jn. 1:18; 3:31-32; Matt. 3:17; Lk. 9:35, for

---

17. Olevianus, *A Firm Foundation*, Q/A 9.
18. Olevianus, *A Firm Foundation*, Q/A 9.
19. SHC XIII.1-3.
20. Bullinger, *Decades*, IV.i (4). In another place Bullinger reiterates this point. He states, "The first and most evident promise of all was made by the very mouth of God unto our first parents, Adam and Evah, . . . Which promise is, as it were, the pillar and base of all christian religion, whereupon the preaching of the gospel is altogether founded, and out of which all the other promises in a manner are derived." *Decades*, IV.i (13-14).

support, and concludes that the preaching of the gospel is "a divine speech, unreprovable, and brought down from heaven: which whosoever believe, they do believe the word of the eternal God; and they that believe it not, do despise and reject the word of God."[21]

In revealing the gospel to human sinners, God works both ways. He works in the human preachers of the gospel, as discussed above, but also in the hearers of the gospel, to make them believe, will, and desire the preached message of the gospel through his Spirit. In the SHC Bullinger quotes II Cor. 3:6 and rightly states that the preaching of the gospel is the ministry of the Spirit, because the Holy Spirit works in the hearts of believers through the preaching of the gospel, making it an effectual means of salvation.[22] In the following chapter of the SHC, Bullinger defines repentance primarily as "the recovery of a right mind in sinful man awakened by the Word of the Gospel and the Holy Spirit."[23] Repentance, that is, the proper response to the gospel, is then the work of God as the Word of the gospel and the Spirit jointly work together in the proclamation of the gospel. To argue for the *sola gratia* principle, Bullinger maintains in his *Decades* the indispensable role of the Holy Spirit in repentance. None are "delivered save those that believe; therefore grace hath somewhat whereby to work in man: for by the pouring of the Holy Ghost into our hearts, the understanding and will are instructed in faith." Without the work of the Holy Spirit inwardly teaching and regenerating the hearers of the gospel, none can believe in the gospel of Christ, repent, and thus be saved. As Bullinger concludes, grace "doth call, justify, save, or glorify the faithful," so that "the whole work of our salvation and all the virtues of the godly do proceed of the only grace of God alone, whose working we do at all times acknowledge and confess."[24]

The CoD also clearly asserts that salvation and thus the proclamation of the gospel are the works of God. "Before the foundation of the world, by sheer grace, according to the free good pleasure of his will, he chose in Christ to salvation a definite number of particular people out of the

---

21. Bullinger, *Decades*, IV.i (4-5).
22. SHC XIII.4.
23. SHC XIV.2.
24. Bullinger, *Decades*, IV.i (9-10, 37).

entire human race." He then "decided to give the chosen ones to Christ to be saved, and to call and draw them effectively into Christ's fellowship through his Word and Spirit."[25] Both the election in Christ and the calling and drawing the elect to Christ are initiated solely by God and carried out through his Word and Spirit. In its second main point of doctrine, the CoD makes explicit what Hoekema calls a kind of *Magna Carta* for missions, that is the mandate to proclaim the gospel to all:

> Moreover, it is the promise of the gospel that whoever believes in Christ crucified shall not perish but have eternal life. This promise, together with the command to repent and believe, ought to be announced and declared without differentiation or discrimination to all nations and people, to whom God in his good pleasure sends the gospel.[26]

Reflecting on this succinct yet apt statement, Hoekema rightly points out the emphatic assertion of the canons that the gospel "must be declared *indiscriminately and without distinction* to all peoples."[27] It should also be noted that, as clearly stated in the same article, the CoD also attributes the sending of the gospel to God. It is God who sends the gospel and reveals his will to all nations and people according to his "free good pleasure and undeserved love."[28] Moreover, the saving power of the gospel belongs to God alone, who "by the power of the Holy Spirit, through the Word or the ministry of reconciliation," accomplishes what "the light of nature" or "the law" cannot do, that is, saving those who sincerely believe the promises proclaimed in the gospel.[29] Those who hear the gospel are said to be "called seriously" by God himself. In the words of the Canons:

---

25. CoD I.7.
26. CoD II.5; Hoekema, "The Missionary Focus," 214.
27. Hoekema, "The Missionary Focus," 214, emphasis his.
28. CoD III/IV.7.
29. CoD III/IV.6.

> Nevertheless, all who are called through the gospel are called seriously. For seriously and most genuinely God makes known in his Word what is pleasing to him: that those who are called should come to him. Seriously he also promises rest for their souls and eternal life to all who come to him and believe.[30]

Consequently, those who reject the gospel reject God himself who calls them.[31]

In line with Hoekema's conclusion in his exposition of the CoD, the Canons are therefore by no means deficient of passion for missions. On the contrary, as Hoekema states, the Canons "do express the missionary focus of the Bible" and have "the *Missio Dei*: God's redemption of the cosmos through Christ" as its main focus. These are things that MacGavran sees as missing in most creeds. Without question, the Canons are deeply concerned with reconciliation between God and humans. As Hoekema states, even though the human responsibility "to bring the gospel message to all, particularly to those nations who have not yet heard it, does not receive equal emphasis" in the Canons, none can doubt the explicit assertion of the canons that "it was God's purpose from eternity to bring about this reconciliation, and that this purpose is being fulfilled in the gathering of the elect by his Word and Spirit from the beginning of the world to the end of time."[32]

The Westminster standards also unwaveringly depict God as active in his mission, calling sinners to himself through the ministry of the Word and the Holy Spirit. Both the outward preaching of the gospel or the ministry of the Word and the inward or effectual calling are the works of God through his Spirit by which God calls and draws sinners to him, and offers his grace to them.[33] Even though the active role of the Holy Spirit is specially identified in the inward and effectual calling of the elect, it is also undoubtedly true in the outward ministry of the Word. When

---

30. CoD III/IV.8.
31. CoD III/IV.9.
32. Hoekema, "The Missionary Focus," 219.
33. WCF X.1-2.

discussing those who are not elected in connection to the effectual calling, the WCF states that "they may be called by the Ministry of the Word; and may have some common operations of the Spirit, yet they never truly come to Christ," denoting that the outward ministry of the Word is never devoid of the operation of the Holy Spirit, who sends, equips with spiritual gifts, and empowers ministers to preach the gospel.[34] Dickson in his commentary on the confession gives a more explicit reference to the Holy Spirit when discussing the effectual calling, especially with regard to the relationship between the outward preaching of the gospel and the inward working of the Spirit. Referring to I Cor. 2: 14, he points out that the preaching of the gospel, grace, and salvation in Jesus Christ are "the things of the Spirit of God," which "the Natural man" can neither know nor believe without the Holy Spirit also working from within.[35]

A similar remark can also be found in the WLC. The catechism defines effectual calling as "the work of God's Almighty power and grace, whereby out of his free and special love to his elect . . . he doth in his accepted time invite and draw them to Jesus Christ by his Word and Spirit."[36] It also explicitly states that the faithful ministry of the Word is the work of the Spirit himself. Those who are called to preach the Word are to preach sound doctrine, "not in the inticing words of mens wisdom, but in demonstration of the Spirit and power," sincerely aiming at God's glory, and people's conversion, edification, and salvation.[37] Commenting on the WSC regarding the effectual calling, Watson insists that both the outward and inward call, that is the twofold vocation of God, are the works of God. "The outward Call brings men to a profession of Christ, the inward to a possession of Christ." Even though Watson seems to attribute the outward call—that is, the outward preaching of the gospel—to human ministers when arguing for the effectual calling, there is no doubt that, for Watson, the outward call is also the means through which the Spirit works to graciously bring believers to salvation, to Christ. Without the Holy Spirit working both

---

34. WCF X.4; XXV.3; WLC Q/A 68; WSC Q/A 89.
35. Dickson, *Truths Victory over Error*, X.2 (70).
36. WLC Q/A 67; WSC Q/A 31.
37. WLC Q/A 159.

outwardly and inwardly, none are effectually called from death to life. As Watson illustrates, "The Ministry of the Word is the Pipe or Organ, the Spirit of God blowing in it, doth effectually change Men's hearts, Acts 10:44."[38]

It is thus evident that for the Reformed confessions, since the very beginning of the church, the proclamation of the gospel has never been primarily a human enterprise. The church's mission to preach the gospel is not merely a human activity of promulgating the good news regarding God and his work of salvation by humans, but instead, the active work of God himself through the Holy Spirit in calling sinners to come to the salvation which God has himself inaugurated and promised in the gospel. He works through the Holy Spirit in both the external calling through the outward preaching of the Gospel and the inward calling of individual believers.

The Propagation of the Gospel by Human Ministries

To propagate the gospel to generations of humankind across all ages and places, God employs human agency. He sends his church, his people, to carry out the mission to proclaim the gospel and to be its living testimony or embodiment to their neighbors. With regard to the church, the mission to bring the gospel to the world can be understood in two senses: institutional and ethical. The church's mission in an institutional sense means that the church as a God-ordained institution is sent to preach the gospel to people through her ministers. The church's mission in an ethical sense means that the church as an organism, that is, the church as God's people, is sent to the world to bear witness to the message of the gospel through the life of faith of her members. Some Reformed confessions teach that God calls some to assume an ecclesiastical office to preach the gospel. God through his Spirit calls these people, furnishes them with necessary gifts, and sends and entrusts them with the ministry of the Word and sacraments. However, a few other confessions also explicitly teach that God through his Spirit calls

---

38. Watson, *A Body of Practical Divinity*, 128.

all his people and enables them to do good works, to testify through their godly lives and conversation so that others may begin to know God and be won to Christ.

The Preaching of the Gospel by the Ministers of the Word

The TC asserts that the sending and the consecration of the ministers of the church for the task of preaching the gospel is the work of the Holy Spirit. The Holy Spirit empowers ministers to undertake the offices to which they are assigned. The confession cites Jn. 20:22, "Receive the Holy Spirit," and states that "what constitutes fit and properly consecrated ministers of the Church, bishops, teachers and pastors, is that they have been divinely sent." As it later describes, being divinely sent means having "received the power and mind to preach the Gospel and to feed the flock of Christ, and also the Holy Ghost who cooperates" in persuading hearts.[39] The church's ministers are thus ministers of Christ insofar as they are endowed by God through his Spirit with his own power and are faithful to God, who sends them to preach the gospel and feed God's people.

The FHC calls the ministers of God's Word "God's co-workers," through whom God "imparts and offers to those who believe in Him the knowledge of Himself and the forgiveness of sins, converts, strengthens and comforts men, but also threatens and judges them."[40] And the highest and chief thing in this office is that "the ministers of the Church preach repentance and sorrow for sins, improvement of life, and forgiveness of sins, and all through Christ."[41] The confession also uses, among others, Jn 20:22 as biblical reference to state that, when the minister performs his tasks, "in all things we ascribe all efficacy and power to God the Lord alone, and only the imparting to the minister." It means that, as far as the human activity in preaching is concerned, the imparting of the knowledge of God and of the forgiveness of sins as promised in the gospel ought to be ascribed to the minister as the agent of God. But the offering of the knowledge of

---

39. TC XIII.
40. FHC XV.
41. FHC XIX.

God and the gospel, along with the converting, strengthening, comforting, threatening, and judging, ought to be understood as God's acts. It is God through the Holy Spirit who is at work in the preaching of the gospel. The fruit that follows from the ministry of the Word is to be attributed to God alone. In the words of the FHC, "It is certain that this power and efficacy never should or can be attributed to a creature, but God dispenses it to those He chooses according to His free will."[42]

As noted earlier, Bullinger in the SHC identifies the preaching of the gospel with the ministry of the Spirit, and thus assumes the integral role of the Holy Spirit in the whole enterprise of propagating the gospel.[43] In the following chapter of the same confession, Bullinger then points out that in accomplishing his mission, God uses human ministers. Further, Bullinger even makes a clear conjunction between the ministry of the gospel and of reconciliation. He affirms the biblical conviction that the church's mission, that is, the proclamation of the gospel, is primarily the ministry of reconciliation. The preaching of the gospel is thus none other than the preaching or teaching of reconciliation. To reconcile people to himself, God calls his ministers to be his ambassadors. Commenting on 2 Cor. 5:18 ff., Bullinger states that "the Lord gave the ministry of reconciliation to his ministers." He then adds that "Christ's ministers discharge the office of an ambassador in Christ's name, as if God himself through ministers exhorted the people to be reconciled to God, doubtless by faithful obedience." To this very purpose it can be said that all properly called ministers "exercise the keys [of the Kingdom of Heaven] when they persuade [men] to believe and repent."[44] Such power and authority of the ministers "to open the Kingdom of Heaven to the obedient and shut it to the disobedient" are certainly not of humans, and therefore can only be correctly understood as the power of God, who by his Spirit works through human ministers. In another place, Bullinger explicitly asserts, "God teaches us by his Word, outwardly through his ministers, and inwardly moves the hearts of his elect to faith

---

42. FHC XV.
43. SHC XIII.3.
44. SHC XIV.8.

by the Holy Spirit."[45] For Bullinger, in carrying out his mission to reconcile humans with himself, God makes use of human ministers. As ambassadors of God, ministers of the Word are commanded and sent with authority and empowered by the Holy Spirit "to preach the Gospel in all the world, and to remit sins," that is, to exercise "the keys of the Kingdom of Heaven."[46] Bullinger asserts more clearly the role of the Holy Spirit in the sending of preachers of the gospel in his *Decades*. Bullinger contends further that the gospel does not cease to be the word of God because it is preached by the ministry of humans. He argues from Matt 10:20 that, when the gospel is preached by human preachers, it is not humans that speak but the Spirit of the Father who is within them. It is certainly the first two chapters of the book of Acts that Bullinger has in mind when he points out that the disciples did not depart from Jerusalem, "until they were first instructed from above, and had received the Holy Ghost."[47] Therefore, for Bullinger, in the preaching of the gospel to humans, it is God who actually preaches. When God uses human preachers as his instruments, the gospel ceases not to be the Word of God, for it is the Holy Spirit who speaks through them.

Other Reformed confessions, such as CC37, the SC, BC, HC, and CoD, also teach that God uses the ministry of men and empowers his ministers to preach the gospel, only without explicit reference to the Holy Spirit.[48] However, the active role of God in the execution of the church's mission by sending his ministers to the world is unquestionable in these confessions. Nor is it downplayed. The CoD's statement might suffice to exemplify and affirm this: "In order that people may be brought to faith, God mercifully sends proclaimers of this very joyful message to the people he wishes and at the time he wishes. By this ministry people are called to repentance and faith in Christ crucified."[49]

---

45. SHC XVIII.2.
46. SHC XIV.8.
47. Bullinger, *Decades*, IV.i (5).
48. CC37 XXX; SC XXII; BC XXIX-XXXI; HC Q/A 84; CoD I.3.
49. CoD I.3.

The Living Testimony of the Gospel by All Believers

Although most of the Reformed confessions discuss the propagation of the gospel as the mission of the church as a God-ordained institution, or particularly the task of the church office which is entrusted with the ministry of the Word, they never deny that the sharing of the gospel is also the mission of the church as God's people. The confessions teach that all individual believers are called to live out their true faith, to live a new life by faith as they are regenerated, justified, and sanctified in Christ by the Holy Spirit. A few confessions even explicitly teach that believers ought to live out the gospel they believe in and be the living testimony of the gospel to their neighbors through the good works they do in their everyday walk. The proclamation of the gospel is the task of all God's people, every one of them.

The TC confesses that the children of God, led by the Spirit of God, should be chiefly devoted to certain actions that are aimed to profit other human beings, their neighbors, which are duly called "the duties of a Christian." These duties are such actions whereby "every one, for his part, may profit his neighbors—first, with respect to life eternal, that they may begin to know, worship and fear God; and then with respect to present life, that they may want nothing required by bodily necessity."[50] Hence believers ought to be concerned with not only their neighbors' well-being with respect to their bodily needs, but also with their well-being with respect to life eternal. The confession, however, does not specify what actions could incite others to "begin to know, worship and fear God." However, the confession points out that believers may show themselves to others as "gods," that is, true children of God, by "love striving for [others'] advantage" as far as they are able.[51] Quoting some biblical references (I Jn. 2:10; 4:7; Gal. 5:14), the confession maintains that works are good, if they proceed out of

---

50. TC VI. HC Q/A 55 might assert the same. The article teaches that each member of "the communion of saints" should consider it a duty to use spiritual gifts "readily and cheerfully for the service and enrichment of the other members." The word *enrichment* in the original German text (*Heil*) can also be translated as *salvation*.

51. TC IV; see also CC45 Q/A 199, where Calvin says that God "requires us to love our neighbors and seek their salvation, and all this with true affection and without simulation;" Calvin, *Institutes*, II.viii.40.

faith through love and that the love of God should be evidenced by the love of others. Good works are acts of faith that are manifested in love toward others. They are works that spring from God's works of regeneration and sanctification that restore the image of God in believers so that they may "supremely love and most earnestly imitate God" in their lives.[52] The confession maintains,

> For whatever the law of God teaches has this end and requires this one thing, that at length we may be reformed to the perfect image of God, being good in all things, and ready and willing to serve the advantage of men; which we cannot do unless we be furnished with virtues of every kind.[53]

Therefore, believers may help others "begin to know, worship and fear God" through their life of love, which is always seeking to serve the advantage of others, since this is the life of the true children of God who are regenerated, being reformed, and led by the Spirit of God. The FHC contends for the same thing when it deals with the message of the entire Scripture, that is, the gospel, that "God is kind and gracious to [humans] and that He has publicly exhibited and demonstrated this His kindness to the whole human race through Christ His Son." The confession then states further that this gospel "comes to us and is received by faith alone, and is manifested and demonstrated by love for our neighbor."[54]

The evangelistic mission of individual believers through good works is also acknowledged and taught by the HC. Opening its third part on "Gratitude," the catechism contends that believers do good works not in order to earn salvation, which they already have by the merit of Christ, but primarily because God through his Spirit is still working in them, renewing them, even when they have been delivered from their misery and redeemed by Christ. The catechism then provides some arguments that further develop the significance of good works in Christian life. With respect to God,

---

52. TC IV.
53. TC IV.
54. FHC V.

good works are believers' sincere expressions of gratitude to God for all that he has done for them, so that in all things, praises are due to God. With respect to themselves, good works may be fruits that assure believers of their faith. With respect to others, good works, or believers' "godly living," are a living testimony of the gospel by which "neighbors may be won over to Christ."[55]

Ursinus discusses further good works as a living testimony of the gospel in his commentary on the HC. For him, good works done for the sake of others has three meanings: First, that "we may be profitable unto our neighbor, and edify him by our example and godly conversation;" second, that "we may not be occasion of offences and scandal to the cause of Christ;" and, third, that "we may win the unbelieving to Christ."[56] Undoubtedly, for Ursinus, this article of the HC refers to personal evangelism. Furthermore, when discussing the necessity of good works to salvation, he maintains that good works are necessary to salvation not as a cause, as if they merited a reward, but as an effect, a consequent, or even as "a means without which we cannot obtain the end." With Augustine he argues that good works are "necessary to righteousness or justification" in those who are justified "as a part of salvation itself; or, as an antecedent of salvation, but not as a cause or merit of salvation."[57] He later adds, "If we do any works which are good, these works are not ours, but God's, who produces them in us by his Holy Spirit." Hence, "if we perform any thing that is good, it is the gift of God, and not any merit on our part."[58] For Ursinus, then, personal evangelism as part of good works, as imperfect as it might be, is also the work of the Holy Spirit in the life of believers. It is part of salvation of all God's people, a necessary fruit of salvation that the Holy Spirit produces in them.

Commenting on the articles of the HC that talk about good works, Ames in his *Sketch* agrees with Ursinus that good works, including zeal for winning neighbors over to Christ, are necessary consequences of salvation

---

55. HC Q/A 86; see also WCF XVI.2, 3, 5.
56. Ursinus, *The Commentary*, 484; see also *The Commentary*, 466; Olevianus, *A Firm Foundation*, Q/A 170.
57. Ursinus, *The Commentary*, 485.
58. Ursinus, *The Commentary*, 486.

as the work of the Holy Spirit.[59] These good works spring up from the renewal of life that the Holy Spirit works in every believer. Ames states, "The operation of the Spirit for the preaching of the gospel is present efficaciously and powerfully for producing the change of a person, which is called the ministry of the Spirit, the law of the Spirit's life, and the arm of God."[60] This "change of a person," visible through good works, distinguishes believers from the rest. Ames states further that the regenerate are "urged and led by the Spirit of God as they walk according to the Spirit;" consequently, they "compose their entire lives according to the revealed will of God in His Word" and are "called to the hope of eternal life, aspire to heaven and to God." In contrast, the unregenerate are "urged and led by their own flesh, " as they "follow their own individual suggestions and corrupt imaginations, or worldly opinions" and "seek this present world and themselves."[61] After laying out this understanding of good works, Ames then urges all believers to "strive more and more to show others . . . the grace of regeneration to which we have been called in Christ." Or, as Klooster righly states in his exposition of the HC Q/A 86, "the Christian by means of his godly life should aim to win his neighbors for Christ."[62]

Resonant with the TC and FHC, Bullinger's SHC insists that true faith is efficacious and active through love (Gal. 5:6). "The same [faith] keeps us in the service we owe to God and our neighbor, strengthens our patience in adversity, fashions and makes a true confession, and in a word, brings forth good fruit of all kinds, and good works."[63] These good works grow "out of a living faith by the Holy Spirit and are done by the faithful according to the will or rule of God's Word."[64] In agreement with the HC, Bullinger also maintains that good works "ought not to be done in order that we may earn eternal life by them, for . . . eternal life is the gift of God." Nor are they to be done for "ostentation" or "gain," but "for the glory of God, to adorn

---

59. Ames, *Sketch*, 122.
60. Ames, *Sketch*, 150.
61. Ames, *Sketch*, 149.
62. Klooster, "Missions," 205.
63. SHC XVI.4.
64. SHC XVI.5.

our calling, to show gratitude to God, and for the profit of the neighbor." Bullinger then cites, among others, a verse in the Gospel: "Let your light shine before men, that they may see your good works and give glory to your Father who is in heaven" (Matt. 5:16).[65]

As discussed above in this chapter, one may agree with Recker, who comments exclusively on the BC, that the Reformed confessions with respect to their genre are not particularly "a rallying call to mission."[66] Therefore, one should not approach these documents anachronistically by imposing on or making judgment about them according to the modern idea or concept of mission. With regard to the modern distinction between home missions and foreign missions, it should be noted that the distinction itself is foreign to the confessions. As evident in the whole discussion of the church's mission in this chapter and in the account of the catholicity of the church discussed in chapter 5, the Reformed confessions never make such a distinction. Rather, the confessions regard the whole world without discrimination—that is, people of all nations, of all places and ages—as the object of the church's mission. In light of this, therefore, while it may be true that the Protestant Reformation deserves to be called "one of the greatest home missionary projects of all history," it does not necessarily lead to seeing the Reformed confessions as documents only for home missions.[67] What Klooster rightly points out in the HC is also true of other confessions, that the message of the confessions "leads inevitably to missions—both home and foreign missions."[68]

As this chapter has demonstrated, and as Recker, Klooster, and Hoekema have argued for the BC, HC, and CoD, the Reformed confessions, when taken as a whole and properly examined, are not in any sense devoid of mission awareness. Nor do they lack a theology of missions. On the contrary, almost all of the confessions present the gospel. Some present it in the form of the doctrine of salvation and other corollary doctrines, others in the exposition of the Apostle's Creed. The confessions also correctly understand

---

65. SHC XVI.6; see also *Decades*, III.9 (356).
66. Recker, "An Analysis of the Belgic Confession," 160.
67. See Klooster, "Missions," 187.
68. Klooster, "Missions," 208.

the church's mission as the mission of God. God is the author and initiator of the church's mission. In fact, he is the first preacher or proclaimer of the gospel. Although in carrying out the mission God calls, sends, and uses the ministries of his church, either as an institution or God's people, the church's mission never ceases to be the *Missio Dei*. God is always the primary actor, and human ministers are merely his instruments. In addition, the confessions place proper emphasis on the role of the Holy Spirit in the whole enterprise of gospel. The Holy Spirit actively works in both the preaching of the gospel and the living testimony of believers. He calls, equips, and sends the ministers of the Word to preach the gospel and also effectually works in the hearers of the gospel, to regenerate, illumine, and renew them from within so that they may come to believe in the message of the gospel. The Holy Spirit also renews the life of believers, leading and guiding them as they walk according to God's will, and enables them to do good works, through which others may be won over to Christ.

PART FOUR

CHAPTER 7

The Holy Spirit and the Doctrine of Good Works

Social Responsibility

The Reformed confessions teach that the Holy Spirit does not cease to work at the conversion or profession of faith of individual believers. Rather, he continues to renew the life of believers in the image of God, sanctifies them, and leads them to live a godly life in obedience to God's revealed will, God's law. As the result of the continuing work of the Holy Spirit, believers produce good works throughout their lives.

Scholars in the past who studied the theology of the Reformed confessions have noted the relations of good works, faith, justification, and sanctification in the Reformed confessions. Barth discusses the doctrine of good works as he comments on several confessions such as the SHC, CC37, GC, BC, SC, IA, WCF, and Erlauthal Confession (1562).[1] Rohls also offers a brief account on the relation of good works and faith in the confessions by putting it in contrast to the Tridentine notion of justification.[2] He rightly summarizes that, according to the confessions, believers cannot be justified "*without* good works," although they are not justified "*on the basis* of good works."[3] He notes that the relationship between good works and

---
1. Barth, *The Theology of the Reformed Confessions*, 92, 93, 100, 101, 113, 115, 131, 135, 143.
2. Rohls, *Reformed Confessions*, 130-135.
3. Rohls, *Reformed Confessions*, 133; emphasis his.

justification is the relationship between "ground and consequence," which can be depicted as "the tree and its fruits."[4] Both Barth and Rohls have also identified the Holy Spirit as the one who effects good works in believers and pointed out that good works proceed from him alone. However, both Barth's and Rohls' presentations lack a clear connection between good works and the love of neighbors, whereas in the Reformed confessions, the connection is often highlighted and exemplified. As a result, the role of the Holy Spirit in the manifold manifestations of Christian love of neighbors is somehow truncated and poorly represented. Therefore, the pneumatological perspective in the confessions on the passion for social responsibility—that is, efforts aimed to profit the surrounding society as one's neighbors—is often overlooked in the confessions.

This chapter will expand the discussion concerning the teaching of the Reformed confessions concerning good works, which was introduced in chapter 6 in its relation to the propagation of the gospel—that is, love of neighbors with respect to their eternal life. This chapter will provide primary source documentation concerning the Holy Spirit as the cause of good works from a wider collection of confessions than the ones that Barth and Rohls use. It will primarily focus on the role of the Holy Spirit in good works. In addition, this chapter will discuss the relationship between good works and Christian duty to love and to profit their neighbors with respect to the present life. Special attention will also be given to the fourth and seventh commandments of the Decalogue, where the catechisms make explicit references to the Holy Spirit. The rest of the chapter then will describe the manifold manifestations of good works that reflect the deep social concerns present in the teachings of the Reformed confessions.

The Holy Spirit as the Cause of Good Works

The Reformed confessions teach in unison the definition and conception of good works. They altogether maintain that true faith does not mitigate

---

4. Rohls, *Reformed Confessions*, 133.

the significance of good works in Christian life. Rather, through the true faith of believers, the Holy Spirit works his way to produce good works in the life of believers.

The TC is very cautious about a notion of faith without works, when it defends the doctrine of justification by faith alone. The confession states,

> These things we will not have men so to understand, as though we placed salvation and righteousness in slothful thoughts of the mind, or in faith destitute of love, which they call faith without form; seeing that we are sure that no man can be justified or saved except he supremely love and most earnestly imitate God.[5]

The confession then continues to assert that in being justified by faith, believers are not only saved, but also made righteous, or "become righteous." Moreover, faith by which believers are justified is the same faith that regenerates and restores the image of God in them. This is certainly not "faith destitute of love," but instead an active faith, that which is "efficacious through love."[6] By this faith believers "become good and upright," loving God, and showing themselves as children of God to others by loving their neighbors. And love is "the fulfilling the whole law," as the entire law of God is summed up in one command: "Thou shalt love thy neighbor as thyself" (Gal. 5:14).[7]

In a chapter that discusses monasticism, the confession also teaches that in using their liberty, believers ought to be "arbitrated and directed by the Holy Spirit of Christ, the bestower of true adoption and liberty, and also to be appointed and bestowed not only for the profit of his neighbors, but also for the glory of God."[8] Good works, therefore, are works that proceed out of true faith through love, according to the law of God, and aim to bring profit to neighbors and glory to God.

---

5. TC IV.
6. TC IV. See Rohls, *Reformed confessions*, 130-131.
7. TC IV.
8. TC XII.

Having defined good works, the TC goes on to enunciate that the ability to do good works cannot be ascribed to human powers but to the Holy Spirit.[9] The Holy Spirit who gives faith and brings believers to Christ is the same Spirit who wholly leads, makes them altogether anew, and works in them both to will and to do (Phil. 2:13), so that there be in them "no lack of good works" for which God has created them. The confession utterly denies that anyone can be saved, nor can anyone fulfill the law of God, unless God, who alone is good, works in him by his Spirit. The children of God are "led by the Spirit of God, rather than that they act themselves (Rom. 8:14)" in such a way that "whatsoever things we do well and holily are to be ascribed to none other than to this one only Spirit, the Giver of all virtues." All good things and works are, therefore, "the mere gifts of God, who favors and loves us of his own accord, and not for any merit of ours."[10]

Other confessions echo the same teaching of good works and the role of the Holy Spirit in them. The FHC confesses that believers do not obtain God's grace and the true sanctification of the Spirit through their "merits or powers but through faith which is a pure gift of God." From this faith spring innumerable good works, which are duly called "fruits of faith." Believers, therefore, ought not to ascribe "the piety and the salvation obtained to such works, but only to the grace of God." "Such a faith is the true and proper service with which a man is pleasing to God."[11]

In his catechisms, Calvin points out that faith is the gift of God through the Holy Spirit and through faith believers are justified and sanctified.[12] Being sanctified, the hearts of believers "are cleansed from their corruption and are softened to obey unto righteousness," to observe the law and do good works.[13] In other words, as Calvin clearly remarks, faith "not only does not make us careless of good works, but is the root from which they are produced."[14] He also states, "Observance of the Law, therefore, is

---

9. TC V.
10. TC V.
11. FHC XIII.
12. CC37 XV; XVI; XVII; CC45 Q/A 112.
13. CC37 XVII.
14. CC45 Q/A 127; Calvin, *Institutes*, III.xiv.8.

not a work that our power can accomplish, but it is a work of a spiritual power," the power of the Spirit.[15] Without being regenerated by the Holy Spirit, none cannot "begin to do the least of the commandments."[16] In his *Institutes*, Calvin states even more clearly that "through his Holy Spirit he dwells in us and by his power the lusts of our flesh are each day more and more mortified; we are indeed sanctified, that is, consecrated to the Lord in true purity of life, with our hearts formed to obedience to the law."[17] Commenting on the article of the Apostles' Creed concerning the Holy Spirit in his CC37, Calvin aptly and passionately teaches that it is the Spirit that "inflames our hearts with the fire and ardent love for God and for our neighbor . . . so that, if there are some good deeds in us, these are the fruits and the virtues of his grace."[18]

The SC maintains that by themselves humans "are not capable of thinking one good thought," but God, who has begun the work in believers through his Spirit, continues to regenerate and sanctify them.[19] The cause of good works, therefore, is not our free will, but "the Spirit of the Lord Jesus who dwells in our hearts by true faith, brings forth such works as God has prepared for us to walk in."[20] These works are those which please God and which he has promised to reward, as commanded in God's holy law.[21]

The BC similarly attributes faith and the good works that it produces to the hearing of God's Word and the work of the Holy Spirit. The confession links the inseparability of justification and sanctification to the Holy Spirit that works in both. The Spirit who produces in a believer the justifying faith by the hearing of God's Word is the same Spirit who "regenerates him and makes him a 'new man,' causing him to live the 'new life' and freeing him from the slavery of sin." The confession contends that "far from making people cold toward living in a pious and holy way, this justifying

---

15. CC37 XVII; XIX.
16. CC45 Q/A 226.
17. Calvin, *Institutes*, III.xiv.9.
18. CC37 XX ("I believe in the Holy Spirit"); see also Calvin, *Institutes*, III.xiv.2, 20.
19. SC XII.
20. SC XIII.
21. SC XIV.

faith, quite to the contrary, so works within them" in such a way that "it is impossible for this holy faith to be unfruitful in a human being." This is what the confession calls "faith working through love." The good works, "proceeding from the good root of faith" and done out of love for God, are "good and acceptable to God and, since they are all sanctified by his grace." Yet these works do not count toward justification, for believers are justified even before they do good works. Good works are the fruits of justification, not the basis of it. The confessions argue that human works "could not be good, any more than the fruit of a tree could be good if the tree is not good in the first place."[22] As certain as good fruits come out of good trees, loving the true God and neighbors should be among the distinguishing marks of Christians. The confession confesses that true Christians are distinguished by the work of the Holy Spirit manifest in their lives, namely by their "faith, and by their fleeing from sin and pursuing righteousness." In consequence, believers actively "love the true God and their neighbors, without turning to the right or left, and they crucify the flesh and its works," and incessantly fight against great weakness that remains in them by the Spirit.[23] Still in connection with the love of God and neighbors, the confession also teaches that being fed by the Holy Spirit at the table of the Lord in the sacrament of the Lord's Supper, "we are moved to a fervent love of God and our neighbors."[24]

The HC fully agrees with the BC and maintains that believers do good works because "Christ by his Spirit is also renewing us to be like himself, so that in all our living we may show that we are thankful to God for all he has done for us, and so that he may be praised through us."[25] Good works are none other than fruits of faith, expressions of genuine gratitude for God's redemption, by which believers may also be assured of their faith. In his exposition on the article, Ursinus enunciates that good works are "the fruits of our regeneration by the Holy Spirit, which are always connected with our free justification" (Rm. 8:30; 1 Cor. 6:11). He then states further,

---

22. BC XXIV.
23. BC XXIX.
24. BC XXXV.
25. HC Q/A 86.

"Those, therefore, who do not perform good works, show that they are neither regenerated by the Spirit of God, nor redeemed by the blood of Christ."[26] For Ursinus, the Holy Spirit is "the first cause," the moving cause of good works. By virtue of his death Christ has merited both the remission of sins and the habitation of God within believers by the Holy Spirit. Ursinus also remarks, "The Holy Spirit, now, is never inactive, but is always efficacious, and so brings it to pass that those in whom he dwells are made conformable to God." The efficacy of the Holy Spirit in producing good works in the life of believers is without a doubt, "for in all those to whom the merits of Christ are applied by faith, there is kindled the love of God, and a desire to do those things which are pleasing in his sight."[27]

Only then the catechism defines good works as those which arise out of true faith, conform to God's law, and are done for his glory. A work may be good and pleasing in the sight of God only if those three conditions are met. Therefore, good works are not those "based on what we think is right or on established human tradition."[28] As Ursinus explains further, by these three conditions the works of the regenerate and the unregenerate are distinguished, and the works of the latter are deemed as sins, and thus are excluded from the category of good works.[29] The catechism also teaches that no one can obey the commandments of God perfectly.[30] Only by the grace of the Holy Spirit, can believers observe the law of God as commanded. In Ursinus' plain words,

> Good works are possible only by the grace and assistance of the Holy Spirit, and that by the regenerate alone, whose hearts have been truly regenerated by the Spirit of God, through the preaching of the gospel, and that not only in their first conversion and regeneration, but also by the perpetual and

---

26. Ursinus, *The Commentary*, 465, 480; see also Olevianus, *A Firm Foundation*, Q/A 170. Olevianus calls good works "fruits worthy of repentance." *An Exposition*, 129.
27. Ursinus, *The Commentary*, 466.
28. HC Q/A 91; see also Ursinus, *The Commentary*, 476-478.
29. Ursinus, *The Commentary*, 478.
30. HC Q/A 114-115.

constant influence and direction of the same Spirit, who works in them a knowledge of sin, faith and a desire of new obedience, and also daily increases and confirms more and more the same gifts in them."[31]

Therefore, the catechism teaches that believers ought to pray to God for the grace of the Holy Spirit and "never stop striving to be renewed more and more after God's image, until after this life we reach our goal: perfection."[32]

A very similar conception and definition of good works can be found in Bullinger's SHC. Having affirmed faith as "a pure gift of God," given to the elect "by the Holy Spirit by means of the preaching of the gospel and steadfast prayer," the confession also asserts that this faith is "efficacious and active through love (Gal. 5:6)."[33] Moreover, the confession avers that the same faith "keeps us in the service we owe to God and our neighbor, . . . brings forth good fruit of all kinds, and good works."[34] The elect are "not created or regenerated through faith in order to be idle," but rather that without ceasing they "should do those things which are good and useful," as a good tree brings forth good fruits.[35] Truly good works, the confession teaches, "grow out of a living faith by the Holy Spirit and are done by the faithful according to the will or rule of God's Word."[36] In his *Decades* Bullinger defines good works as "deeds, or actions, wrought of those which are regenerate by the Spirit of God, through faith, and according to the word of God, to the glory of God, the honesty of life, and the profit of neighbour."[37] Good works, therefore, must have their beginning not of humans but of God himself, "the well-spring of all goodness." Having regenerated believers, God renews them. He does this "by his Spirit and by faith in Christ Jesus," so that believers "do no longer their own, that is,

---

31. Ursinus, *The Commentary*, 479.
32. HC Q/A 115.
33. SHC XVI.2, 4.
34. SHC XVI.4.
35. SHC XVI.7.
36. SHC XVI.5.
37. Bullinger, *Decades*, III.ix (321-322).

the works of the flesh, but the works of the Spirit, of grace, and of God himself." Moreover, the good works of the regenerate "do grow up by the good Spirit of God that is within them; which Spirit, even as the sap giveth strength to trees to bring forth fruit, doth in like manner cause sundry virtues to bud and branch out of us men."[38]

While stressing the role of the Holy Spirit as the giver of faith and the cause of good works, Bullinger also stresses that good works are also the works of believers and thus call for the active engagement of believers in good works. In his *Decades* Bullinger already states that, even though good works proceed from God and are justly called the fruits of the Spirit and of faith, good works are also said to be the works of believers, "the works of faithful men."[39] They are such "partly because God worketh them by us, and useth our ministry in the doing of the same; and partly because we are by faith the sons of God, and are therefore made the brethren and joint-heirs with Jesus Christ."[40] For Bullinger, the key link between the two notions—good works as the works of God and of the faithful—is the Holy Spirit himself. When discussing the inseparable relationship between faith and good works, Bullinger states, "For the same Holy Spirit which giveth faith doth therewithal also regenerate the understanding and will, so that the faithful doth ardently desire, and do his endeavour in all things, to do service to God his maker."[41] Accordingly, the SHC passionately states,

> And so we diligently teach true, not false and philosophical virtue, truly good works, and the genuine service of a Christian. And as much as we can we diligently and zealously press them upon all men, while censuring the sloth and hypocrisy of all those who praise and profess the Gospel with their lips and dishonor it with their disgraceful lives.[42]

---

38. Bullinger, *Decades*, III.ix (322).
39. Bullinger, *Decades*, III.ix (321-324).
40. Bullinger, *Decades*, III.ix (324).
41. Bullinger, *Decades*, III.ix (335).
42. SHC XVI.9.

In affirming the relationship between good works and the law, Bullinger again attributes good works to the Holy Spirit. In the SHC Bullinger teaches that the law of God, his expressed will, is "the pattern of good works" prescribed for the elect.[43] Thus, "works and worship which we choose arbitrarily are not pleasing to God."[44] Insofar as the good works that the elect do are done by faith and approved by God, they are "done from God's grace through the Holy Spirit" and are "pleasing to God."[45]

The WCF sets forth a similar teaching to that of the other confessions discussed above, albeit one that is more pointed and concentrated. The confession highlights on the need of the law of God in guiding good works before it discusses the rootedness of faith in good works. "Good works are only such as God hath commanded in his holy Word, and not such as, without the warrant thereof, are devised by men, out of blind zeal, or upon any pretence of good intention."[46] The positioning of the doctrine of good works—immediately after the chapters on the saving faith and repentance and before the chapter of the perseverance of the saints—gives more bearing to what the confession is arguing throughout the chapter on good works, that good works, done in obedience to God's commandments, are "the fruits and evidences of a true and lively faith"—the same Spirit-given faith, by which the elect believe to be true whatever is revealed in the Word and accept Christ for justification.[47] The confession even explicitly states that the Holy Spirit subdues and enables the human will to freely and cheerfully do the will of God, which is revealed in the law and required to be done by all true believers.[48] By doing good works, believers manifest "their thankfulness, strengthen their assurance, edify their Brethren, adorn the profession of the Gospel, stop the mouths of the adversaries, and glorifie God, whose workmanship they are."[49] The affirmation for the mandatory

---

43. Bullinger also calls the Decalogue "a most sure and absolute platform of good works." *Decades*, III.ix (353).
44. SHC XVI.5
45. SHC XVI.9.
46. WCF XVI.1.
47. WCF XVI.1-2; see also XIV.1-2.
48. WCF XIX.7.
49. WCF XVI.2.

nature of good works by the confession can also be found in the discussion of the life of the communion of the saints. Being blessed with manifold gifts and graces by the Holy Spirit, all saints "have communion in each others gifts and graces, and are obliged to the performance of such duties publick and private, as do conduce to their mutual good, both in the inward and outward man."[50] Furthermore, saints are "bound to maintain an holy fellowship and communion in the worship of God and in performing such other spiritual service as tend to their mutual edification; as also, in relieving each other in outward things, according to their several abilities; and necessities."[51]

In discussing the doctrine of good works, the WCF also pointedly argues against the notion of salvation by works on two fronts. On the one hand, the confession maintains that the ability of the elect to do good works is "not at all of themselves, but wholly from the Spirit of Christ."[52] On the other hand, the confession also argues that even the best works of human beings do not merit pardon of sin, or eternal life. Besides the infinite unbridgeable distance between human beings and God, human works are always "defiled, and mixed with so much weakness and imperfection that they can not endure the severity of God's judgment." Even when humans do what they can and have done their duty, they are merely "unprofitable servants," because as the works are good "they proceed from his Spirit."[53] To be noted, both arguments which the confession brings forth point to the same thing—the indispensable role of the Holy Spirit in good works. The Holy Spirit is the root or the cause of good works, without whom none is able to do any good work. To emphasize this, the confession even contends that works done by the unregenerate are "sinful and cannot please God, or make a man meet to receive grace from God," because they "proceed not from a heart purified; nor are done in a right manner, according to the word nor to a right end, the glory of God."[54]

---

50. WCF XXVI.1.
51. WCF XXVI.2.
52. WCF XVI.3.
53. WCF XVI.5.
54. WCF XVI.6.

Acts of Good Works as the Manifestation of Social Concerns

Having defined good works and affirmed the Holy Spirit as the cause of them, some Reformed confessions go on to describe believers' acts of good works that profit their neighbors. In describing these acts of good works, the confessions never limit the recipients of good works to fellow believers. Even though sometimes some confessions only mention fellow believers, acts of good works indiscriminately aim to profit believers and non-believers alike. Moreover, the confessions regard good works toward neighbors—namely, familial duty, care for the poor, afflicted, and the oppressed—as Christian duties not only for individual believers, but also for the church and civil magistracy as institutions.

The common and natural place where the acts of good works toward others are discussed is the exposition of the Decalogue in the Reformed catechisms. The teaching of the Decalogue, mainly its second table, in the Reformed catechisms exemplifies the attention or concern to social issues that the Reformed of the sixteenth and seventeenth centuries had. The catechisms do not understand the commandments as containing only prohibitions on certain human acts that may violate or bring any detriment to others. Rather, they also teach that inherent in the negative commandments are positive moral obligations or duties toward others. Since the treatment of the fourth and seventh commandments in the Reformed catechisms often contain explicit references to the Holy Spirit, they will be dealt with first, while leaving the other commandments and the general assertions concerning social concerns from the Reformed confessions for later in this chapter.

Keeping the Sabbath and Marriage Holy

That the Holy Spirit is the cause of good works that enables believers to observe the law of God is already affirmed. However, discussions concerning other aspects of the work of the Holy Spirit are also present in the treatment of the fourth and seventh commandments in the Reformed catechisms, namely CC37, CC45, and the HC.[55] While the fourth commandment pertains to the work of the Holy Spirit in relation to keeping the Sabbath holy, the seventh pertains to that in relation to holy matrimony.

The Reformed catechisms teach that the main reason behind the giving of the command to observe the Sabbath is that the people of God may submit their lives more to the leading and guidance of the Holy Spirit. Also inherent in the same commandment is concern for others, namely the relief of servants. It is to be noted that even though the fourth commandment falls well into the category of the first table of the Decalogue, which deals mainly with the duty toward God, the Reformed catechisms acknowledge that concern for others is also present in the commandment. Apparently, the catechisms simply follow and explain what the Scripture itself teaches in Ex. 20:8-11 concerning the prohibition on the imposed work or labor of servants on the Sabbath day.

In his catechisms Calvin states that there are three reasons for giving the fourth commandment: "To represent spiritual rest, in aid of ecclesiastical polity, and for the relief of servants."[56] While admitting that the sabbath as "a shadow of a reality yet to be" has ceased in Christ, and therefore "superstitious observance of days must remain far from Christians," by spiritual rest Calvin means that "we meditate all our life on a perpetual sabbath from our works so that the Lord may operate in us by his spirit."[57] It is "to cease from our own works, that the Lord may work in us," to put "ourselves under His government."[58] "How is that done?," Calvin asks. It is by "mortifying our flesh, that is renouncing our own nature, so that God may govern us by His Spirit." And this is to be done continually, and certainly every day for the rest of believers' life.[59] One day, that is, the seventh day, is specially appointed because of human weakness, so that the people of God are reminded to meditate continually on the works of God.

---

55. The WLC and WSC do not give explicit reference to the Holy Spirit in their expositions of the fourth and seventh commandments.
56. CC45 Q/A 171; CC37 VIII.4.
57. CC37 VIII.4; see also Calvin, *Institutes*, II.viii.34.
58. CC45 Q/A 172, 184.
59. CC45 Q/A 173-174, 178.

The day is sanctified so that they can observe the order constituted in the church, to listen to the word of God preached and taught, to participate in the sacraments, to engage in public prayers, and to bear witness to their faith and religion, activities which are instituted or commanded by God for the church, his people, in which God himself works through his Spirit.[60] Furthermore, this commandment is also given "to provide for the relief of servants," namely, to give one day for rest to those who are under the power of others.[61] In other words, believers are commanded to avoid any form of oppression toward others by imposing work when due rest should be given to them. They ought not to "oppress inhumanly with work" those who are subject to them.[62]

The HC clearly follows Calvin in explaining the meaning and application of the fourth commandment, albeit with different arrangement of thoughts. The fourth commandment is given to God's people for two reasons. First, God wills that "the gospel ministry and education for it be maintained" so that they may attend the assembly of God's people. Second, God also wills that they may cease from their evil ways by letting God work in them "through his Spirit." Implied in the first reason are the opportunities of the believers "to learn what God's Word teaches, to participate in the sacraments, to pray to God publicly, and to bring Christian offerings for the poor."[63] The catechism also affirms, as Calvin does, that the commandment primarily directs believers' thoughts to the eternal Sabbath, which already begins in this life.

If in the treatment of the fourth commandment the Reformed catechisms testify to the governing and leading of believers by the Holy Spirit, then the treatment of the seventh commandment reveals another aspect of the work of the Holy Spirit, namely, the indwelling of the Spirit in believers. In their explication of the commandment, the catechisms teach that what underlies the command against all sort of unchastity and adultery is the view of a Christian, body and soul, as a temple of the Holy Spirit.

---

60. CC37 VIII.4; CC45 Q/A 178-179, 183.
61. CC45 Q/A 180.
62. CC37 VIII.4.
63. HC Q/A 103; see also Ursinus, *The Commentary*, 557, 566; WCF XXI.8.

In CC37 Calvin discusses the seventh commandment exclusively in the context of marriage. Any kind of lewdness and immodesty, or unfaithfulness within the bond of marriage, that occurs against the sacredness of holy matrimony instituted by God violates the union between man and woman that God himself binds by his authority, and thus is cursed.[64] But in his CC45 Calvin discusses the commandment from its wider scope, as to apply to both the married and single. He teaches that from the commandment it could be derived that all fornication is cursed by God, assuming that the commandment applies to all, both to the married and single. The command to abstain from any form of unchastity rests on the fact that "our bodies and souls are temples of the Holy Spirit (I Cor. 3:16; 6:15; 2 Cor. 6:16)."[65] The command, however, does not "halt at the outward act," namely physically or sexually abstaining from unchastity, but "requires the pure affection of the heart."[66] Looking at individual believers holistically as temples of the Holy Spirit, Calvin then asserts that believers ought to strive to live in holiness, to embody his holiness in their everyday life, that is to "preserve [their bodies and souls] in uprightness," not only "in deed, but also in desire, word and gesture."[67]

The explication of the seventh commandment in the HC bears much resemblance to that in CC45. "God condemns all unchastity," therefore all believers, married or single, should "thoroughly detest it" and "live decent and chaste lives."[68] In answering the question whether the commandment forbids only such scandalous sins as adultery, the catechism reveals the reason behind the giving of the commandment. God "forbids everything which incites unchastity, whether it be actions, looks, talk, thoughts, or desires," because "we are temples of the Holy Spirit, body and soul, and God wants both to be kept clean and holy."[69]

---

64. CC37 VIII.7.
65. CC45 Q/A 201.
66. CC45 Q/A 202.
67. CC45 Q/A 203. See pp. 88-91 in chapter 3 for more discussion on sanctification as the mortification of the old self and the vivification of the new self.
68. HC Q/A 108.
69. HC Q/A 109; see also Ames, *Sketch*, 185.

Care for the Common Good, the Poor, and the Afflicted

Although the Reformed confessions do not often give explicit references to the Holy Spirit when discussing the rest of the commandments, especially those of the second table of the Decalogue, the Spirit is already presupposed to be the cause of the acts of good works by virtue of what has been laid out in the doctrine of good works in general. The Spirit enables, leads, and even creates desire in believers to observe God's commandments, the revealed will of God, without whom no one can observe even the least of the commandments. The confessions teach that the church as the people of God is obliged to demonstrate their love toward neighbors through the observance of the law. As one looks at the confessions and catechisms, one may find that the manifestation of good works is discussed in different places. The catechisms in general, as mentioned earlier, discuss the manifestation of good works—the application of the law, or the Decalogue to be specific—as an obligation for the church as the people of God, which all confessed individual believers are obliged to follow. But in some Reformed confessions, the manifestation of good works is also discussed in relation to the church and civil magistracy as institutions, in addition to its relation to the obligation of individual believers. The manifestation of good works is also the obligation that duly rests on the shoulders of those who assume ecclesiastical functions and those others who undertake the role of magistrates in societies.

In his catechisms, Calvin teaches that believers ought to have concern for the welfare of others indiscriminately, from parents and magistrates to the weak, poor, and afflicted. He maintains that believers are commanded to owe all reverence, obedience, and gratitude, and to render all possible services to fathers and mothers, and also to those who are above them, such as princes and magistrates, insofar as not transgressing the Law of the Lord is concerned.[70] Believers also ought to see their neighbors as fellow human beings who are created in the image of God. They must hold their neighbors as "holy and sacred," so that any violation against them is

---

70. CC37 VIII.5; CC45 Q/A 186, 194.

a violation against the image of God in them.[71] Instead, for Calvin, God requires believers to "love their neighbours and seek their salvation, and all this with true affection and without simulation."[72] All robberies, frauds, and false witnesses, by which the weak and the innocent are aggravated, oppressed, deceived, and wound, should be "very far from [God's] people."[73] Calvin also adds that since the Lord "exacts indeed an extraordinary affection, sovereignly ardent with love, for the brethren," believers must be so affectionate that they are "no longer even solicited by any cupidity contrary to the law of love, and ready to render most willingly to each one that which is his."[74]

The HC follows Calvin in displaying concrete love and concern for others in its teaching of the Law of God. The catechism teaches that individual believers ought to "honor, love, and be loyal" to parents and all those in authority over them, as is proper.[75] It also maintains that, by forbidding envy, hatred, and anger, "God tells us to love our neighbors as ourselves . . . to protect them from harm as much as we can, and to do good even to our enemies."[76] The catechism also asserts that believers ought to do whatever they can for their neighbor's good and that they work faithfully so that they "may share with those in need."[77] Moreover, believers are obliged to do what they can to "guard and advance" their neighbor's good name.[78]

The WLC starts its discussion of the second tablet of Decalogue with an affirmation of the sum of the six commandments as the overarching moral principle toward fellow human beings. The catechism states clearly that "our duty to man" is "to love our neighbour, and to do to others what we would have them do to us" (Matt. 22:39; 7:12).[79] In the spirit of this overarching principle, the catechism proceeds to explicate the six commandments of the

---

71. CC37 VIII.6.
72. CC45 Q/A 199.
73. CC37 VIII.8-9; CC45 Q/A 205-212.
74. CC37 VIII.10; CC45 Q/A 213-214.
75. HC Q/A 104.
76. HC Q/A 107.
77. HC Q/A 111.
78. HC Q/A 112.
79. WLC Q/A 122.

second tablet. Regarding the fifth commandment, the catechism affirms that the commandment does not only pertain to familial relationship between parents and their children, but also to several other human relationships that involve others who are superior in age and gifts, and "especially such as by Gods Ordinance are over us in place of Authority, whether in family, Church, or Common-wealth."[80] It then asserts that mutual love ought to inspire and mark believers' "performance of those duties which we mutually owe in our severall relations, as Inferiours, Superiours, Equals."[81] Similarly, the sixth commandment consists of the duties to "preserve the life of ourselves, and others," to comfort and succor the distressed, and to protect and defend the innocent.[82] Among the duties required in the eighth commandment is "an endeavour by all just, and lawfull meanes, to procure, preserve, and further, the wealth and outward estate of others, as well as our own."[83] The duties required in the ninth commandment include "the preserving and promoting of truth between man and man, and the good name of our neighbour," as well as "a charitable esteem of our neighbours; loving, desiring, and rejoycing in their good name; sorrowing for, and covering of their infirmities; . . . defending their innocency."[84] As for the tenth commandment, believers are required to have "such a charitable frame of the whole soul toward our neighbour, as that all our inward motions and affections touching him tend unto and further all that good which is his."[85]

Whereas the Reformed catechisms address the acts of good works in their exposition of the Decalogue, some Reformed confessions usually discuss it in several places, such as the doctrine of good works and sanctification. The confessions also frame their discussions in relation not only to individual believers but also to ecclesiastical functions and the magistrates, as well as individual believers.

---

80. WLC Q/A 124; WSC Q/A 64.
81. WLC Q/A 125.
82. WLC Q/A 135; WSC Q/A 68.
83. WLC Q/A 141; WSC Q/A 74.
84. WLC Q/A 144; WSC Q/A 77.
85. WLC Q/A 147; WSC Q/A 80.

The TC asserts that the duties to which a Christian should be chiefly devoted are those whereby one may profit one's neighbors, with respect to both life eternal and the present life. Besides what has been discussed in chapter 6 concerning the duties with respect to life eternal, the confession also teaches Christian duties that pertain to the present life. One ought to devote herself to profit her neighbors that "they may want nothing required by bodily necessity."[86] For the confession, acts of good works may include various acts that span across the boundaries of societies, from the service of the family and the magistracy to ecclesiastical functions, to vocational callings of individuals. Besides "ecclesiastical functions" and "the administration of the government," the confession lists among the chief duties of individual Christians:

> obedience to magistrates (for these are of importance for the common profit), the care which is devoted to wife, children and family, and the honor which is rendered parents, because without these the life of men cannot subsist; and, lastly, the professions of good arts and all honorable branches of learning since without the cultivation of these we would necessarily be destitute of the greatest blessings, and those which are peculiar to mankind.[87]

As far as the human liberty is concerned, the confession urges every Christian to engage in vocational callings or professions, "whereby he may confer the greatest advantage upon men."[88] The confession reiterates the same urge when discussing the vocational calling of monks. It teaches that in discerning his vocational calling, one should endeavor to "be of service to magistrate, parents, relatives and all others whom God has made nearest to him and brought to him for assistance, in what place, time or manner soever their profit demands," according to his ability and as God's law

---

86. TC VI.
87. TC VI.
88. TC VI.

requires. It then continues to assert, "Then let him embrace that mode of living whereby he may chiefly provide for the affairs of his neighbors."[89]

Discussing good works, the SC asserts that works, which are counted good before God, are of two kinds: "The one is done to the honour of God, the other to the profit of our neighbour, and both have the revealed will of God as their assurance."[90] Regarding the second kind, the confession offers a similar list to that in the TC but with an explicit concern for social justice. Acts of good works that exemplify the second kind are:

> To honour father, mother, princes, rulers, and superior powers; to love them, to support them, to obey their orders if they are not contrary to the commands of God, to save the lives of the innocent, to repress tyranny, to defend the oppressed, to keep our bodies clean and holy, to live in soberness and temperance, to deal justly with all men in word and deed, and finally, to repress any desire to harm our neighbour, are the good works of the second kind.[91]

The list undoubtedly reflects acts which are implicated by the commandments in the second tablet of the Decalogue. The list also reveals the urge of the confession for believers to engage in social justice issues in concrete ways.

The FC does not give a list of acts that can be reckoned as good works as the TC does. However, the FC provides a description of good works in terms of ecclesiastical functions that the TC only mentions. The FC maintains that the true church, governed according to the order established by Christ, should have "pastors, overseers, and deacons," so that "true doctrine may have its course, that errors may be corrected and suppressed, and the poor and all who are in affliction may be helped in their necessities; and that assemblies may be held in the name of God, so that great and small may be edified."[92] In other words, ecclesiastical offices are established and

---

89. TC XII.
90. SC XIV.
91. SC XIV.
92. FC XXIX.

meant to profit others with respect to things that pertain to both the right worship of God and love of neighbors, or in the words of the TC, eternal life and the present life.

The same is also true of Bullinger's SHC. In his confession, Bullinger does not give a list of acts in the chapter where he discusses faith and good works as the TC and SC do.[93] However, he shows explicit concerns for the sick, the poor, and the afflicted in various places in the confession and discusses them particularly in relation to the life and function of the church. Among ecclesiastical offices, the office of a bishop is dedicated primarily to meet the needs of the church with regard to the present life, to "administer the food and needs of the life of the Church."[94] A pastor is also assigned to care for the needs of the church with regard to both the present life and eternal life. In a chapter on catechizing and comforting the sick, Bullinger assigns to pastors the tasks of both catechizing young people and visitation of the sick. Concerning the care for the sick, he strongly contends that pastors ought "to watch more carefully for the welfare of their flocks" who are "sick and weakened by diseases of both soul and body." He states that

> surely it is never more fitting for pastors of the churches to watch more carefully for the welfare of their flocks than in such diseases and infirmities. Therefore let them visit the sick soon, and let them be called in good time by the sick, if the circumstance itself would have required it. Let them comfort

---

93. But in his *Decades* Bullinger does provide a list of acts through which good works and the application of the law are manifested. The list includes "the moderate conservation of the ecclesiastical ceremonies, the preaching of God's word, public prayers, and whatsoever else doth belong to the outward service or external worship due to God," "the natural love of children toward their parents, of men toward their country and kinsfolks, the due obedience that we owe to the magistrates and all in authority, and lastly, the offices of civil humanity," "the protection of widows and orphans, the delivering of the oppressed and afflicted, well-doing to all men, and doing hurt to no man," "the faith of wedded couples, the offices of marriage, the honest and godly bringing up of children, with the study of chastity, temperance, and sobriety," the "upright dealing in contracts, liberality, bountifulness, and hospitality," "the study of truth through all our life-time, faith in words and deeds," and the promotion of "good affections, holy wishes, with all holy and honest thoughts." Bullinger, *Decades*, III.ix (354).

94. SHC XVIII.5.

and confirm them in the true faith, and then arm them against the dangerous suggestions of Satan.[95]

Bullinger also teaches that the possession of the church ought to be properly, even especially, used for, among other things, "the succor and relief of the poor." He also states that "schools and institutions which have been corrupted in doctrine, worship and morals must be reformed, and that the relief of the poor must be arranged dutifully, wisely, and in good faith."[96]

In describing the duties of magistrates, the Reformed confessions point out that magistrates are obliged according to God's law to preserve and care for the welfare of their subjects as they bring into action their love of neighbors. Christian magistrates or governments are certainly what the framers of the confessions had in mind when they wrote articles concerning magistracy. The TC teaches that next to ecclesiastical functions as the chief duties of a Christian is "the administration of the government," because this vocation may potentially confer the greatest advantage upon people.[97] The FHC also confesses that, receiving their powers from God alone, a government is not to be tyrannical, but to "protect and promote the true honor of God and the proper service of God." Furthermore, the confession maintains that a good government "should rule the people according to just, divine laws."

> It should sit in judgment and administer justice, preserve the public peace and welfare, guard and defend the public interest, and with fairness punish wrong-doers according to the nature of their crimes against life and property. And when a government does this, it serves God its Lord as it ought to do and is obligated to do.[98]

---

95. SHC XXV.2.
96. SHC XXVIII.1-2.
97. TC VI.
98. FHC XXVI.

In the GC, Calvin states that in defending the afflicted and innocent, or in correcting and punishing the malice or the perverse, magistrates perform their office, "serve God and follow a Christian vocation."[99] The SC similarly confesses that civil magistrates are "appointed and ordained by God" for the manifestation of God's own glory and for "the good and well being of all men." The confession also states that magistrates are ordained to maintain justice and peace for the good and welfare of their subjects. They are "the judges and princes to whom God has given the sword for the praise and defence of good men and the punishment of all open evil doers."[100]

Bullinger's SHC echoes the same concern. With the power endowed by God, a magistrate rules according to the Word of God and is against anything contrary to it. In the light of this the confession states,

> Let him exercise judgment by judging uprightly. Let him not respect any man's person or accept bribes. Let him protect widows, orphans and the afflicted. . . . Therefore, let him draw this sword of God against all malefactors, seditious persons, thieves, murderers, oppressors, blasphemers, perjured persons, and all those whom God has commanded him to punish and even to execute.[101]

In addition, a magistrate may wage war to preserve the safety of the people when necessary, provided "he has first sought peace by all means possible, and cannot save his people in any other way except by war." And when a magistrate does these things in faith, "he serves God by those very works which are truly good, and receives a blessing from the Lord."[102]

Similar to the SC, the WCF holds that civil magistrates are ordained by God "to be under him, over the people for his own Glory and the publick good." The confession adds that to that end God has "armed them with the power of the sword, for the defence and encouragment of them that

---

99. GC XXI.
100. SC XXIV.
101. SHC XXX.3.
102. SHC XXX.4.

are good, and for the punishment of evil doers."[103] Moreover, according to the confession, Christians are lawful to accept and execute the office of a magistrate when they are called. This is so because embedded in the office is an opportunity to serve people for the advancement and preservation of their welfare, their common good, by maintaining "Piety, Justice, and Peace." Even so, toward that end, they may lawfully "wage War, upon just and necessary occasion."[104]

To such governments that do things according to the law of God, maintaining order and striving for the common good, the Reformed confessions teach that believers should show their obedience and be "ready to serve" with their "lives, goods, and possessions."[105] Believers ought to accord such magistrates "honour and reverence, to render respect and subservience, to execute their commands, to bear the charges they impose on us, so far as we are able without offence to God."[106]

As discussed above, therefore, it may be concluded that the Holy Spirit that enables believers to do good works is the same Spirit that leads and directs them to manifest those good works in concrete acts of love toward their neighbors by fulfilling the law of God. In so doing they display concern and love for their neighbors. The Reformed confessions teach that believers ought to give themselves to be led by the Holy Spirit to care for and engage actively in the preservation and furtherance of the well-being and good of others. This active engagement may manifest itself in such acts as the conservation of ecclesiastical ministries, the preservation of order in the family and society, the protection and care for the poor, the defense of the oppressed and afflicted, the upholding of the sacredness of marriage along with chastity, sobriety, and temperance, the promotion of honesty and justice, and the cultivation of good affections toward others. Far from keeping the concern to themselves, or being individualistic Christians, the Holy Spirit leads believers to seek out ways to care for and help others.

---

103. WCF XXIII.1.
104. WCF XXIII.2.
105. FHC XXVI.
106. GC XXI; see also SHC XXX.5; WCF XXIII.4.

CHAPTER 8

Conclusion

This dissertation has been an attempt to bridge a gap in the history of scholarship concerning the doctrine of the Holy Spirit in Reformed orthodoxy. It explores and provides a systematic account of the person and some aspects of the work of the Holy Spirit as treated in the confessions. It does so with a critical analysis of some major Reformed confessions and catechisms of the sixteenth and seventeenth centuries, both of the structure of these confessional documents and of the content of articles that teach explicitly or implicitly the aspect of the doctrine of the Holy Spirit being discussed in each chapter. The critical analysis was done by setting the doctrine in both the historical context of the documents and the context of scriptural reference that lie behind the doctrine, with the help of ancillary documents such as treatises and sermons mainly written by the framers of the confessional documents or their comtemporaries.

This final chapter will recapitulate the conclusions of each preceding chapter and reiterate how comprehensive the doctrine of the Holy Spirit presented in the Reformed confessions is. It will also provide some final reflections on the treatment of the doctrine of the Holy Spirit in the Reformed confessions.

The Doctrine in Review

In light of the treatment of the Holy Spirit in the Reformed confessional documents in the preceding chapters, it must be clear that the doctrine of the Holy Spirit is of paramount importance in the Reformed tradition, as the Holy Spirit is discussed in relation to almost all other doctrines. The Holy Spirit is presented in the Reformed confessions as playing an indispensable role not only in doctrines that have been identified by scholars who studied the theology of the confessions in the past, such as the doctrines of Scripture, the Trinity, Christ, salvation, the church in general, and sacraments, but also in other doctrines such as creation, providence, the church's unity, diversity of spiritual gifts, mission, and good works.

In relation to the doctrine of Scripture, the Reformed confessions depict the Holy Spirit as the divine author who inspired the biblical authors to write the canonical books of Scripture. Scripture is the Word of God because God through his Spirit speaks through it. Besides the divine author and revealer, he is also the teacher and interpreter of Scripture, without whose light or illumination one may never arrive at the true knowledge of God revealed in the Word of God, in Scripture.

In their treatment of the doctrine of the Trinity, the confessions provide quite extensive discussions of the Holy Spirit—especially of his divinity and personhood. They unanimously hold to the orthodox belief in one only, true, living and almighty God, in three persons: the Father, Son, and Spirit. The Spirit, as one of the three distinct subsistences or persons in the one sole and simple divine essence, is consubstantial, and thereby equal in divinity, with the Father and the Son. He is, therefore, worthy of receiving the same honor, glory, and worship with the Father and the Son. Moreover, decidedly adhering to the Western trinitarian tradition's view of *filioque*, the confessions contend for the divinity and equality of the Son and the Holy Spirit with the Father by arguing that the *ad intra* distinction, that is, the begetting of the Son and the procession of the Holy Spirit, denotes personal distinctions in the same divine essence, not separation or inferiority. The *ad extra* distinction of the Son and the Holy Spirit, namely their distinct offices in divine works toward the creation, similarly testifies to the equal divinity of the Son and the Holy Spirit with the Father. In their operations *ad intra* and *ad extra*, the unity of the three divine persons of the Trinity and their equality are fully exhibited.

The Reformed confessions teach that, just as all three persons of the Trinity work together in every divine work and are undivided in their operations, the three divine persons also jointly worked together in the incarnation of Christ. The role of the Holy Spirit in the redemptive acts of Christ does not go unnoticed in the confessions. The Holy Spirit plays a sanctifying role in the conception of Christ. He also anointed Christ to undertake his offices as Prophet, Priest, and King throughout his life, death, and resurrection. There is no single work that Christ carried out on earth in which the Holy Spirit was not upon him and empowering him.

A thorough account of the Holy Spirit can also be found in the doctrine of salvation. The Reformed confessions teach that whereas the Father has planned redemption from eternity and the Son has accomplished the redemption objectively in history, the Holy Spirit applies the redemption fully and subjectively in the hearts and lives of believers. This application of redemption by the Holy Spirit is nonetheless multifaceted. The Holy Spirit actively works in all aspects of the application of redemption—calling, regeneration, faith, repentance, justification, sanctification, and perseverance—in the life of believers. He permeates every aspect of Christian life.

The fingerprints of the Holy Spirit evident in the gathering of all believers, the church, are also acknowledged by the Reformed confessions when they discuss the doctrine of the church. The Holy Spirit gives identity and marks the true church. He is involved in the church from its inception, even before the constitution of the world. The whole existence of the church and its continuation—its being and *raison d'être*, its identity and action—come from God, who works through his Spirit.

The confessions also assert that the Holy Spirit invigorates the church by the use of sacraments. The sacraments are divinely ordained to be outward means expedient for the faith of the godly, the people of God. Through them God by his Spirit nourishes and confirms the faith of believers. Therefore, the sacraments, duly observed, can become efficacious and profitable only to the faithful, not to the unfaithful, because at the very heart of the sacraments lies faith and the work of the Holy Spirit confirming faith. Both the requisite faith for sacraments and the growth of faith resulting from the observance of the sacraments are the fruits of the work of the Holy Spirit.

In relation to the doctrine of creation and providence, the confessions strongly affirm that both creation and providence are not the works of one or two, but of all three divine persons of the Trinity. However, the unique role of the Spirit in both creation and providence is acknowledged, despite the strong affirmation of the indivisibility of the divine works *ad extra*. To the Holy Spirit is attributed the power or virtue of the Father. He is the one through whom the Father and Christ not only created, but also do all things. He is the creator Spirit, and he creates the world and faith alike. He transfuses his energy into all things, and gives life to animate creatures and beauty to all that he once created. Without him nothing was created or is able to exist and live by itself. In providence, the Holy Spirit is seen as the infinite power of God that fills, strengthens, vivifies, preserves, and governs all things. With regard to the special providence over the church, the confessions teach that the Holy Spirit is the one who brings salvation to the elect, preserves their faith amidst spiritual warfare against the wicked and the devils, and with the Word rules the elect. In preserving and governing his church, God uses his ministers and their ministries as outward means. God through his Spirit calls his ministers, bestows upon them necessary gifts for their offices, and gives power, authority, and efficacy to their ministries. The power and presence of the Holy Spirit are always with the ministers who carry out their ministries faithfully according to the Word of God.

There are roles of the Holy Spirit in some aspects of the doctrine of the church in the Reformed confessions that have not been adequately treated by scholars in the past who studied the theology of the confessions. These aspects are the unity of the church, the diversity of spiritual gifts, and the evangelistic mission of the church. The Reformed confessions are not destitute of fundamentals on which the church's unity ought to be built, nurtured, and developed. At the same time, the confessions also note how the Holy Spirit is deeply involved in this endeavor. The Spirit establishes the church's unity, as he leads, gathers, and unites all believers with Christ and with each other. The holy catholic church, namely, the communion of the saints, finds its true unity only in the shared experience of the Holy Spirit, as the Spirit applies Christ's redemption in the lives of believers along with its corollary benefits. The Holy Spirit is the undergirding basis of the church's unity. This unity is manifest in the universality of the church that goes beyond the boundaries of geography, ethnicity, language, and time, as the work of the Holy Spirit is not subject to those boundaries. This unity is expressed in worship and service as believers are led by the Spirit to worship and serve one God. There will always be one church of God, a holy congregation and gathering of true Christian believers, which Christ as the Head himself rules and governs through his Word and Spirit. To preserve this unity, God also ordains sacraments as outward means, in which the Holy Spirit works, preserving and fostering the unity that believers have with each other as well as with Christ. Moreover, God through his Spirit endows the church with various spiritual gifts of ministry so that the church may unite under Christ as her head, experience growth, and worship and serve God in the world.

Regarding the diversity of spiritual gifts, the Reformed confessions teach that gifts are God's means to build up and unite his church. God unites his church through his Spirit working inwardly in the lives of believers, as well as working outwardly through the ministry of all members of the same body, on whom he bestows various spiritual gifts of ministry, each according to his own will. The confessions teach that the gifts of ministry are not given for individual purposes. Instead, they are lavishly distributed for the building up of the church so that believers may have communion in each other's gifts and graces and thus be united.

A careful reading of the confessions also demonstrates that the confessions do not lack in passion for evangelism when it is understood as the propagation of the gospel of salvation. Nor do they neglect the role of the Holy Spirit in the proclamation of the gospel, that is, the evangelistic mission of the church. For the Reformed confessions, since the very beginning of the church, the proclamation of the gospel has never been primarily a human enterprise. The church's mission to preach the gospel is not merely a human activity of promulgating the good news regarding God and his work of salvation by humans, but instead the active work of God himself through the Spirit in calling sinners to come to the salvation which God has himself inaugurated and promised in the gospel. He works through the Holy Spirit in both the external calling through the outward preaching of the Gospel and the inward calling of individual believers. God through his Spirit calls some people, furnishes them with necessary gifts, and sends and entrusts them with the ministry of the Word and sacraments. However, a few other confessions also explicitly teach that God through his Spirit calls all his people and enables them to do good works, to testify through their godly lives and conversations so that others may begin to know God and be won to Christ.

As God ever renews believers in the image of God, he also by his Spirit enables them to do good works, leading and directing them to manifest those good works in concrete acts of love toward their neighbors by fulfilling the law of God. In so doing they display concern and love for their neighbors. Far from keeping the concern to themselves, or being individualistic Christians, the confessions teach that believers ought to give themselves to be led by the Spirit to care for and actively promote the preservation, well-being, and good of others. The manifestation of good works is the obligation which duly rests on the shoulders of individuals, as well as of those who assume ecclesiastical offices and those others who undertake the role of magistrates in societies.

Final Reflections on the Treatment of the Doctrine in the Reformed Confessions

After a careful analysis on the treatment of the doctrine of the Holy Spirit in the Reformed confessions, some theological reflections on the characteristics of the treatment and the content of the doctrine are now in order. Seven critical reflections will be offered in this section. The first three pertain to characteristics of the treatment of the doctrine and the last four pertain to the content of the doctrine.

First, with regard to the placement of the doctrine of the Holy Spirit in the Reformed confessions, a careful reading of the confessions reveals that they do not usually discuss the Holy Spirit in one independent or exclusive *locus* or chapter. Rather, they treat the doctrine of the Holy Spirit in several *loci*, that is, always in relation to other doctrines. Even when some confessions, such as the SC, BC, and TNA, have a separate article or chapter on the Holy Spirit and seemingly treat the doctrine as an independent *locus*, they do not exclude the Holy Spirit from being discussed in relation to other doctrines. When such an article or chapter on the Spirit is present, it usually only contains the main doctrinal statement regarding the deity of the Holy Spirit, or in a few cases also some major aspects of the work of the Holy Spirit, such as faith, assurance of salvation, sanctification, and regeneration. This kind of treatment is also true of several other doctrines in the confessions, especially the doctrines of God and Christ. However, while the doctrines of God and Christ often do have independent chapters or sets of articles that contain a great deal of doctrinal material, the doctrine of the Holy Spirit does not. This is partly due to the pervasive nature of the work of the Holy Spirit. The manifold aspects of the work of the Holy Spirit are so many and overlap with so many other doctrines that the authors of the confessions always chose to treat the doctrine of the Holy Spirit—his personhood and work—in relation with other doctrines. Otherwise, an immense redundancy was inevitable. Therefore, to look for the teaching of the Holy Spirit only in an independent chapter or article of faith in the confessions not only does an injustice to the way the doctrine has been treated in the confessions, but will also eventually prove unfruitful. The conclusion of such study will often be misleading since it fails to recognize so many materials on the doctrine of the Holy Spirit scattered throughout other doctrines in the confessions.

Second, a careful reading of the Reformed confessions also unveils the trinitarian framework within which the doctrine of the Holy Spirit is developed and ramified. This leads to the relatively infrequent explicit references given to the Spirit. However, rarely mentioning the Holy Spirit does not necessarily mean a neglect of the Holy Spirit or the doctrine of the Holy Spirit. As demonstrated in some of the preceding chapters, especially in chapters 2 and 4, the confessions generally use the inclusive term "God" to denote all three persons in the Godhead, Father, Son, and Holy Spirit. When the term is used, as is often the case in the general assertion of any doctrine, all three persons in the Godhead are referred to. Unless the names of the trinitarian persons are mentioned or clearly referred to in light of the context, it is justifiable to read the inclusive term "God" as denoting all three persons in the Godhead, including the Holy Spirit. The strong affirmation of the indivisibility of the divine works *ad extra* as present and evident in the Reformed confessions provides sufficient substantiation for this way of reading.

Third, the Reformed confessions teach clearly that the Holy Spirit permeates every aspect of Christian life. Even though different confessional documents offer different levels of emphasis on the doctrine of the Holy Spirit, the confessions, taken as a whole, evidence the comprehensiveness of the treatment of the doctrine of the Holy Spirit in the Reformed tradition. The discussions of the Spirit were set against the backdrop of threats coming from heresies of the day as well as the affairs of everyday Christian life, such as worship, service and ministry, personal piety, evangelism, and care for others. As such, the doctrine presented in the confessions not only reflects the Reformed concern for orthodoxy (the right teaching), but also for orthopraxy (the right *praxis* or practice). The doctrine of the Holy Spirit in the confessions is not only apologetic, but also pedagogical, confessional, and pastoral in nature. It serves as a standard of orthodoxy, expressing what the Reformed church believes and teaches, as well as a standard of piety, teaching and urging believers to go beyond their mere sacramental profession of faith into concrete acts of faith in their daily walk.

Once the pervasive nature of the work of the Holy Spirit is acknowledged, and the way that the confessions treat the doctrine of the Holy Spirit—that is, always in relation to other doctrines—is recognized, it is evident that the confessions contain far more doctrinal statements regarding the Holy Spirit and offer richer materials for theological reflection on the doctrine of the Spirit than scholars in the past have identified and perceived.

The reflection on the many facets and aspects of the doctrine of the Holy Spirit in the Reformed confessions presented throughout the preceding chapters leads to a balanced and comprehensive view of the Holy Spirit. The confessions exhibit this balanced and comprehensive view by employing some important theological distinctions—such as personal distinctions in the Godhead, natural-supernatural, immediate-mediate works of the Holy Spirit—and identifying different realms that the doctrine of the

Holy Spirit embraces—personal, social, and political realms. The following four reflections spring from these distinctions and different realms that the doctrine of the Holy Spirit in the confessions employs and covers.

First, the Reformed confessions clearly acknowledge the distinction between the persons of the Trinity. Yet, the distinct persons of the Trinity indivisibly work together in all of divine operations. In light of this, the Holy Spirit is seen as always working indivisibly with the Father and the Son. On the one hand, this should increase cognizance of, appreciation for, and perhaps also further reflection on the roles of each trinitarian person in every divine work toward, in, and through creatures, particularly the role of the Holy Spirit. Certain roles of the Spirit in some divine works not commonly associated with him, such as Christ's incarnation, creation, providence, church's unity, mission, social responsibility, are now here brought forth and highlighted, instead of being neglected. On the other hand, other roles of the Spirit in divine works that are commonly associated with him are affirmed and put into the proper perspective within the trinitarian theological framework. Seeing from this perspective, it is justifiable to regard the Holy Spirit as of paramount importance in the whole theological structure in the Reformed tradition. All things considered, therefore, Christians should offer worship, service, and prayer, duly and equally, to all persons of the Trinity.

Second, with regard to nature, the Reformed confessions use the *opus naturae* (the divine work through the natural operation of things) and the *opus gratiae* (the divine work of grace conferred on the elect) distinction and teach that the Triune God works in both. God works in the natural operation of created things and confers grace on the elect. In his providence, God works by his Spirit either according to, above, or even against the nature of things, at his pleasure. The distinction is also made between the general and special providence with respect to the object. The former has all creatures and the whole created order as the objects of providence, while the latter the elect in particular. However, these distinctions are not meant to denigrate nature and the natural order of things at any sense. Instead, it is the same God who, by the same Spirit, his infinite power, works in all things so that to him alone all glory is due. The cosmic work of the Spirit in creation and providence, including the sustenance and preservation of things according to its created order, form, and being is never taught by the confessions as less significant than his work in applying redemption. Both are distinguished merely with respect to the recipients and the grace conferred, not the agent who carries both works out. The Spirit works in the natural operation of things as much as in redemptive operation of grace. Both the natural order of things and miracles are means through which the Holy Spirit executes divine plan. Thus, both should inspire the same awe and wonder in believers to render worship to the Triune God.

Third, regarding the way the Holy Spirit works, namely, through the use of means, the confessions acknowledge that the Holy Spirit may work with or without the use of means. He works both mediately and immediately. There are outward means that God by his Spirit uses to carry out his plan of redemption. On the one hand, God has ordained Scripture, sacraments, ministers of the Word, civil magistrates, the ministry of fellow believers, his church, and others to be outward means through which the Holy Spirit works to usher the elect into his plan of salvation, to be built up, to be renewed in the image of the Son, and to be united with Christ and with one another. On the other hand, God by his Spirit also works immediately, without the use of outward means, in creating faith, regenerating, bringing to repentance, and justifying believers. Insofar as the work of God by his Spirit is the focal point, none of the works is superior or inferior to each other. Appreciation and gratitude are due to God alone upon recognizing and receiving both works.

Finally, the Reformed confessions teach that the work of the Holy Spirit is by no means limited to the individual realm, but extends to social and political realms as well. The Holy Spirit does not cease to work at the conversion or profession of faith of individual believers, but continues to renew the life of believers in the image of God, sanctifies them, and leads them to live a godly life in obedience to God's revealed will, God's law. As the result of the continuing work of the Holy Spirit, believers produce good works throughout their lives. The life-giving and empowering Spirit that enables believers to do good works is the same Spirit that leads and directs them to display concern and love for their neighbors. Far from keeping the concern to themselves, or being individualistic Christians, the Reformed confessions teach that believers ought to give themselves to be led by the Holy Spirit to care for and engage actively for the preservation and furtherance of the well-being and goodness of others. The Holy Spirit even calls some and lavishes upon them necessary gifts to serve their neighbors as ecclesiastical officers or civil magistrates. As a result, the work of the Holy Spirit extends beyond the individual realm to social and political realms. This Spirit who works in all things will also bring everything to completion according to the will of God, so that in all things God may be glorified—*in omnibus glorificetur Deus.*

Bibliography

Sixteenth- and Seventeenth-Century Reformed Confessions and Catechisms

"The Augsburg Confession A.D. 1530." In *The Creeds of Christendom with a History and Critical Notes*, vol. 3, edited by Philip Schaff, 3-73. Grand Rapids: Baker, 1984.

"The Belgic Confession." In *Ecumenical Creeds and Reformed Confessions*, 78-120. Grand Rapids: CRC Publications, 1988.

Beza, Theodorus. *A Confession of Faith, Made by Common Consent of Diuers Reformed Churches beyond the Seas*. London: Henry Bynneman, 1571.

———. *A Briefe and Piththie [sic] Sum of the Christian Faith, Made in Forme of a Confession, with a Confutation of All Such Superstitious Errours, as are Contrarie Thereunto*. Translated by R. F. London: William How, 1572.

———. *A Little Catechisme*. London: Hugh Singleton, 1579.

"Calvin's Catechism (1537)." In *Reformed Confessions of the 16th and 17th Centuries in English Translation: Volume 1, 1523-1552*, compiled by James T. Dennison, Jr., 354-401. Grand Rapids: Reformation Heritage Books, 2008.

"Calvin's Catechism (1545)." In *Reformed Confessions of the 16th and 17th Centuries in English Translation: Volume 1, 1523-1552*, compiled by James T. Dennison, Jr., 468-519. Grand Rapids: Reformation Heritage Books, 2008.

"The Canons of Dort." In *Ecumenical Creeds and Reformed Confessions*, 122-145. Grand Rapids: CRC Publications, 1988.

"The Confession of Faith." In *The Confession of Faith and the Larger and Shorter Catechism*, 3-74. Edinbourg: George Swintoun and Thomas Brown, 1683.

"The Confession of the English Congregation at Geneva (1556)." In *Reformed Confessions of the Sixteenth Century*, edited by Arthur Cochrane, 131-136. Louisville: Westminster John Knox Press, 2003.

"The First Confession of Basel (1534)." In *Reformed Confessions of the 16th and 17th Centuries in English Translation: Volume 1, 1523-1552*, compiled by James T. Dennison, Jr., 287-296. Grand Rapids: Reformation Heritage Books, 2008.

"The First Confession of Basel (1534)." In *Reformed Confessions of the Sixteenth Century*, edited by Arthur Cochrane, 91-96. Louisville: Westminster John Knox Press, 2003.

"The First Helvetic Confession (1536)." In *Reformed Confessions of the Sixteenth Century*, edited by Arthur Cochrane, 100-111. Louisville: Westminster John Knox Press, 2003.

"The French Confession of Faith (1559)." In *Reformed Confessions of the Sixteenth Century*, edited by Arthur Cochrane, 144-158. Louisville: Westminster John Knox Press, 2003.

"The Geneva Confession." In *Reformed Confessions of the Sixteenth Century*, edited by Arthur Cochrane, 120-126. Louisville: Westminster John Knox Press, 2003.

"The Heidelberg Catechism." In *Ecumenical Creeds and Reformed Confessions*, 12-77. Grand Rapids: CRC Publications, 1988.

"The Irish Articles of Religion A.D. 1615." In *The Creeds of Christendom with a History and Critical Notes*, vol. 3, edited by Philip Schaff, 526-544. Grand Rapids: Baker, 1984.

"The Larger Catechism." In *The Confession of Faith and the Larger and Shorter Catechism*, 75-166. Edinbourg: George Swintoun and Thomas Brown, 1683.

"The Lausanne Articles (1536)." In *Reformed Confessions of the Sixteenth Century*, edited by Arthur Cochrane, 115-116. Louisville: Westminster John Knox Press, 2003.

"Report 34: Neo Pentecostalism." In *Acts of Synod 1973*, 398-493. Grand Rapids: CRC, 1973.

"The Scottish Confession of Faith (1560)." In *Reformed Confessions of the Sixteenth Century*, edited by Arthur Cochrane, 163-184. Louisville: Westminster John Knox Press, 2003.

"The Second Helvetic Confession (1566)." In *Reformed Confessions of the Sixteenth Century*, edited by Arthur Cochrane, 224-301. Louisville: Westminster John Knox Press, 2003.

"The Shorter Catechism." In *The Confession of Faith and the Larger and Shorter Catechism*, 167-192. Edinbourg: George Swintoun and Thomas Brown, 1683.

"The Tetrapolitan Confession (1530)." In *Reformed Confessions of the Sixteenth Century*, edited by Arthur Cochrane, 54-88. Louisville: Westminster John Knox Press, 2003.

"The Thirty Nine Articles of the Church of England." In *The Creeds of Christendom with a History and Critical Notes*, vol. 3, *The Evangelical Protestant Creeds with Translations*, edited by Phillip Schaff, 486-516. Reprint, Grand Rapids: Baker Books, 1984.

Books, Articles, and Essays

Ames, William. *The Marrow of Theology*. Edited by John D. Eusden. Grand Rapids: Baker Books, 1968.

————. *A Sketch of the Christian's Catechism*. Translated by Todd M. Rester. Grand Rapids: Reformation Heritage Books, 2008.

Barth, Karl. *Church Dogmatics*. Translated and edited by G. W. Bromiley and T. F. Torrance. Vols. 1-4. Edinburgh: T&T Clark, 2004.

————. *Theology of the Reformed Confessions*. Translated by Darrel L. Guder and Judith J. Guder. Louisville: Westminster John Knox Press, 2005.

Bavinck, Herman. *Reformed Dogmatics*. Translated by John Vriend and edited by John Bolt. 4 vols. Grand Rapids: Baker Academics, 2003-2008.

Beaver, R. Pierce. "The Genevan Mission to Brazil." In *The Heritage of John Calvin*, ed. John H. Bratt, 55-73. Grand Rapids: Eerdmans, 1973.

Beeke, Joel R., and Sinclair B. Ferguson, eds. *Reformed Confessions Harmonized*. Grand Rapids: Baker Books, 1999.

Bergema, Hendrik. "De betekenis van Calvijn voor de Zending en de Missiologie." *Vox Theologica* 20 (November 1958): 44-54.

Berkhof, Louis. *Systematic Theology*, New edition. Grand Rapids: Eerdmans, 1996.

Bloesch, Donald G. *The Holy Spirit: Works and Gifts*. Downers Grove: InterVarsity Press, 2000.

Bolt, John. "The Characteristic Work of the Holy Spirit: Sanctification, Sabbath Glory, Beauty." *Stulos Theological Journal* 3/1 (May 1995): 1-11.

Bucanus, Gulielmus. *Institutions of Christian Religion*. Translated by Robert Hill. London: 1659.

Bulgakov, Sergius. *The Comforter*. Translated by Boris Jakin. Grand Rapids: Eerdmans, 2004.

Bullinger, Heinrich. *Commonplaces of Christian Religion*. London: Tho. East and H. Middleton, 1572.

———. *The Decades of Henry Bullinger*. 4 vols. Translated by H. I. and edited by Thomas Harding. Cambridge: The University Press, 1849-1852.

Bultmann, Rudolf. *Theology of the New Testament*. Translated by Kendrick Grobel. New York: Charles Scribner's Sons, 1951.

Burgess, Stanley M. *The Holy Spirit: Eastern Christian Traditions*. Peabody: Hendrickson, 1989.

———. *The Holy Spirit: Medieval Roman Catholic and Reformation Traditions*. Peabody: Hendrickson, 1997.

———. *The Spirit and the Church: Antiquity*. Peabody: Hendrickson, 1984.

Calvin, John. *Commentaries on the Book of Genesis*. Vol. 1. Translated by John King. Grand Rapids: Eerdmans, 1948.

———. *Commentary on a Harmony of the Evangelists, Matthew, Mark, and Luke*. Vol. 1. Translated by William Pringle. Grand Rapids: Baker, 2003.

———. *Commentary on the Epistles of Paul the Apostle to the Corinthians*. Vol. 1. Translated by John Pringle. Grand Rapids: Baker Books, 2003.

———. *Commentary upon the Acts of the Apostles*, ed. Henry Beveridge, vol. 2. Grand Rapids: Eerdmans, 1949.

———. *Institutes of the Christian Religion*. 2 vols. Translated by Ford Lewis Battle and edited by John T. McNeill. Philadelphia: Westminster Press, 1960.

Catholic Church. *Catechism of the Catholic Church*. 2nd ed. Vatican City: Libreria Editrice Vatican, 2000.

Cazelles, H., P. Evdokimov, and A. Greiner. *Le Mystére de l'Esprit-Saint*. Tours: Maison Mame, 1968.

Chaney, Charles. "Missionary Dynamics in the Theology of John Calvin." *Reformed Review* 17 (1964): 24-38.

Chung, Paul (Seung Hoon). *Spirituality and Social Ethics in John Calvin: A Pneumatological Perspective*. Lanham: University Press of America, 2000.

Coalter, Milton J., John M. Mulder, and Louis B. Weeks, eds. *The Confessional Mosaic: Presbyterians and Twentieth-Century Theology*. Louisville: Westminster John Knox Press, 1990.

Cochrane, Arthur C., ed. *Reformed Confessions of the Sixteenth Century*. Louisville: Westminster John Knox Press, 2003.

Congar, Yves. *I Believe in the Holy Spirit*. 3 vols. Translated by David Smith. New York: Crossroad, 1997.

The Council of Trent. *The Canons and Decrees of the Sacred and Oecumenical Council of Trent*. Translated by J. Waterworth. Chicago: The Christian Symbolic Publication Society, 1848.

De Ridder, Richard R. *Discipling the Nations*. Grand Rapids: Baker, 1975.

Dennison, James T., Jr., comp. *Reformed Confessions of the 16th and 17th Centuries in English Translation: Volume 1, 1523-1552*. Grand Rapids: Reformation Heritage Books, 2008.

Drews, Paul. "Die Anschauungen reformatorischer Theologen über die Heidenmission," *Zeitschrift für praktische Theologie* 28 (1897): 1-26, 193-223, 289-316.

Erickson, Millard J. *Christian Theology*. 2nd ed. Grand Rapids: Baker Book House, 1983

Evdokimov, Paul. *La Nouveaute de l'Esprit*. Bégrolles en Mauges: Abbaye de Bellefountaine, 1977.

———. *Présence de l'Esprit Saint dans la tradition orthodoxe*. Paris: Cerf, 1969. Reprint, 1977.

———. *The Sacrament of Love*. Translated by Anthony P. Gythiel and Victoria Steadman. Crestwood: St. Vladimir's Seminary Press, 1985.

———. *The Struggle with God*. Translated by Sister Gertrude. Glen Rock: Paulist, 1966.

Farley, Benjamin Wirt. *The Providence of God*. Grand Rapids: Baker, 1988.

Fee, Gordon D. *God's Empowering Presence: The Holy Spirit in the Letters of Paul*. Peabody: Hendrickson, 1994.

Ferguson, Sinclair B. *The Holy Spirit*. Downers Grove: InterVarsity Press, 1996.

Hall, Peter. *The Harmony of Protestant Confessions: Exhibiting the Faith of the Churches of Christ Reformed after the Pure and Holy Doctrine of the Gospel, throughout Europe*. New edition. London, J. F. Shaw, 1844.

Heideman, Eugene P. "God the Holy Spirit." In *Guilt, Grace, and Gratitude: A Commentary on the Heidelberg Cactechism*, ed. Donald J. Bruggink, 111-135. New York: Half Moon Press, 1963.

Hendry, George S. *The Holy Spirit in Christian Theology*, 2nd ed. Philadelphia: Westminster, 1965.

Heppe, Heinrich. *Reformed Dogmatics: Set Out and Illustrated from the Sources*. Translated by G. T. Thomson. Grand Rapids: Baker Book House, 1978.

Hesselink, I. John. *Calvin's First Catechism: A Commentary*. Louisville: Westminster John Knox, 1997.

———. "Calvin's Use of *Doctrina* in His Catechisms." In *Calvinus sacrarum literarum interpres*, ed. Herman J. Selderhuis, 70-87. Göttingen: Vandenhoeck & Ruprecht, 2008.

———. "The Charismatic Movement and the Reformed Tradition." In *Major Themes in the Reformed Tradition*, ed. Donald K. McKim, 377-385. Grand Rapids: Eerdmans, 1992.

———. "Governed and Guided by the Spirit: A Key Issue in Calvin's Doctrine of the Holy Spirit." In *Reformiertes Erbe: Festschrift für Gottfried W. Locher zu seinem 80 Geburtstag*, vol 2, ed. Heiko A. Oberman, 161-171. Zurich: Theologischer Verlag, 1993.

———. "Pneumatology." In *Calvin Handbook*, ed. Herman J. Selderhuis, 299-312. Grand Rapids: Eerdmans, 2009.

Hodge, Charles. *Systematic Theology*. 3 vols. New York: Charles Scribner's Sons, 1888.

Hoekema, Anthony A. "The Missionary Focus of the Canons of Dort." *Calvin Theological Journal* 7, no. 2 (November, 1972): 209-220.

———. *Saved by Grace*. Grand Rapids: Eerdmans, 1989.

Hoeksema, Herman. *The Triple Knowledge of God: An Exposition of the Heidelberg Catechism*. 3 vols. Grand Rapids: Reformed Free Publishing Association, 1970-72

Holl, Karl. "Luther und die Mission," *Neue Allgemeine Missionszeitschrift* 1 (1924): 36-49.

Holsten, Walter. "Reformation und Mission." *Archiv für Reformationsgeschichte* 44 (1953): 1-32.

Jansen, John F. *Calvin's Doctrine of the Work of Christ*. London: James Clarke, 1956.

Jongeneel, Jan A. B. "The Missiology of Gisbertus Voetius: The First Comprehensive Protestant Theology of Missions." *Calvin Theological Journal* 26, no. 1 (April 1991): 47-79.

Jun, Ho-Jin. "Reformation and Mission: A Brief Survey of the Missiological Understanding of the Reformers." *ACTS Theological Journal* 5 (1994): 160-178.

Kane, J. Herbert. *Understanding Christian Missions*, 3rd ed. Grand Rapids: Baker, 1982.

Kärkkäinen, Velli-Matti. *Pneumatology: The Holy Spirit in Ecumenical, International, and Contextual Perspective*. Grand Rapids: Baker Academic, 2002.

———. *Toward a Pneumatological Theology: Pentecostal and Ecumenical Perspectives on Ecclesiology, Soteriology, and Theology of Mission*. Edited by Amos Yong. Lanham: University Press of America, 2002.

Kasdorf, Hans. "The Reformation and Mission: A Bibliographical Survey of Secondary Literature." *Occasional Bulletin of Missionary Research* 4, no. 4 (October 1980): 169-175.

Kim, Myung Yong. "Reformed Pneumatology and Pentecostal Pneumatology." In *Reformed Theology: Ecumenicity and Identity*, ed. Wallace M. Alston and Michael Welker, 170-189 Grand Rapids: Eerdmans, 2003.

Klauber, Martin I. "The Helvetic Formula Consensus (1675): An Introduction and Translation." *Trinity Journal* 11, no. 1 (Spring, 1990): 103-123.

Kline, Meredith. *Images of the Spirit*. Grand Rapids: Baker, 1980.

Klooster, Fred H. *A Mighty Comfort: The Christian Faith according to the Heidelberg Catechism.* Grand Rapids: CRC Publications, 1990.

———. "Missions—The Heidelberg Catechism and Calvin." *Calvin Theological Journal* 7, no. 2 (November, 1972): 181-208.

———. *Our Only Comfort: A Comprehensive Commentary on the Heidelberg Catechism,* 2 vols. Grand Rapids: Faith Alive, 2001.

Knapp, Henry M. "Understanding the Mind of God: John Owen and Seventeenth-Century Exegetical Methodology." Ph.D. diss., Calvin Theological Seminary, 2002.

Kreeft, Peter J. *Catholic Christianity: A Complete Catechism of Catholic Beliefs.* San Francisco: Ignatius Press, 2001.

Krusche, Werner. *Das Wirken des Heiligen Geistes nach Calvin.* Göttingen: Vandenhoeck & Ruprecht, 1957.

Kuiper, Herman. *By Grace Alone: A Study in Soteriology.* Grand Rapids: Eerdmans, 1955.

Kuyper, Abraham. *The Work of the Holy Spirit.* Translated by Henri De Vries. Grand Rapids: Eerdmans, 1975.

Kuyvenhoven, Andrew. *Comfort & Joy: A Study of the Heidelberg* Catechism. Grand Rapids: Faith Alive, 1988.

Latourette, Kenneth Scott. *A History of Christianity,* First edition. New York: Harper & Brothers, 1937-1945.

———. *A History of the Expansion of Christianity,* Vol. 3. New York: Harper & Brothers, 1939.

Linde, Simon van der. *De Leer van den Heiligen Geest bij Calvijn.* Wageningen: Veenman, 1943.

Loetscher, Lefferts A. *The Broadening Church: A Study of Theological Issues in the Presbyterian Church since 1869.* Philadelphia: University of Pennsylvania, 1957.

MacGavran, Donald. "A Missionary Confession of Faith." *Calvin Theological Journal* 7, no. 2 (November, 1972): 133-145.

McBrien, Richard P. *Catholicism.* 2 vols. Minneapolis: Winston Press, 1980.

McIntyre, John. *The Shape of Pneumatology: Studies in the Doctrine of the Holy Spirit.* Edinburgh: T&T Clark, 1997.

Migliore, Daniel L. *Faith Seeking Understanding: An Introduction to Christian Theology*. 2nd ed. Grand Rapids: Eerdmans, 2004.

Möhler, Johann Adam. *Symbolism: Exposition of the Doctrinal Differences between Catholics and Protestants as Evidenced by Their Symbolic Writings*. Translated by James Burton Robertson. New York: The Crossroad Herder Book, 1997.

Moltmann, Jürgen. *The Church in the Power of the Holy Spirit*. Translated by Margaret Kohl. San Francisco: Harper & Row, 1977.

———. *The Coming of God: Christian Eschathology*. Translated by Margaret Kohl. Minneapolis: Fortress Press, 1996.

———. *God in Creation: A New Theology of Creation and the Spirit of God*. Translated by Margaret Kohl. Minneapolis: Fortress Press, 1993.

———. *The Spirit of Life: A Universal Affirmation*. Translated by Margaret Kohl. Minneapolis: Fortress Press, 1992.

———. *Trinity and the Kingdom*. Translated by Margaret Kohl. San Francisco: Harper & Row, 1981.

Mudge, Lewis S. *One Church: Catholic and Reformed*. Philadelphia: The Westminster Press, 1963.

Muller, Richard A. "Calvin on Sacramental Presence, in the Shadow of Marburg and Zurich." *Lutheran Quarterly* 23, no. 2 (Summer 2009): 147-167.

———. "The Holy Spirit in the Augsburg Confession: A Reformed Definition." *Concordia Theological Quarterly* 61, no. 1-2 (January-April 1997): 53-78.

———. *God, Creation, and Providence in the Thought of Jacob Arminius: Sources and Directions of Scholastic Protestantism in the Era of Early Orthodoxy*. Grand Rapids: Baker, 1991.

———. *Post-Reformation Reformed Dogmatics*, 4 vols. Grand Rapids: Baker Academic, 2003.

———. "Reformed Confessions and Catechisms." In *The Dictionary of Historical Theology*, ed. Trevor A. Hart, 466-485. Grand Rapids: Eerdmans, 2000.

———. "'To Grant This Grace to All People and Nations': Calvin on Apostolicity and Mission." In *For God So Loved the World: Missiological reflections in Honor of Roger S. Greenway*, ed. Arie C. Leder, 211-232. Belleville: Essence Publishing, 2006.

Murray, Andrew. *Redemption, Accomplished and Applied*. Grand Rapids: Eerdmans, 1955.

Niemeyer, H. A. *Collectio confessionum in ecclesiis reformatis publicatarum.* Leipzig: Klinkhardt, 1840.

Niesel, Wilhelm. *Reformed Symbolics: A Comparison of Catholicism, Orthodoxy, and Protestantism.* Translated by David Lewis. Edinburgh: Oliver and Boyd, 1962.

Olevianus, Caspar. *An Exposition of the Apostles' Creed.* Translated by Lyle D. Bierma. Grand Rapids: Reformation Heritage Books, 2009.

———. *A Firm Foundation: An Aid to Interpreting the Heidelberg Catechism.* Translated by Lyle D. Bierma. Grand Rapids: Baker Books, 1995.

Osterhaven, M. Eugene. *The Faith of the Church: A Reformed Perspective on Its Historical Development.* Grand Rapids: Eerdmans, 1982.

Ott, Ludwig. *Fundamentals of Catholic Dogma.* Translated by Patrick Lynch. Rockford: Tan Books and Publishers, 1974.

Owen, John. *PNEUMATOLOGIA.* Chancery Lane: J. Darby, 1674.

Pannenberg, Wolfhart. *Systematic Theology.* 3 vols. Translated by G. W. Bromiley. Grand Rapids: Eerdmans, 1991, 1994, 1998.

———. *Theology and the Kingdom of God.* Philadelphia: Westminster Press, 1969.

Pelikan, Jaroslav. *Credo: Historical and Theological Guide to Creeds and Confessions of Faith in the Christian Tradition.* New Haven: Yale University Press, 2003.

Pelikan, Jaroslav, and Valerie Hotchkiss, eds. *Creeds and Confessions in the Reformation Era.* Vol. 2 of *Creeds and Confessions of Faith in the Christian Tradition.* New Haven: Yale University Press, 2003.

Pinnock, Clark H. *Flame of Love: A Theology of the Holy Spirit.* Downers Grove: InterVarsity Press, 1996.

Plantinga, Cornelius, Jr. "Gregory of Nyssa and the Social Analogy of the Trinity." *The Thomist* 50 (1986): 325-352.

———. "Social Trinity and Tritheism." In *Trinity, Incarnation, and Atonement,* eds. Ronald J. Feenstra and Cornelius Plantinga, Jr., 21-47. Notre Dame: University of Notre Dame Press, 1989.

Prenter, Regin. *Spiritus Creator.* Translated by John M. Jensen. Philadelphia: Fortress, 1953.

Pruett, Gordon E. "Protestant Doctrine of the Eucharistic Presence." *Calvin Theological Journal* 10, no. 2 (November 1975): 142-174.

Quick, Oliver Chase. *Doctrines of the Creed: Their Basis in Scripture and Their Meaning To-day.* New York: Charles Scribner's Sons, 1938.

Quistorp, H. "Calvin's Lehre vom Heiligen Geist." In *De Spiritu Sancto*, ed. J. de Graf, 109-150. Utrecht: Drukkerij V/H Hemink & Zoon, 1964.

Recker, Robert. "An Analysis of the Belgic Confession as to Its Mission Focus." *Calvin Theological Journal* 7, no. 2 (November, 1972): 158-180.

Richardson, Herbert W. *Toward an American Theology.* New York: Harper & Row, 1967.

Robertson, O. Palmer. "The Holy Spirit in the Westminster Confession." In *The Westminster Confession into the 21st Century*, vol. 1, ed. J. Ligon Duncan, III, 57-100. Fearn: Mentor, 2003.

Robinson, H. Wheeler. *The Christian Experience of the Holy Spirit.* London: Nisbet & Co., 1928.

Rohls, Jan. *Reformed Confessions: Theology from Zurich to Barmen.* Translated by John Hoffmeyer. Louisville: Westminster John Knox Press, 1998.

Rooy, Sidney H. *The Theology of Missions in the Puritan Tradition.* Delft: W. D. Meinema, 1965.

Rorem, Paul. *Calvin and Bullinger on the Lord's Supper.* Bramcotte: Grove Books Limited, 1989.

Salvard, Jean François. *Harmonia confessionum fidei, orthodoxarum et reformatarum ecclesiarum.* Geneva: Apud Petrum Santandreanum, 1581.

Schaff, Phillip, ed. *The Evangelical Protestant Creeds with Translations.* Vol. 3 of *The Creeds of Christendom with a History and Critical Notes.* Reprint, Grand Rapids: Baker Books, 1984.

Scheffczyk, Leo. *Creation and Providence.* Translated by Richard Strachan. New York: Herder and Herder, 1970.

Sherry, Patrick. *Spirit and Beauty: An Introduction to Theological Aesthetics.* Oxford: Clarendon, 1992.

Shults, F. LeRon, and Andrea Hollingsworth. *The Holy Spirit.* Grand Rapids: Eerdmans, 2008.

Streeter, B. H., ed. *The Spirit.* New York: The Macmillan Co., 1921.

Swete, H. B. *The Holy Spirit in the Ancient Church.* London: Macmillan & Co., 1912.

Tillich, Paul. *Systematic Theology*. Vol. 3. Chicago: University of Chicago Press, 1963.

Torrance, Thomas F. *The School of Faith: The Catechisms of the Reformed Church*. London: J. Clarke, 1959.

Turretin, Francis. *Institutes of Elenctic Theology*. Translated by George Musgrave Giger and edited by James T. Dennison, Jr. 3 vols. Philipsburg: P&R, 1992-1997.

Ursinus, Zacharias. *The Commentary of Dr. Zacharias Ursinus on the Heidelberg Catechism*. Translated by G. W. Williard. Phillipsburg: P&R, 1985.

Van Dusen, Henry P. *Spirit, Son and Father: Christian Faith in the Light of the Holy Spirit*. New York: Charles Scribner's Sons, 1958.

Vanden Berg, J. "Calvin and Missions." In *John Calvin: Contemporary Prophet*, ed. Jacob T. Hoogstra, 167-183. Grand Rapids: Baker, 1959.

Vincent, Thomas. *An Explicatory Catechism*. Glasgow: Robert Sanders, 1692.

Warfield, Benjamin Breckinridge. *Calvin and Augustine*. Philadelphia: Presbyterian and Reformed Publishing, 1956.

Warneck, Gustav. *Outline of a History of Protestant Missions from the Reformation to the Present Time*. 3rd English edition. Translated from the 8th German edition by George Robson. Edinburgh: Oliphant Anderson & Ferrier, 1906.

Watkin-Jones, Howard. *The Holy Spirit in the Medieval Church*. London: Epworth, 1922.

Watson, Thomas. *A Body of Practical Divinity*. London: Thomas Parkhurst, 1692.

Weber, Otto. *Foundations of Dogmatics*. Translated by Darrell L. Guder. Vol. 2. Grand Rapids: Eerdmans, 1981-83.

Welker, Michael. *God the Spirit*. Translated by John F. Hoffmeyer. Minneapolis: Fortress, 1994.

———, ed. *The Work of the Spirit: Pneumatology and Pentecostalism*. Grand Rapids: Eerdmans, 2006.

Williams, J. Rodman. *The Era of the Spirit*. Plainfield: Logos International, 1971.

———. *The Pentecostal Reality*. Plainfield: Logos International, 1972.

———. *Renewal Theology*. Grand Rapids: Zondervan, 1990.

Yong, Amos. *Beyond the Impasse: Toward a Pneumatological Theology of Religions*. Grand Rapids: Eerdmans, 2001.

———. *Spirit-Word-Community: Theological Hermeneutics in Trinitarian Perspective*. Burlington: Ashgate, 2002.

———. *The Spirit Poured Out on All Flesh: Pentecostalism and the Possibility of Global Theology*. Grand Rapids: Baker Academic, 2005.

Zizioulas, John D. *Being as Communion*. Crestwood: St. Vladimir's Seminary Press, 1985.

———. *Community and Otherness: Further Studies in Personhood and the Church*. Edited by Paul McPartlan. Edinburgh: T&T Clark, 2006.

———. "The Doctrine of the Holy Trinity: The Significance of the Cappadocian Contribution." In *Trinitarian Theology Today: Essays on Divine Being and Act*. Edited by Christoph Schwöbel, 44-60. Edinburgh: T&T Clark, 1995.

www.ingramcontent.com/pod-product-compliance
Lightning Source LLC
Chambersburg PA
CBHW051539230426
43669CB00015B/2661

Finally a book on this so important topic! The doctrine of the Holy Spirit has been characteristic of Reformed Theology and has been one of the causes for the lasting influence, mainly through the Reformed confessions that were preached and taught to the congregations. Now with this study not only the influence of the pneumatology in Reformed confessions is demonstrated, but also its relevance for church and theology today. Dr. Adhinarta has served us with a well structured and source based study that I wish to be read and used by many.

Herman J. Selderhuis,
Director Refo500, Professor of Church History,
Theological University Apeldoorn, Netherlands

Reformed Christianity revolves around the triune God. The work of this God and our communion with Him comes from the Father through the Mediator, Jesus Christ. Yet that work and communion is permeated with the presence of the Holy Spirit. In a masterful piece of research, Yuzo Adhinarta demonstrates from major confessions and catechisms that the doctrine of the Spirit truly fills the Reformed tradition. He investigates the pervasive place of the Spirit not only in the doctrines of the Trinity, Christ, salvation, and the means of grace, but also in the doctrines of creation, providence, church life, missions, and social justice. Though most of the Reformed standards did not devote a separate article to the Holy Spirit, the Spirit's work is pervasive to their witness. Adhinarta's dissertation reminds us, as Calvin once said, that it is only by "the secret energy of the Spirit" that "we come to enjoy Christ and all his benefits," for "the Holy Spirit is the bond by which Christ effectually unites us to himself" (Institutes, 3.1.1).

Joel R. Beeke,
President and Professor of Systematic Theology, Church History, and Homiletics,
Puritan Reformed Theological Seminary, Grand Rapids, Michigan

Yuzo Adhinarta's study of the doctrine of the Holy Spirit in the Reformed Confessions is a major contribution to Reformation studies. As far as I know, there is nothing quite like it in any language. The author has made a thorough and careful examination of all the major confessions and catechisms of the sixteenth and seventeenth centuries and has read widely in the relevant secondary literature. The analysis is balanced and perceptive and reads so well that non-specialists can also benefit from this excellent study.

I. John Hesselink,
Past President and Emeritus Professor of Theology,
Western Theological Seminary, Holland, Michigan

The Holy Spirit did not go to sleep between Montanus and Azusa Street and not only did churches of the Reformation experience the power of the Holy Spirit, they also proclaimed it to the world in their confessions. Yuzo Adhinarta's careful textual study of the major Reformed Confessions of the sixteenth and seventeenth centuries will help put to rest for good the oft-repeated mischaracterization of the Reformation that it practically and theologically neglected the work of the Holy Spirit. It is a much needed corrective that will benefit both the church and the academy.

John Bolt,
Editor of Herman Bavinck's Reformed Dogmatics in English translation, Professor of Systematic Theology, Calvin Theological Seminary, Grand Rapids, Michigan

After the Azusa Street revivals it has seemed to Pentecostal and charismatic evangelicals that Reformed theology, piety, and practice lacks sufficient appreciation of the person and work of the Holy Spirit. To Roman Catholic critics it seems as if the Reformed do not appreciate the centrality of the church and sacraments in the Spirit's operation. Others have tried to refashion it after the image of Karl Barth. The present work by Yuzo Adhinarta clarifies the picture treating the confessional documents on their own terms and by calling attention to the dynamic, mysterious, Trinitarian, and churchly character of the confessional Reformed understanding of the person and work of the Holy Spirit. Those inside and outside the Reformed tradition will benefit from Dr. Adhinarta's account of the confessional Reformed teaching.

R. Scott Clark,
Professor of Church History and Historical Theology,
Westminster Seminary California, Escondido, California